Work, Employm and Development

MIKE MAYES · KEITH SMALLEY

Series editor:
ROBERT PROSSER

COLLINS INSIGHT GEOGRAPHY

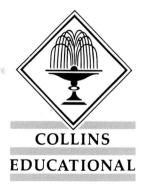

COLLINS
EDUCATIONAL

CONTENTS

Glossary words are highlighted in SMALL CAPITALS in the text the first time they appear in any Unit.

Location of case studies

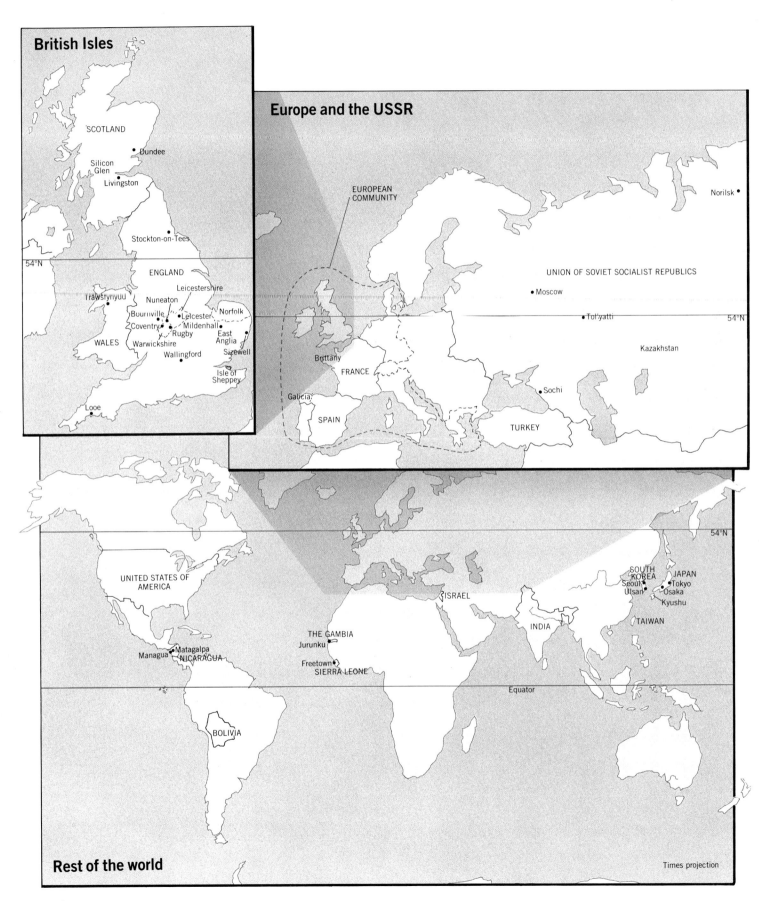

British Isles

SCOTLAND
- Dundee
- Silicon Glen
- Livingston
- Stockton-on-Tees

54°N

ENGLAND
- Trawsfynydd
- Leicestershire
- Nuneaton
- Leicester
- Norfolk
- Bournville
- Mildenhall
- Coventry
- Rugby
- East Anglia
- Warwickshire
- Wallingford
- Sizewell
- WALES
- Isle of Sheppey
- Looe

Europe and the USSR

EUROPEAN COMMUNITY

- Norilsk

UNION OF SOVIET SOCIALIST REPUBLICS
- Moscow
- Tol'yatti   54°N
- Kazakhstan
- Sochi

- Brittany
- FRANCE
- Galicia
- SPAIN
- TURKEY

Rest of the world

54°N

UNITED STATES OF AMERICA

SOUTH KOREA
- Seoul
- Ulsan
- JAPAN
- Tokyo
- Osaka
- Kyushu

ISRAEL

INDIA

TAIWAN

THE GAMBIA
- Jurunku

- Managua
- Matagalpa
- NICARAGUA

- Freetown
- SIERRA LEONE

Equator

BOLIVIA

Times projection

WHAT IS WORK?

Digging on allotments in Southall, Middlesex

Employment and leisure

WORK is often contrasted with leisure. Leisure includes the things we choose to do for fun, while work includes all those things we do to get by in everyday life. One aspect of work is paid EMPLOYMENT. However we also talk about *working* in the garden, in the allotment, or in the kitchen. The distinctions between work and leisure are difficult to draw because some aspects of work may *also* be things we choose to do for fun. For example we may be working in the kitchen but also think of cooking as a leisure activity.

1 In pairs look at the activities listed below and decide:
   a) whether all of them involve work.
   b) how far any of them could be described as leisure.

- Cooking the family dinner
- Baking a cake for a children's tea party
- Cooking dinner for yourself and six friends
- Cooking dinner for someone else's small dinner party as part of your catering business
- Sailing a small boat for fun
- Going out in a fishing boat to catch fish to sell
- Going out in a lifeboat to rescue people

Types of work

2 Study Source A and Source B. Show the type of work done in the Parsons family (and by whom) by completing a copy of the table below Source A.
3 The Parsons' work is *daily, weekly* and *seasonal*. List the work that each person in the family does under each of these headings.
4 Source B shows how the Parsons family work in both the formal economy and the domestic (informal) economy. Think about the work done by all the people in your household. Draw a similar diagram to show this work.

The Parsons Family

Mr Parsons was made redundant five and a half years ago. He was lucky enough to be young and fit enough to be taken on as a postman, a job which he much enjoys. Now that his children are older he can afford to accept a much lower wage, particularly as his wife works full-time in a wallpaper shop. He was trained in the army as an electrician and he can do most jobs around the house himself. As he finishes his work as a postman at 1 p.m. he has the rest of the day to work for himself and this he does very vigorously. As he says, 'I'm a gardening fanatic'.

Mrs Parsons uses her deep freeze to store the vegetables which come in, from the January Brussels sprouts to the October runner beans. When she was interviewed she was just finishing the rhubarb and starting on the gooseberries. They both enjoy the pressure of their work and see it as fun. When the last vegetables are frozen they turn, in November, to decorating.

Mrs Parsons gets a 40% discount through working in the wallpaper shop and the couple agree on an annual work programme for keeping their house, rented from the council, immaculate. Machines to help cut and wash the vegetables and a pressure cooker to reduce cooking time are much prized. Since Mrs Parsons works until 5.30, it is her husband who often cooks the meals.

The Parsons household is a mini vegetable factory: 'I think I could supply this whole road,' says Mrs Parsons, and Mr Parsons admitted that he sold vegetables. 'It's nothing for me to go and pick twelve cucumbers in one day and obviously I can't eat twelve cucumbers in a day', he said.

The domestic economy ties Mr and Mrs Parsons to their home for most of the year. Even Sunday mornings are fully occupied as Mr Parsons is chairman of the Allotment Society and sells HORTICULTURAL supplies at discount rates from a shed. As Mr Parsons said, 'We try to arrange it to have every other Sunday off but it doesn't always work.' Mrs Parsons explained, 'Then he's on his allotment and he's there if they want him. The phone has been ringing quite busily lately for chrysanthemum plants which he sells as well.' All the goods and tools for the Allotment Society are delivered to the Parsons' home. He uses his carport as a store.

Mr Parsons' work in the formal economy is poorly paid but it provides him with a social position – 'I poke letters in the same letter boxes every day, but I enjoy it. Because I'm out in the air, I've got nobody to govern me'. The money he gets pays for gas and electricity and rent. His wife's pay helps towards the extras: they go away for a holiday each year and they are both keen on buying machinery to support their domestic economy.

Their daughter, who is just about to leave school, earns money by babysitting for her married sister or cutting someone's hair (she is hoping to be a hairdresser). The local coalman keeps horses and she helps him and gets more money delivering dung in a barrel to the allotment. But sometimes the dung is paid for in vegetables.

Family member	Domestic work	Formal work
Mr Parsons		
Mrs Parsons		
Miss Parsons		

Divisions of Labour. R. Pahl (Blackwell)

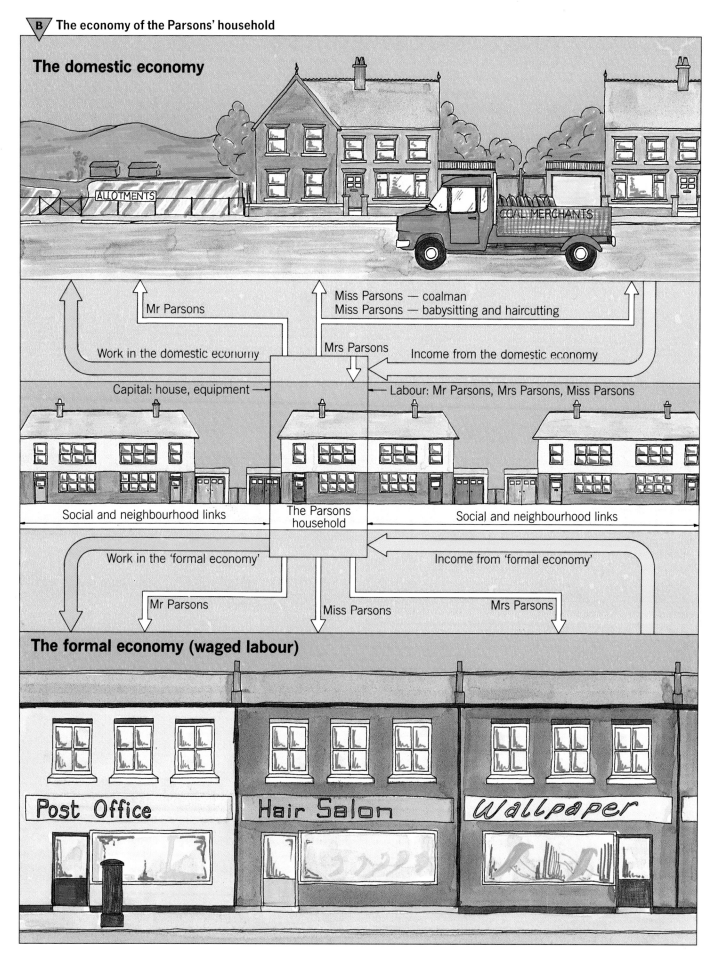

The domestic economy

Mr Parsons

Miss Parsons — coalman
Miss Parsons — babysitting and haircutting

Mrs Parsons

Work in the domestic economy

Income from the domestic economy

Capital: house, equipment

Labour: Mr Parsons, Mrs Parsons, Miss Parsons

Social and neighbourhood links

The Parsons household

Social and neighbourhood links

Work in the 'formal economy'

Income from 'formal economy'

Mr Parsons

Miss Parsons

Mrs Parsons

The formal economy (waged labour)

Post Office

Hair Salon

Wallpaper

1.2 SEPARATE ECONOMIES?

Working informally

Ray Pahl is a researcher who studied work patterns on the Isle of Sheppey in Kent. He investigated work in the formal or wage economy. (Mr Parsons' job as a postman is an example of formal employment.) He also wanted to find out about work in the informal economy – activities such as Mr Parsons' work on his allotments.

1 Sources B, C and D show surveys Ray Pahl used to find out how much informal work is done on the Isle of Sheppey and by whom.
a) Complete each survey for your own household.
b) Share your information with the rest of the class.

2 a) Now present your results as tables and bar graphs.
b) Discuss and analyse your findings.

3 Ray Pahl was impressed by the amount of work members of individual households did for themselves in Sheppey. Do the results of your class show a similar pattern?

A

Repairing bikes – an example of informal work on the Isle of Sheppey

Helping other people

B

Are there any tasks that members of your household do for other people?	For relatives		For non-relatives		Totals	
	By M	By F	By M	By F	By M	By F
Shopping						
Babysitting						
Housework						
Washing clothes						
Visiting people						
Hairdressing						
Pet care						
Gardening						
Dressmaking						
Decorating						
Provision of transport						
Repairs, carpentry, etc.						
Local activities						
Voluntary work						
Other help						
Total						

Who does the work?

C

Copy and complete the table by ticking the relevant box.

	Work done by the household			Work done using 'formal' services, eg. garage, builders	Work done by others informally	
	By male	By female	By child		Paid	Unpaid
1 House maintenance						
1 Indoor painting						
2 Plastering						
3 Mending a broken window						
2 Home improvement and decoration						
4 Double glazing						
5 Putting in a bathroom						
6 Building a garage or extension						
7 Putting in central heating						
3 Routine housework						
8 Washing up						
9 Tidying house or flat						
10 Cleaning outside windows						
11 Cooking family meals						
12 Getting a take-away meal						
13 Shopping						
14 Washing clothes and sheets						
15 Ironing clothes and sheets						
4 Domestic production						
16 Baking a cake						
17 Making clothes						
18 Knitting						
19 Repairing clothes						
20 Growing vegetables						
21 Making jam						
22 Making bread						
23 Making beer or wine						
5 Car maintenance						
24 Washing the car						
25 Checking the oil etc.						
26 Tuning the engine						
6 Child care						
27 Bathing child						
28 Changing nappies						
29 Looking after a sick child						
30 Collecting child from school						
31 Seeing schoolteacher about child						
32 Taking child to doctor						
33 Getting child's hair cut						

D-I-Y in the household	
Which of these tasks have one or more members of your household carried out? Put a tick or cross in the boxes opposite.	✓
Painting	
Plastering	
Mending a broken window	
Putting in double glazing	
Putting in a new bathroom	
Building a garage	
Building an extension to the home	
Converting an attic	
Putting in central heating	
Total	

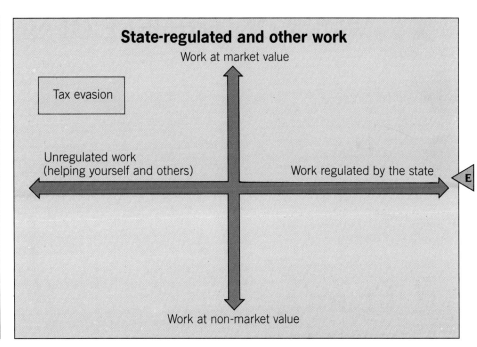

State-regulated and other work

Work at market value

Tax evasion

Unregulated work (helping yourself and others)

Work regulated by the state

Work at non-market value

Categorising work

There are many different types of work. These can be grouped in two different ways. Look at Source E. One axis shows how the value of work may be measured. This can be calculated by the money gained or by its use to individuals and to others. The other axis shows the role of the State. Some work is regulated by the State. Other work is not known of by the State and is unlikely to appear in national statistics.

4 a) In pairs draw a large copy of Source E. Mark the examples of work from Source F in the appropriate place. Tax evasion has been done for you.

b) Lightly shade in the three quarters of Source E which could be labelled INFORMAL WORK.

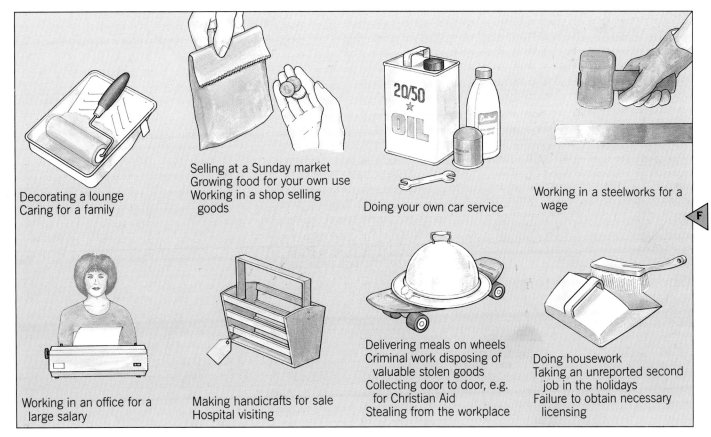

Decorating a lounge
Caring for a family

Selling at a Sunday market
Growing food for your own use
Working in a shop selling goods

Doing your own car service

Working in a steelworks for a wage

Working in an office for a large salary

Making handicrafts for sale
Hospital visiting

Delivering meals on wheels
Criminal work disposing of valuable stolen goods
Collecting door to door, e.g. for Christian Aid
Stealing from the workplace

Doing housework
Taking an unreported second job in the holidays
Failure to obtain necessary licensing

1 Read Source A which describes informal work on the Isle of Sheppey since the last century.

a) List the types of informal work mentioned in Source A.

b) Use Source B to give grid references for where this work might be found.

c) What other informal work, not mentioned in Source A, might be taking place in Source B?

From Smuggling to Tourism

In the early nineteenth century smuggling was common. Today, many islanders go fishing and shoot and trap duck and rabbits on the marshes. Much of the island gives a remote and desolate impression and, until recently, wildlife was abundant. For nearly a century, holidaymakers have doubled the population of the island in the summer, bringing money and the opportunity for quick-witted ENTREPRENEURS to make small fortunes out of food, drink and 'amusements'. Leysdown-on-Sea attracted hustlers and cowboys and provided apprenticeships in mild crookery for generations of school leavers who, in the 1950s, 1960s and early 1970s, went 'down Leysdown' to work as cheap labour, cleaning the chalets in the holiday camps, serving in cafes and bars and minding stalls and (later) machines in the fairgrounds and amusement arcades.

Opportunities for formal work

As well as being involved in the informal economy, many people on the Isle of Sheppey also work hard in the formal economy of paid employment. This page and page 7 examine existing employment opportunities in the formal economy for the 33,000 inhabitants of the Isle of Sheppey.

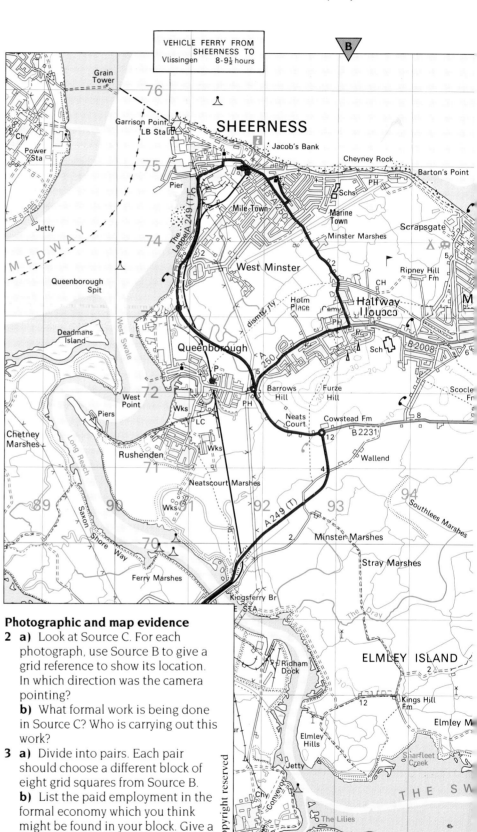

Photographic and map evidence

2 a) Look at Source C. For each photograph, use Source B to give a grid reference to show its location. In which direction was the camera pointing?

b) What formal work is being done in Source C? Who is carrying out this work?

3 a) Divide into pairs. Each pair should choose a different block of eight grid squares from Source B.

b) List the paid employment in the formal economy which you think might be found in your block. Give a grid reference for its location.

c) Suggest possible reasons why the employment might be found there.

4 a) Now draw an employment opportunities map for the Isle of Sheppey. On graph paper draw a rectangle the size of 10 by 15 grid squares. On it put in the outline of the Isle of Sheppey.

b) Use what you have learnt on this page and page 6 to shade in your grid squares according to the following key:

- Green – agricultural employment opportunities
- Red – industrial employment opportunities
- Brown – transport employment opportunities
- Yellow – holiday service employment opportunities.
- Orange – other service employment opportunities.

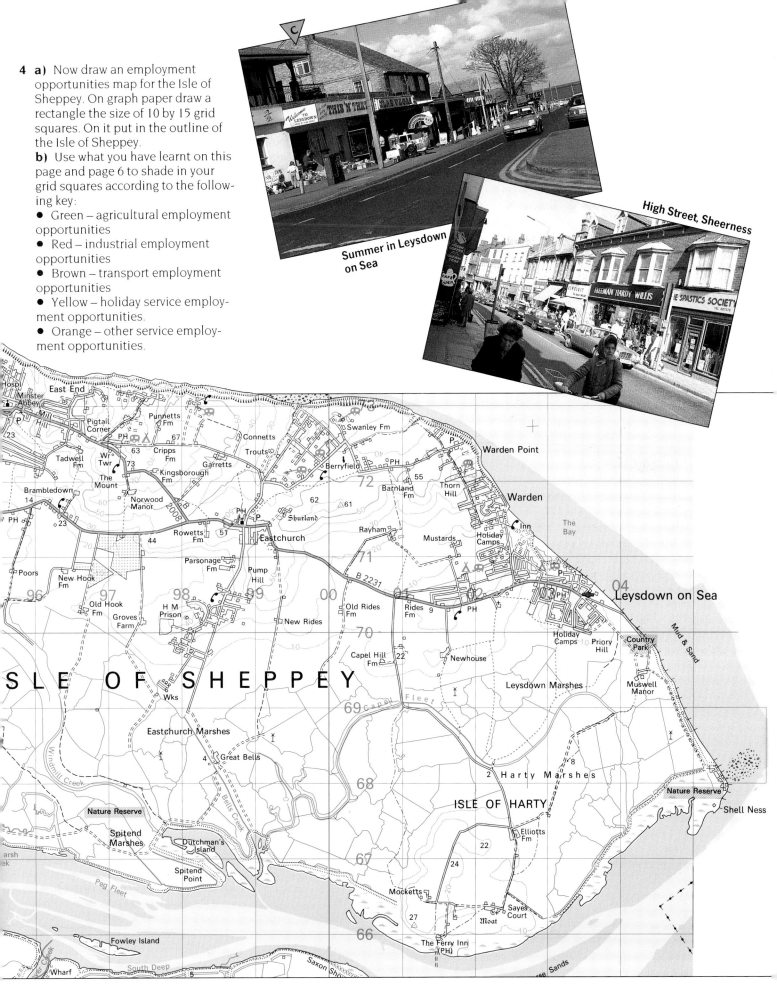

Summer in Leysdown on Sea

High Street, Sheerness

ISLE OF SHEPPEY

Leysdown on Sea

ISLE OF HARTY

The importance of investment

Any local area offers some paid employment opportunities. But the chances of getting a paid job depend on where firms decide to invest. Companies invest capital to make a product (or provide a service) in order to make a profit. Different firms invest at different times in areas. Over the years these decisions provide job opportunities for people locally. Individuals compete for jobs in the local labour market. This page and page 9 examine employment trends on the Isle of Sheppey.

A

'Our class went to Sheppey to do some fieldwork. It was part of our GCSE coursework. I was interested to see what job opportunities there were for people. What choices of work did they have? I knew that firms invested capital and that this created jobs. My teacher told us that you could look at capital investment like waves washing over the area. Waves of capital washing over Sheppey created different job opportunities at different times.

During our stay on the island we visited some of the larger industrial firms to see what jobs they offered. From what we saw, many of them were foreign firms. They were investing in new technology and creating jobs.'

Joanne Roberts

1 Use Source A to describe the different job opportunities which have existed on the Isle of Sheppey over the past hundred and fifty years. Do this by completing an enlarged copy of the table below Source A.

Changing patterns of employment

Before 1900

In the seventeenth century the Admiralty invested in the naval dockyards. They were rebuilt in the nineteenth century. Workers came from miles around to make iron ships and steam engines. There was little employment for women. The town grew quickly from 1857 to 1861.

Around 1900

Some private capital was invested in industries, particularly at Queenborough. The Sheppey Glue and Chemical Works was set up in 1888 and still exists today as Sheppey Fertilisers. There is pottery making and a bottle works. Holidaymakers were attracted to Sheerness. A light railway was built from Queenborough to Leysdown.

1960

The Admiralty Dockyards were closed. This put 700 dockyard workers out of work. Even today 7.6% of Sheerness people are unemployed, whereas the average unemployment rate in the South-East of England is 5.5%.

Since 1960

Later, Sheerness deep-water port, cross-Channel ferry and docks were developed. Since 1975 it has been one of the main ports for importing Japanese cars. Port activities employ 380 people.

Private industry invested in the island. It was attracted by government grants, lots of cheap land, and low-cost labour. Canadian, Japanese, Italian, American and German investments have all brought jobs to the area. Half of the main industrial employment is controlled from outside the UK.

School leavers don't have many employment opportunities. There are few service industries. Married women compete for semi-skilled factory work, more and more on a part-time basis. The holiday industry is declining.

A chronological summary of jobs on Sheppey

Date	Name of industry	Source of capital (public, private, foreign)	Type and number of jobs created
Before 1900			
Around 1900			
1960			
Since 1960			

B

The Toyota car factory at Queenborough

An increase in foreign firms?

2 What evidence is there in Source A and Source B that foreign investment is becoming important in providing employment?

The Sheerness steel company

The Sheerness steel plant began production in 1972 on the old army playing fields. Today, it employs 800. It uses scrap metal from London. Car bodies are crushed at the fragmentation plant nearby. Metal billets are cast to produce reinforcing bars and rods and steel bars for general engineering. Half a million tonnes of steel are produced each year. This is a high yield, low cost, high quality process.

The products are sold in South East England and the firm looks to a future market when the Channel Tunnel is built. They increasingly export to Algeria, France, Iran, the Soviet Union, Belgium, Germany, Nigeria, Sweden, Dubai, Holland, Romania and Switzerland.

The plant is part of Co. Steel, Inc., a privately owned Canadian steelmaker. Their turnover in the UK is £57 million each year. Planning and policy decisions are made in Canada. Day-to-day control is in the hands of each plant.

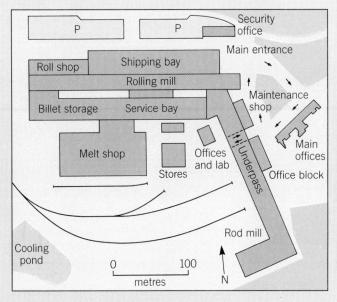

An aerial view of the plant

Inside the plant

Job opportunities

3 **a)** Study Source C. Use the layout plan to identify the buildings shown in the aerial photograph.
   b) Draw a flow diagram to show the processes involved from raw material to finished product.
   c) Say which products are sold and where they are sold.
4 **a)** Who owns the Sheerness steel plant?
   b) Who makes the major decisions affecting the whole company?
   c) Where are these decisions made?

Job opportunities
5 **a)** On your flow diagram indicate the employment opportunities you think exist.
   b) Why do you think that fewer than 11% of the workforce in this plant are women?

KLIPPON ELECTRICAL
* Located in Sheerness
* Makes electrical and electronic goods (terminals, enclosures etc.)
* Came in 1959 and has expanded since (£1·4 million)
* Employs 400 in the UK; 30% of production exported
* Member of the Weidmiller group of companies (21 companies in 15 different countries)
* Turnover £32 million

6 Other students in Joanne's group visited another large firm, Klippon Electrical. Their findings are shown in Source D. What similarities and differences are there between Klippon Electrical and the Sheerness steel plant?

Local investigation
7 Using your local area show how different investments of capital have affected employment opportunities in your community. Visit a local firm so that you can write a case study like Joanne's.

WHAT AFFECTS EMPLOYMENT OPPORTUNITIES?

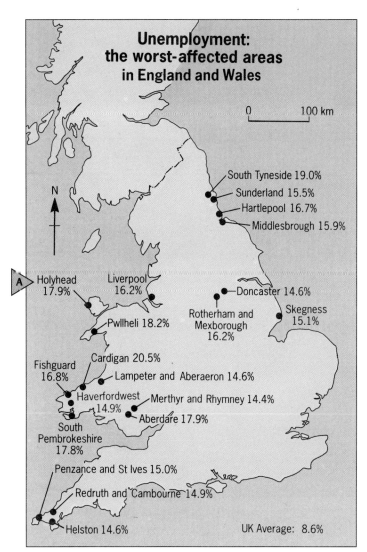

Unemployment: the worst-affected areas in England and Wales

0 _____ 100 km

N

South Tyneside 19.0%
Sunderland 15.5%
Hartlepool 16.7%
Middlesbrough 15.9%

A

Holyhead 17.9%
Liverpool 16.2%
Doncaster 14.6%
Pwllheli 18.2%
Rotherham and Mexborough 16.2%
Skegness 15.1%
Cardigan 20.5%
Fishguard 16.8%
Lampeter and Aberaeron 14.6%
Haverfordwest 14.9%
Merthyr and Rhymney 14.4%
South Pembrokeshire 17.8%
Aberdare 17.9%
Penzance and St Ives 15.0%
Redruth and Cambourne 14.9%
Helston 14.6%

UK Average: 8.6%

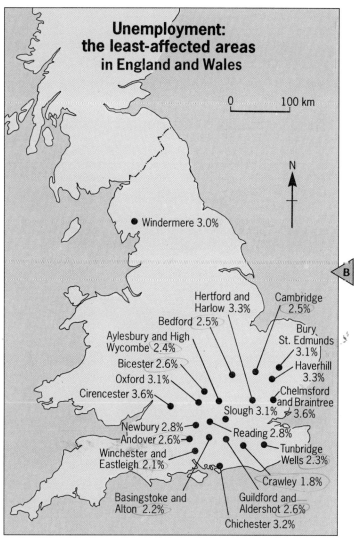

Unemployment: the least-affected areas in England and Wales

0 _____ 100 km

N

Windermere 3.0%

B

Hertford and Harlow 3.3%
Cambridge 2.5%
Bedford 2.5%
Bury St. Edmunds 3.1%
Aylesbury and High Wycombe 2.4%
Bicester 2.6%
Haverhill 3.3%
Oxford 3.1%
Cirencester 3.6%
Chelmsford and Braintree 3.6%
Slough 3.1%
Newbury 2.8%
Reading 2.8%
Andover 2.6%
Winchester and Eastleigh 2.1%
Tunbridge Wells 2.3%
Crawley 1.8%
Basingstoke and Alton 2.2%
Guildford and Aldershot 2.6%
Chichester 3.2%

In the Isle of Sheppey capital has been withdrawn, resulting in job losses. But capital has also been invested and this has created jobs. The same process has occurred to a greater or lesser extent in other areas. Some places have many job opportunities; others have few. Your chances of getting paid employment depend a great deal on where you live.

Regional influences

1 a) Look at Source A. List the ten worst places for job opportunities in rank order.
b) On a traced copy of Source A, draw lines (ISOPLETHS) to link those places having 15%, 17% and 19% unemployment.

c) Complete the following sentence from the list below: 'The unemployment rate in England and Wales is highest in . . .'

- Coastal areas
- Inland areas
- The South
- The North
- The West
- Places distant from London
- The East
- Places near to London

Where are the best employment prospects?

2 a) From Source B list the ten best places for job opportunities, starting with the top one.

b) On a traced copy of Source B, draw isopleths to show those places with 2% and 3% unemployment.
c) Complete the following sentence from the list below question 1(c): 'Places having the lowest unemployment rate in England and Wales are in . . .'

3 Look again at Source A. In groups, share your general knowledge to try to explain why the places shown have such high unemployment rates. Refer to text books to find out how people in these places earn their living.

4 What is the unemployment rate where you live? Suggest reasons for this situation.

Who is most likely to find a job?

5 Imagine a firm has decided to invest in an area and therefore create job opportunities. Some people still may not be able to gain employment. In groups discuss how each of the factors shown in Source C might help or limit someone's chances of getting a job.

6 Look at Source D, which comes from a government publication.
 a) What work is being done and by whom?
 b) Use Source E to judge whether the caption to Source D is correct.

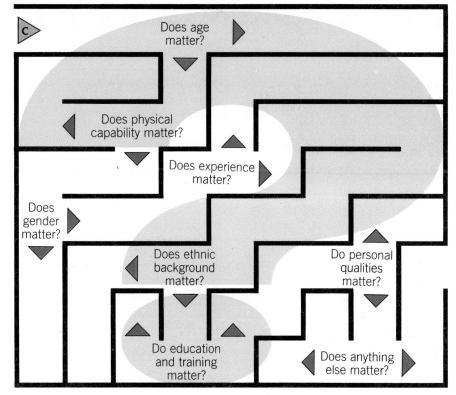

On the buses: people from ethnic minorities are stongly represented in the transport industry

7 **a)** In groups of four study Source E to investigate the jobs that different people do. One person should look at the figures for white male employment, another at those for white female employment, a third at the ethnic minority male employment and the fourth at the ethnic minority female employment.

b) Present your data individually in the form of a pie-chart and a table ranking employment by type of industry from one to ten.
c) Display your data. Discuss the differences between male and female employment and white and ethnic minority employment. How great are these differences?

E

Employment by industry and ethnic origin 1984–86 (thousands)

Standard industrial classification (type of industry)	Males				Females			
	White	%	Ethnic minorities	%	White	%	Ethnic minorities	%
All industries	12,911	100	493	100	9,414	100	325	100
Agriculture, forestry, fishing	415	3	—	—	114	1	—	—
Energy and water supply	560	4	—	—	91	1	—	—
Extraction of minerals	593	5	15	3	173	2	—	—
Metal goods, engineering and vehicles	1,914	15	79	16	494	5	24	7
Other manufacturing industries	1,369	11	71	14	899	10	48	15
Construction	1,505	12	26	5	151	2	—	—
Distribution, hotel and catering	2,017	16	131	27	2,435	26	78	24
Transport and communication	1,072	8	57	12	268	3	14	4
Banking, finance, etc	1,095	8	30	6	963	10	24	7
Other services including:	2,322	18	84	17	3,781	40	140	43
Education	527	4	12	3	1,049	11	19	6
Medical/health/vet services	272	2	25	5	978	10	55	17

Employment Gazette (adapted), March 1988

11

Some people work by growing things or extracting minerals from the ground. Others make products to sell, or earn their living through building. Many people provide services for others, such as in banks or hospitals. The UK government collects figures about the type of work people do in what it calls the *Standard Industrial Classification* (SIC). These figures are calculated by civil servants who use CENSUSES. There are around 21 million people in the UK who are in formal employment.

1 Using Source E on page 11, copy and fill in Source A to show the *total* numbers employed in each Standard Industrial Classification group. Calculate the percentage for each group.

These types of jobs are often grouped into sectors of the economy. The PRIMARY sector includes those people working in agriculture, forestry and fishing. The SECONDARY sector includes those working in jobs making goods. The TERTIARY sector consists of people in jobs which provide services to other people and to industries.

2 Complete Source A by ticking the sector you think each Standard Industrial Classification group belongs to.

3 Use Source B to work out the percentage of people employed in the following: agriculture, services, construction and mining, manufacturing. How have these percentages changed since 1946?

4 What types of work are not recorded by the Standard Industrial Classification? (Think about the different varieties of work you have studied in this Unit.)

▽ A

Sectors of industry

SIC number	Standard Industrial Classification group	Total number	Percentage	P	S	T
0	Agriculture, forestry, fishing					
1	Energy and water supply					
2	Extraction of minerals					
3	Metal goods, engineering and vehicles					
4	Other manufacturing industries					
5	Construction					
6	Hotels and catering					
7	Transport and communication					
8	Banking, finance etc.					
9	Other services					
	Total					

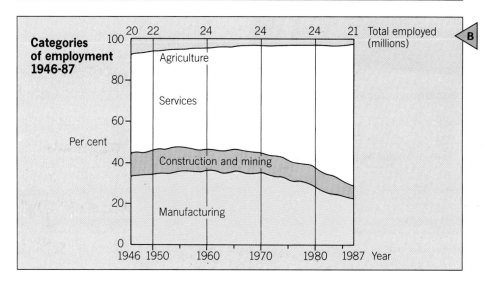

Categories of employment 1946-87

Per cent. Agriculture, Services, Construction and mining, Manufacturing. Years 1946, 1950, 1960, 1970, 1980, 1987. Total employed (millions): 20, 22, 24, 24, 24, 21.

▷ B

The structure of this book: study questions

This book is in two parts. The first is about work and employment. The Units investigate employment opportunities in different industries as the contents page shows.

As you study these Units you should have three main questions in mind:
● What work and employment is done where?
● What processes have produced this pattern?
● Who gains, who loses?

The second part of this book is about CHANGE, PROGRESS, and DEVELOPMENT. It looks at the way three countries (The Gambia, South Korea, and Nicaragua, in different continents) have taken different paths to development.

As you study these Units you should have three main questions in mind:
● What is development?
● What processes bring about this development?
● Who gains, who loses?

At the end of each Unit you are asked to follow up the ideas raised in earlier pages in assignments, investigations and decision-making exercises.

High Street, Lewes, Sussex

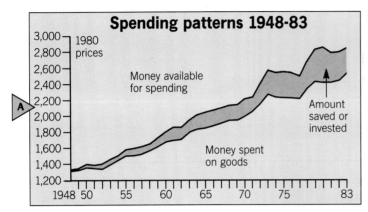

Spending patterns 1948-83

1980 prices

Money available for spending

Amount saved or invested

Money spent on goods

3,000
2,800
2,600
2,400
2,200
2,000
1,800
1,600
1,400
1,200

1948 50　55　60　65　70　75　83

Year	A How much money each person has	B How much money each person spends	Spending as % of income $\left(\frac{B}{A} \times 100\right)$
1950			
1970			
1980			
1983			

Service industries

In Unit 1, we learned that jobs have been growing in the tertiary sector of industry in the UK. The photograph on page 13 shows some of the service industries which have been growing most rapidly during the past 20 years or so. The growth has happened because of changes in our lifestyles – in the money we have, how we spend it and in our expectations. These changes have caused job losses, but they have also led to new opportunities. This Unit looks at:

● who is creating the jobs.
● why these jobs are being created.
● what sort of jobs they are.
● where job opportunities are growing.

1　Jobs in service industries can only grow if people have money to spend.
a) Using Source A, copy and complete the table next to it.
b) Describe briefly what your figures and Source A tell you. Say how they help to explain the growth of service industries.
2　Look at Source B. What sort of service industry jobs are we likely to create by the way we spend our money?
3　From the photograph on page 13, list the service industries shown and suggest which of these have been growing.

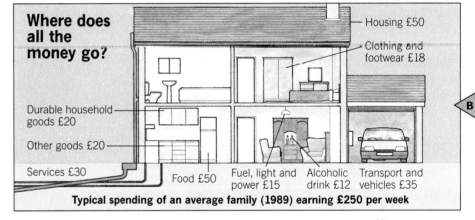

Where does all the money go?

Housing £50
Clothing and footwear £18
Durable household goods £20
Other goods £20
Services £30
Food £50
Fuel, light and power £15
Alcoholic drink £12
Transport and vehicles £35

Typical spending of an average family (1989) earning £250 per week

A 1930s Tesco store

Tesco: From stall to superstore

One growth area has been retailing (selling goods). Sir Jack Cohen, former President of Tesco, is part of a huge success story.

4　Look at Source C. With a partner, discuss:
a) the business risks Jack Cohen took.
b) the land, labour and capital he needed.
c) why you think his business enterprises have succeeded.

'I always wanted to be a businessman. In 1920, I invested £30 in buying groceries and sold them from a stall in the East End of London. Later, I worked in a number of markets, and started to sell to other market traders. By the Second World War in 1939, I had opened a chain of grocery shops – 113 to be exact. To raise the money, I founded a PRIVATE LIMITED COMPANY and people invested their money in it by buying shares. This meant I had less choice in what I did, but I needed the capital.'

'When the war ended in 1945, I was sure economic conditions would improve. People in the UK were likely to earn more and to spend their money on better food, clothes and so on. I had to take risks if I was to benefit and make profits for my shareholders. So, I took on partners, raised more money by selling shares and invested. I had to gamble on forecasting what was going to happen and get into the market first.'

Sir Jack Cohen

Re-organisation

Between 1971 and 1984 the total number of shops in the UK fell from 471,000 to 342,000. There has been a 'retail revolution' which has transformed our high streets. Tesco is a successful retail organisation. It satisfies consumer demands. It has grown by taking over smaller shops. Tesco has been successful by RATIONALISATION. By changing the location, number and size of its stores, the company affected job opportunities.

5 a) Using Source D, draw a graph to show how Tesco has developed since 1947. Plot the total number of stores, the number of self-service supermarkets and the number of superstores.
b) Add notes to your graph to show significant events in Tesco's development.
c) On a second graph show how employment has changed at Tesco.
d) Using your two graphs and Source D, compare changes in sales areas, number of stores and number of employees. Do there seem to be any connections between any of these statistics?

6 Using your knowledge about Tesco, try to explain the fall in the number of shops in the UK between 1971 and 1984.

Jobs

Tesco is investing £500 million in new developments. It is building new stores which will provide 10,000 new jobs. The new Tesco superstore at Leicester Road, Rugby, is one of these stores.

7 Before 1988, many Tesco stores were in locations similar to that shown in Source E. Describe this location. What were some of the advantages and disadvantages of situating a store there?

8 a) Look at the photo in Source E. Does the new store look as though it will appeal to shoppers? Give reasons.
b) How many jobs have been created by this development?
c) Who benefits most from these new jobs?
d) What advantages does the new location have?

Tesco over forty years

Year	The Company	Total no. of stores	Self-service supermarkets	Superstores	Employees
1947	Tesco became a public limited company	113	1		
1949	Company grows by buying up				
1950	smaller retail groups		20		
1955		120	100		1,500
1959		380			
1964		477	194		
1967		600			
1968	First superstore opened beginning the superstore revolution. Covered 2,323 square metres of selling space. Sold food and other goods.	880	292	1	
1970	Trading stamps introduced. Some			53	
1983	smaller stores sold.	500		80	40,000
1985				100	
1987		343		117	45,750
1988		379			50,192

Average sales area: 1975 – 550m²; 1980 – 975m²; 1985 – 1,600m²

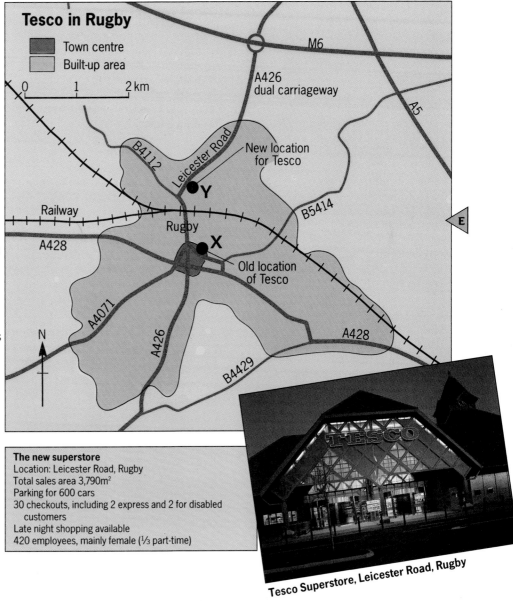

Tesco in Rugby

■ Town centre
■ Built-up area

0   1   2 km

M6
A426 dual carriageway
A5
B4112
Leicester Road
New location for Tesco
Y
Railway
Rugby
A428
X
B5414
Old location of Tesco
N
A4071
A426
A428
B4429

The new superstore
Location: Leicester Road, Rugby
Total sales area 3,790m²
Parking for 600 cars
30 checkouts, including 2 express and 2 for disabled customers
Late night shopping available
420 employees, mainly female (⅓ part-time)

Tesco Superstore, Leicester Road, Rugby

MONEY, JOBS AND HOMES

On pages 14 and 15 we saw that, in the last 20 years, many people have had more money to spend or to save. By saving or investing, people are helping to create jobs – in banks, investment companies, insurance companies and building societies.

As well as being places for saving people's money, the main purpose of banks and building societies is to invest or lend that money at interest. In all, 1.3 million people work in the insurance, banking and financial sector of industry in the UK.

How can saving create Jobs?

1 Look at Source A. How many jobs have been created in building societies since 1970?
2 a) What proportion of building society jobs were full-time and what proportion part-time in 1970, 1980 and 1988?
   b) Can you suggest reasons for the changes?
3 Draw *one* graph from Source A to show how jobs have grown from 1970 to 1988. Remember to select the type of graph which will tell you most about the figures.
4 a) Study Source B. Imagine you want to buy a house. Explain how you would go about getting a mortgage.
   b) How do building societies get money to help people with mortgages?

The process of saving, lending and borrowing

This process creates office jobs directly in local and national offices servicing customers

| Investors choose to invest capital in a building society | UK building societies have 160 million of assets | The customer takes out a mortgage. In the UK 62% of people own their own home |

Investment

Interest

A borrower is loaned money so that he/she can buy a house

Mortgage loan for house

Pays back capital and interest (15%)

B

Local investigation

There are 130 building societies in the UK, ranging from household names like the Halifax, Abbey National, Nationwide Anglia, and the Alliance and Leicester, to smaller ones like the Rugby and Hinckley or Shepshed Building Society.

5 Find out which building societies have branches in your area:
   a) For your nearest three towns, draw a table like the one on the right. Rank the towns in order of population.
   b) Using the Yellow Pages, list the building societies in your area.
   c) Work out the number of branches for each town. Complete the total.

d) Assume that there are eleven people employed in each branch. How many jobs are there in building societies in each town?
6 Draw a scatter graph and map to see whether there is a connection between the population of a town and the number of people working in building societies. Are there more branches and a greater variety of societies in the larger towns?
7 What other information about the population would you need to know to explain the distribution of these branches?

Staff employed in building societies 1970–88			
Year	Total staff	Full-time	Part-time
1970	25,000	24,000	1,000
1972	29,000	28,000	1,000
1974	33,000	31,000	2,000
1976	38,000	35,000	3,000
1978	45,000	41,000	4,000
1980	52,000	46,000	6,000
1982	58,000	49,000	9,000
1984	63,000	52,000	11,000
1986	69,000	56,000	13,000
1988	63,910	47,684	16,226

A

The distribution of building society branches			
Town	Leicester	Hinckley	Loughborough
Population	272,000	55,000	48,000
Abbey National	2	0	1
Bradford and Bingley	1	0	1
Total number of branches	59	12	14
Total number of jobs	649	132	154

From June 1989, the Abbey National ceased to operate as a building society.

Does bigger mean better?

Building societies in the UK have been changing rapidly. As in so many other industries a small number of very large companies now dominates. This has been caused by a process of mergers and TAKEOVERS. Consider the examples of Mr Jones and Mrs Smith, of Margate in Kent. In 1950, they both invested some savings in a local company – the Isle of Thanet Building Society. Source C shows what has happened to their investment.

8 a) Use Source C to make a diary of the merger and takeover events which led to the situation by 1987.
b) What percentage of all building society assets did Nationwide Anglia hold in 1987?
c) What difference did developments in 1987 make to its structure? (Think of size and ranking with other building societies.)
9 Look at Source D. In pairs:
a) List the points that Mr Jones and Mrs Smith make.
b) Use the information on this page to provide evidence which supports each of their opinions.
c) Whose opinion do you think is nearer the truth?

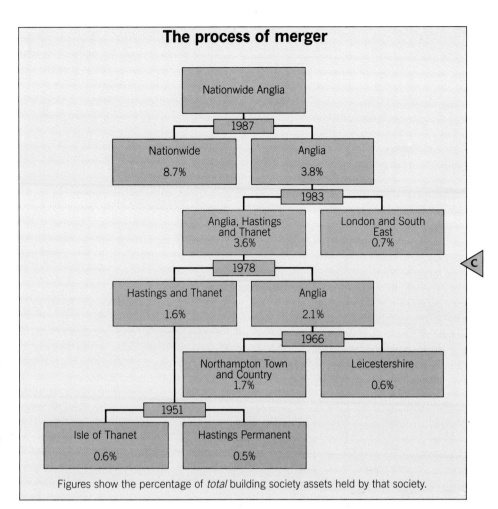

The process of merger

Figures show the percentage of *total* building society assets held by that society.

C

Building societies 1970–88		
Year	Number of building societies	Total number of branches
1970	481	2016
1972	456	2522
1974	416	3099
1976	364	3696
1978	316	4595
1980	273	5684
1982	227	6480
1984	190	6816
1986	151	6954
1988	130	6915

Building societies: the distribution of assets		
Location of head office	Percentage of societies	Percentage of total assets
Yorkshire and Humberside	8	36.2
Greater London	15	42.6
Midlands	22	7.7
South East (excluding Greater London)	21	3.0
South West	9	6.1
North and North West	14	3.0
East Anglia	3	0.5
Wales	3	0.4
Scotland	2	0.3
Northern Ireland	2	0.1

D

◄ **Mr Jones's view**

'I've saved with the Thanet for years and watched it change into the Anglia and then the Nationwide Anglia. But I'm worried about what has happened to building societies over my lifetime. They've got bigger and there are fewer of them. This means less choice for both the savers and the borrowers. There must be fewer jobs. As building societies become bigger, they become less efficient and less friendly to customers. What also worries me is that assets get concentrated into the four big powerful building societies. That centre of power is likely to be in London.'

Mrs Smith's view ►

'I don't agree. Money makes money. The bigger the building society, the better it can use its assets. This gives higher interest to investors. People have more choice, not less. Look at your local High Street. With so many branches, there must be more jobs. Big building societies can afford computers, word processors and all the modern technology. This makes them more efficient. You have only to look at the names of the big building societies to know that mergers and the concentration of power benefits other areas apart from London.'

10 Suppose these trends continue to the year 2000. What do you think might happen to:
a) the number of building societies?
b) the number of branches?
c) The distribution of assets (capital and property)?
d) What implications do these factors have for the number and distribution of jobs?

Interior of an accountant's office in London

Consumers buy goods in shops like Tesco. People save in and borrow money from places like the Nationwide Anglia. All this creates jobs in retailing and in building societies. Such jobs are examples of CONSUMER SERVICES. Other firms produce goods. They employ large firms of accountants and solicitors to help them. Such firms are examples of PRODUCER SERVICES. Read on to find out how these producer services achieve their efficiency.

Efficiency and the office

1 Source A shows work in an accountant's office. In pairs answer the following questions:
   a) How many people are working in the office? What is their sex and approximate age?
   b) What work do the people seem to be doing? What equipment are they using?
   c) What sort of qualifications and personal qualities do you think you would need to work in this office?
   d) Do the working conditions seem good?
   e) Where might you find this office?
2 Now use your findings to write a paragraph describing the main characteristics of the work, the people employed and the qualities of the working environment in Source A.

New technology

3 **a)** The modern office uses a great deal of electronic equipment. Read Source B and on a copy of the diagram, add information about the equipment and activities now found in an office.
   b) How might this modern technology increase efficiency?
   c) What effect has it had on jobs?
4 Do we really need to go out to work at all? The office of the future could be in people's homes.
   a) Explain why this might happen.
   b) Draw a diagram to show how an office at home might be best planned.

The electronic office

External data bank		Work stations		
	Central processing unit	Local area network	Electronic mail	
Link to external computer				

Shops and Offices, M. Bateman (John Murray)

Advances in computer technology have created the possibility of a totally electronic office. Instead of sitting at an ordinary desk, the individual office worker has a work station – an electronic desk top. At this he/she receives information which can be processed or be used to make decisions. As the workers are linked to other work stations, they can pass information amongst themselves. Messages can be received or sent by the electronic mail system. The link with the central processing unit enables workers to carry out complex calculations or use the word processor equipment. Links to external data banks such as Prestel enable sources of financial information to be accessed (obtained). There are also links to external computers to access information from other branches of the firm elsewhere in the country.

New equipment has led to:

● higher productivity
● fewer skilled professionals
● division of the workforce into highly skilled professionals and support staff

Financial Times; firm directories

C ▷ The big ten: the ten largest accountancy firms in the UK

Firm (1986)	Fee income (£ million)	Number of offices	Total staff
Coopers and Lybrand	119.4	37	4704
Peat Marwick Mitchell & Co	114.4	42	4728
Price Waterhouse & Co	108.9	20	3706
Deloitte Haskins and Sells	99.3	28	4141
Ernst and Whinney	82.9	23	3544
Touche Ross and Co	76.5	22	2807
Arthur Young	75.0	23	3544
Arthur Anderson and Co	67.1	16	2181
Grant Thornton	58.0	55	3066
KMG Thomson McLintock	52.5	22	2412

All the firms shown above have expanded overseas and have become international accountancy firms.

D ▷ Where the jobs are in Price Waterhouse

Office	Population of town	Number of jobs (1966)	Number of jobs (1986)
London	6,756,000	652	2056
Liverpool	492,000	22	71
Newcastle/Middlesbrough	1,140,000	891	200
Leeds	711,000	38	178
Cardiff	279,000	12	44
Manchester	451,000	60	180
Birmingham	1,008,000	166	304
Glasgow	744,000	29	58
Bristol	394,000	91	130
Nottingham	279,000	121	127
Leicester	283,000	—	66
Southampton	203,000	—	97
Edinburgh	440,000	—	42
Windsor	133,000	—	134
Total		2082	3687

Price Waterhouse & Co

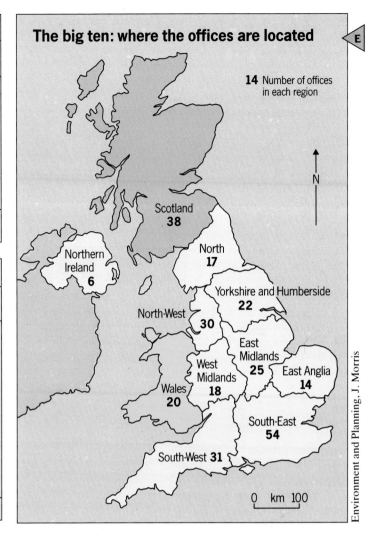

The big ten: where the offices are located   E

14 Number of offices in each region

N

Scotland **38**

Northern Ireland **6**

North **17**

Yorkshire and Humberside **22**

North-West **30**

East Midlands **25**

West Midlands **18**

East Anglia **14**

Wales **20**

South-East **54**

South-West **31**

0   km   100

Environment and Planning, J. Morris

Price Waterhouse

Source A on page 18 is of Price Waterhouse, a major accountancy firm. Price Waterhouse makes money by checking the accounts of large firms and by dealing with tax returns. It also offers help to the managers of other firms. Such services are known as management consultancy. The firm might, for example, show a manager how to computerise his or her business. Price Waterhouse also deals with the assets of bankrupt firms.

Efficient accountancy firms like Price Waterhouse locate in the towns and regions where most business is generated.

5 Use Source C and the information on this page to answer the following questions:
  a) How many offices does Price Waterhouse have?
  b) What is the average number of people per office?
  c) What does Price Waterhouse do to make its money?
  d) How has the firm added to its work in recent years?
  e) How does its fee income compare with its rivals?

6 Price Waterhouse has tried to become more efficient. It has opened offices in many UK towns and cities in order to gain new business. Using Source D and an atlas, draw a map of the UK to show the location of Price Waterhouse offices.

7 The larger the town, the more business will be generated. This should open up more job opportunities for Price Waterhouse. Draw a scatter-graph to test this idea. Plot the numbers employed on the vertical axis and the size of the town on the horizontal axis.

The move from London

8 Many other accountancy firms have opened offices away from London. Look at Source E.
  a) Present the data shown in Source E as a choropleth map.
  b) Suggest some reasons which may help to explain this distribution of offices. You may think, for example, that the number of accountancy offices increases with the size of population, or the amount of business activity.
  c) Test your ideas. You can collect information from the latest edition of *Regional Trends*, published by HMSO and found in your local library.

Inside the Leicester Royal Infirmary

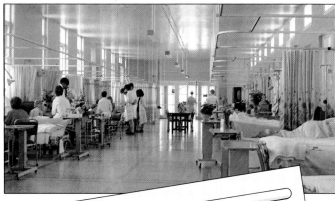

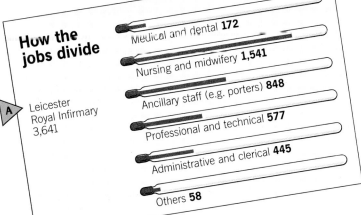

How the jobs divide

Leicester Royal Infirmary 3,641

- Medical and dental **172**
- Nursing and midwifery **1,541**
- Ancillary staff (e.g. porters) **848**
- Professional and technical **577**
- Administrative and clerical **445**
- Others **58**

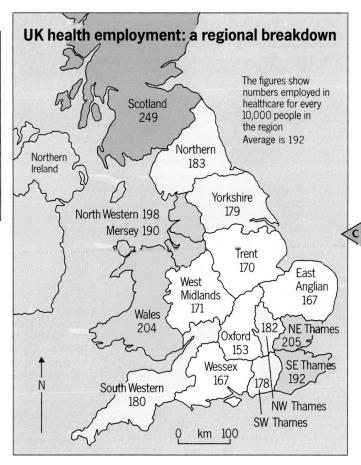

UK health employment: a regional breakdown

The figures show numbers employed in healthcare for every 10,000 people in the region
Average is 192

- Scotland 249
- Northern Ireland
- Northern 183
- North Western 198
- Mersey 190
- Yorkshire 179
- Trent 170
- West Midlands 171
- Wales 204
- East Anglian 167
- Oxford 153
- Wessex 167
- 182 NE Thames 205
- SE Thames 192
- 178 NW Thames
- SW Thames
- South Western 180

N

0 km 100

C

The National Health Service

In the UK the National Health Service exists to serve a population of 56 million. The NHS began in 1948. The service was intended to meet all recognised medical needs and conditions, acute and chronic. It was to be free to all UK residents and funded from general taxation. There was to be professional independence for the medical groups in the service.

B

The NHS was set up by the Labour party, although today all political parties recognise the importance of providing health care in this way. But there are disagreements between political parties over the amount of money to be spent and how it should be spent and over whether private hospitals should be encouraged. The amount spent on the NHS makes up 13% of total public expenditure, compared with 12% on defence, 29% on social security and 12% on education.

Health employment

1952 – 641,000	1973 – 1,105,000
1956 – 701,000	1975 – 1,220,000
1960 – 761,000	1978 – 1,280,000
1966 – 931,000	1981 – 1,249,000
1971 – 1,036,000	1984 – 1,255,000

(Figures for N. Ireland not available)

The National Health Service

1 Look at Source A and work through the following:
   a) List the types of jobs being done.
   b) What other jobs are likely to exist in a hospital?
   c) Rank the jobs in order of importance. How can you judge 'importance'?

2 **a)** Now rank the jobs in Leicester Royal Infirmary in order of the numbers employed. What work might be involved in each of these jobs?
   b) Approximately two thirds of the jobs in Leicester Royal Infirmary are carried out by women. Which jobs do you think these might be?
   c) Which jobs might be part-time and which full-time?

3 The National Health Service is an example of a public service. Study Source B and answer the following questions:
   a) In what year was the National Health Service set up?
   b) Who set it up?
   c) What were (and remain) its aims?
   d) Is the National Health Service free?
   e) What percentage of total public expenditure goes on health care? How does this compare with other public expenditure?

4 **a)** Employment in health care has grown since 1948. Using Source B, draw a line graph to show this.
   b) By how much has employment grown? Has the increase been an even one?

The regional picture

5 Look at Source C. Draw a map of the UK to show the number of health workers per 1,000 of the population. Shade those areas which are above the UK average in one colour, and those below in another. Comment on what your map shows.

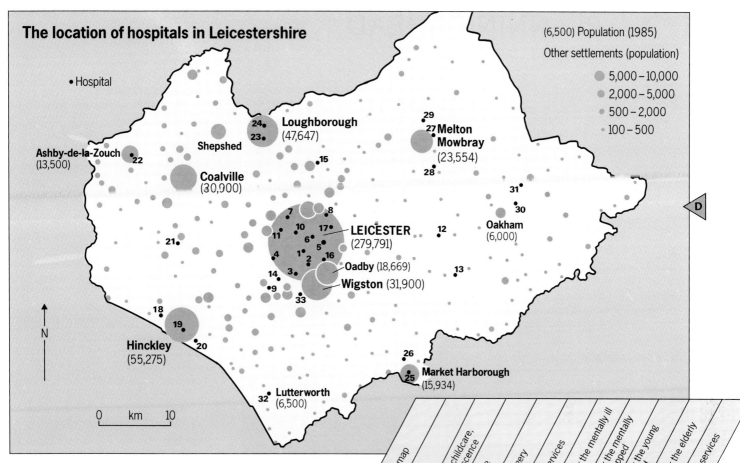

The location of hospitals in Leicestershire

• Hospital

(6,500) Population (1985)

Other settlements (population)

● 5,000 – 10,000
● 2,000 – 5,000
● 500 – 2,000
· 100 – 500

Loughborough (47,647)
Shepshed
Ashby-de-la-Zouch (13,500)
Coalville (30,900)
Melton Mowbray (23,554)
Oakham (6,000)
LEICESTER (279,791)
Oadby (18,669)
Wigston (31,900)
Hinckley (55,275)
Market Harborough (15,934)
Lutterworth (6,500)

N

0   km   10

Hospitals in Leicestershire

Leicestershire District Health Authority is part of the Trent Regional Health Authority. Like other health authorities it has to make decisions about the future of its health care facilities.

6 Source D shows the present hospital situation in Leicestershire. For each town named, calculate the number of hospitals.
7 Does there seem to be a connection between the number of hospitals and size of settlement?
8 What is the pattern of service provision within the hospitals in Leicestershire? Using Sources D and E, list the types of service available in each town.

Hospital provisions in Leicestershire — Name of hospital	Number on map	Total beds	Others; e.g. childcare, convalescence	GP medicine	General surgery	Maternity services	Services for the mentally ill	Services for the mentally handicapped	Services for the young disabled	Services for the elderly	Emergency services
Leicester Royal Inf.	1	845	40		174	244				137	290
Fielding Johnson	2	39			22	6					11
Westcoles	3	22					22				
Roundhills	4	30			—	30					
Leicester General	5	901	13		83	153	148		26	285	193
Groby Road	6	243								47	196
Glenfield Community	7	168								168	
The Towers	8	498					498				
Carlton Hayes	9	653					653				
Leicester Frith	10	296						296			
Gorse Hill	11	96						96			
Stretton Hall	12	126						126			
Kibworth Hall	13	33						33			
Glengate	14	54						54			
Mountsorrel	15	87						87			
Stoneygate	16	22						22			
Montrose Court	17	24						24			
Higham Grange	18	54	54								
Hinckley & District	19	37		12	9	8				8	
Sunnyside	20	38								38	
Bosworth Park	21	118								118	
Ashby	22	29		16		13					
Regent	23	73								73	
Loughborough General	24	73			26	8				5	34
Market Harborough	25	25		14		11					
St. Luke's	26	52								52	
Melton	27	47	10	26	4	3				4	
St. Mary's	28	106				21			9	76	
Framland	29	41								41	
Rutland Memorial	30	34		17	3	13				1	
Catmose Vale	31	42								42	
Fielding Palmer	32	15		15							
Blaby	33	20								20	

D

E

Decisions

Leicestershire District Health Authority has to take decisions about health care. It needs to plan the number of hospitals it wants to run and the services it aims to provide.

1 Imagine it is your responsibility to take health care decisions. Turn back to page 21 and look again at Sources D and E. In small groups, discuss how you would act in the following situations:

a) The plan is to close 15 hospitals between 1990 and the year 2000, as part of a rationalisation programme.

Which 15 hospitals would you close and why? Think about the services offered and the size and location of the hospitals.

b) The idea is to keep the facilities of the remaining hospitals roughly the same, but to expand two of them, one by 250 beds and the other by 50. Which two hospitals would you expand and why?

c) The plan is to open a new 600-bed hospital. Where would you locate it? Give reasons for your decision. Compare your proposals with another group.

d) Briefly summarise your three decisions.

Money and services

2 Think about how you will provide specific health services. From the list below, outline what you think should be provided and where this care should be centred.

- Health education and disease prevention
- Services for the mentally ill
- Services for the mentally handicapped
- Services for children
- Maternity services
- Acute hospital specialities – e.g. kidneys, limbs

Now present your proposals to the class.

3 Your plans will involve money. Imagine the Leicestershire Health Authority is planning to spend an additional £20 million between 1990 and the year 2000. Source B shows how much has recently been spent by the Leicestershire Health Authority. Where would you allocate the additional £20 million? Give reasons.

4 Health Authorities have been encouraged to increase their efficiency. Some suggestions for doing this are:
- To renegotiate existing contracts.
- To increase the number of patients dealt with.
- To give work such as cleaning and laundering to outside firms.

What effect do you think these proposals, if put into practice, will have on jobs within the National Health Service?

5 Your plans will involve additional workers. Look at Source C.

a) How many extra workers are needed?

b) How are they distributed amongst the services offered?

c) What problems might there be in obtaining these workers?

The Leicester Royal Infirmary, the largest hospital in Leicestershire

A

Leicestershire Health Authority: expenditure 1983–84

Description of spending	£ (million)	% of total expenditure
Basic acute (emergency etc.)	50	40.5
Ambulance	4	3.3
Regional specialities	10	7.6
Community care and illness prevention	12	9.8
Services for the elderly	11	8.9
Services for the younger disabled	0.5	0.4
Services for the mentally handicapped	7	5.4
Services for the mentally ill	16	12.5
Maternity services	10	7.6
Administration	5	4.0

B

Additional workers needed 1984–94

Acute	810
Community	90
Elderly	410
Maternity	30
Mental handicap	100
Mental illness	200
Physically disabled	30
Other	1

C

Jobs in private health care

Most people in the UK receive their health care in hospitals provided by the National Health Service. However, some choose to pay for private consultation, treatment and accommodation. This is paid for by taking out private medical insurance which can be done either by an individual or in a group scheme. Group insurance is usually arranged through employers.

6 Source D is taken from private health care publicity material. What advantages of private care are being emphasised?
7 **a)** Using Source E, write down the economic groups which use private health care the most and those which use it the least.
b) Why might private health care not be available to everyone in the UK?
8 Look at Source F. What does it show about the availability of private health care throughout the UK?

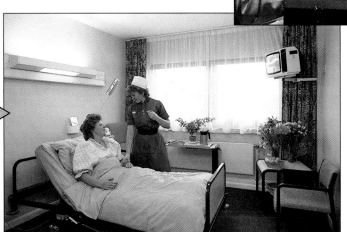

The above photographs are from advertisements for private health care. The three biggest groups providing health insurance are BUPA (British United Provident Association), P.P.P. (Private Patients Plan) and W.P.A. (Western Provident Association). There are 4.5 million people in the UK who have taken out private medical insurance. Some private patients are treated in National Health Service hospitals.

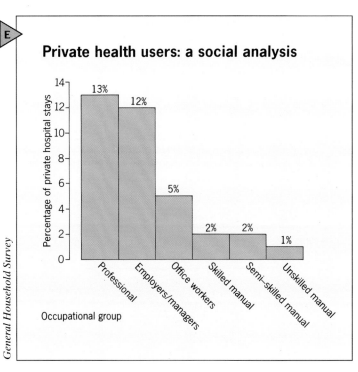

Private health users: a social analysis

General Household Survey

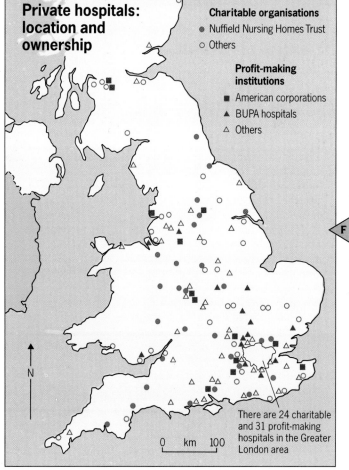

Private hospitals: location and ownership

There are 24 charitable and 31 profit-making hospitals in the Greater London area

SHOULD A PRIVATE HOSPITAL BE BUILT?

A
> We're here to discuss this proposal to build a new hospital. Should we go ahead with it? If so, where?

> We've got to be clear. We need to fill 50 to 60 beds to make it profitable. That's a large number. We need to draw on about 21,000 people in the catchment area. But this is a rich area. There are lots of people who have taken out private insurance to help them pay for private health care. If we advertise, we could persuade others as well.

> We must be careful. A lot of private hospitals have been built in the last ten years. I hope there will not be too many beds left empty for too long. We have to think about other things too – this report gives us more details.

A role-play exercise

1 Read Source A, in which the possibility of building a new hospital is being talked about by a private hospital company. Imagine you are directors of this company. Divide into groups of four. You are about to discuss whether or not to build the hospital. Each person has a role:
- One is a director talking about whether there is a demand for a hospital.
- Another director talks about the capital and finance needed.
- Another director gives information about labour and equipment.
- A fourth director is concerned about the site for the hospital.

a) Prepare what you will say at the meeting. (Use Source A and Source B to help you.)

b) Role-play the meeting.

2 **a)** Do you think the hospital will get the go-ahead? If so, where do you think it will be built?

b) Who might benefit and who might lose if the hospital is built?

c) What values lie behind the views your group put forward?

Report on new hospital proposal

Finance	• It costs £100,000 to provide one bed in a private hospital.
	• The company needs to interest local businesses so that they provide financial backing.
	• The company needs to persuade local firms to provide insurance shares for their workers.
	• Firms should be made aware of the tax allowances available to them if they pay medical insurance for their employees.
Labour and equipment	• The hospital will need up to 200 specialist consultants and surgeons.
	• Consultants working in the National Health Service can now earn up to 10% of their salary in private work.
	• Most of the specialist staff will also be involved with the NHS.
	• The hospital will need a lot of support staff.
	• The company can pay attractive wages and offer flexible working hours and good conditions.
	• There will be competition for workers from the NHS.
	• Specialist equipment such as radiology laboratories in NHS hospitals will be available to the company.
Location	• The ideal site would be in a quiet, secluded area.
	• Local councils are not in favour of building on GREEN BELT sites which make the best locations.
	• Local planners would rather see hospitals on old NHS sites near city centres than in rural areas.

B

RECREATION, TOURISM AND JOBS

Aerial view of Looe, Cornwall

The photograph on page 25 is of Looe in Cornwall. Many people go there on holiday. Its popularity as a holiday resort creates jobs in the leisure and tourist industry. There are 1.4 million people employed in the leisure industry in the UK. Leisure is one of the most rapidly growing sectors of industry in the country. In 1986, £11.1 billion was spent on UK tourism. Between 1975 and 1985 there was a 41% increase in hotel and catering jobs. Read on to find out more about how the jobs have been created and who has benefited.

A holiday resort

1 **a)** Mrs Foxton had definite reasons for wanting to set up her guest house in Looe. Using Source A, give her three main reasons.
   b) Briefly describe a guest house.
2 Using Source B, draw a sketch map of Looe. Add explanatory notes to your map to show:
   a) the natural attractions of Looe.
   b) the artifically created attractions of Looe as a holiday resort.

Why join the leisure industry?

3 Other hotel and guest house owners including the owner of the property in Source C were also asked why they set up their leisure business in Looe. Their responses are shown in Source D. Are Mrs Foxton's reasons typical of the other owners?
4 Source D also shows why other leisure industries came to Looe.
   a) From the information given, rank the economic reasons.
   b) Now rank the social reasons.
   c) Which reasons seem to be more important?

Mrs Foxton

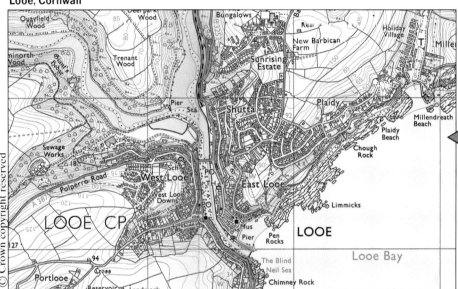

Looe, Cornwall

© Crown copyright reserved

I used to work in London before I bought the Glenavon Guest House in 1982 and came to live in Looe. I find it an attractive place. I like the small town – the sea, the coast and the houses seem to fit together. It's such a contrast to the hectic life in London. I was unhappy working for others and wanted to be my own boss.

The Leward Guest House, Looe

Why join the leisure industry?

Reasons given	Hotels and guesthouses	Self-catering accommodation	Restaurants, cafes and public houses	Shops	Total
Economic					
To be self-employed	1	1	3	4	9
Made redundant in previous job	1	1	1	2	5
To make more money	1	0	1	1	3
Return to previous employment	0	1	2	0	3
Total	3	3	7	7	20
Social					
To get out of the 'rat race'	0	2	1	0	3
To come to Looe or to Cornwall	6	2	1	5	14
Family or personal reasons	1	4	3	3	11
Semi or early retirement	5	2	1	0	8
Total	12	10	6	8	36
Other	4	6	3	4	17
Total	19	19	16	19	73

Who benefits from tourism?

5 Look at Source E. Complete a copy of the table to show where those who have set up leisure businesses in Looe have come from.

6 a) From Source F, write down *total* male and female employment in the leisure industry in Looe.
b) How many female workers are there for every male worker?
c) Is this pattern the same in each individual part of the leisure industry?

Seasonal difficulties

7 a) Using Source F, draw a bar graph to show *total* part-time and full-time employment in the leisure industry in Looe.
b) For every full-time job, how many part-time jobs are there?
c) Is this pattern the same throughout the year?

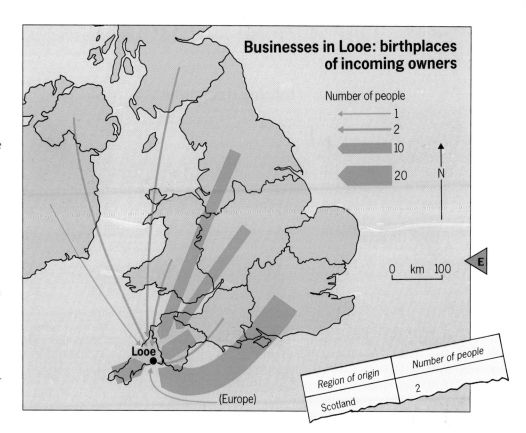

Businesses in Looe: birthplaces of incoming owners

Number of people
— 1
— 2
10
20

N

0   km   100

E

Region of origin	Number of people
Scotland	2

Looe: employment patterns in the leisure industry						
Employment breakdown	Hotels and guesthouses	Self-catering accommodation	Restaurants, cafes and public houses	Shops	Total	% of total
Total employed	92	188	105	64	449	100
Male	18	44	29	9	100	22
Female	74	144	76	55	349	78
Full-time	34	33	34	19	120	27
Part-time	58	155	71	45	329	73

Seasonal breakdown of employment			
Month	Full-time	Part-time	Total
June	150	400	550
July	175	395	570
August	155	405	560
September	155	395	550
October	75	175	225
November	65	90	155
December	60	90	150
January	60	85	145
February	70	80	150
March	75	85	160
April	100	200	300
May	130	335	465

F

LOCAL ECHO

Outside connections
A council survey shows many Londoners own leisure businesses in the town.

OCTOBER: the town closes for the winter

Leisure workforce dominated by women
'More effort is needed to bring jobs for men in the town,' says local councillor.

Lack of full-time jobs in Looe
Local councillor Jack Askew declares 'We are a town of part-time workers.'

G

8 From your findings, do you think the statements in Source G are justified?

9 a) Work with a partner. Using the information on this page and page 26, write a letter to the local newspaper stating why Looe should not rely too heavily on tourism.
b) Suggest two ways in which Looe could lengthen the tourist season.

Holiday decisions

Rebecca

I would like somewhere with reliable weather. I'm attracted to quiet places and would also like to explore the area's history and culture.

Paul

I'm the only one with a car, but I don't want to spend my holidays driving. I haven't been abroad before and I'd like to try some different foods.

Winston

I want to go somewhere warm and sunny. I don't mind where as long as I don't have to cook. I must say, I'm not very keen on flying.

Alice

I like active holidays with lots of water sports. I'd like to fly – it's something I've never done before. I haven't got a great deal of money to spend.

About six in every ten people in the UK take at least one holiday a year. Tourism has become a major industry. Many other countries have caught on to this and in 1987, for the first time, UK holiday-makers spent more money abroad than they did on holidays in their own country. Wherever you take your holidays, your decisions will affect job opportunities and economic development.

1 Source A shows a discussion between four students about where to go for a summer holiday. Having sorted through piles of brochures, they finally narrow the choice down to Brittany (France) or Turkey. They want to find a place they can all enjoy. In small groups list the preferences of each student.

2 From Source B, match up which area suits each student best.

3 Now decide which holiday you think the group should take.

4 What else would the group need to know to make a more informed choice?

5 In deciding where to go on holiday, the students used the information and services available. Make a list of the various people and the jobs which are done to help holiday-makers decide where to stay.

Camping in Brittany

This year, why not try a camping holiday in Brittany? The sites are completely up-to-date. There are showers, washing facilities, shops on site and play areas for children.

Brittany is warm in summer, with cooling sea breezes. There are good sandy beaches, safe for children and ideal for bathing and water sports. Sea food is plentiful and delicious. With the freedom of a camping holiday you can be as active or lazy as you want. You can visit prehistoric sites, picturesque fishing villages or just stay on the clean, sandy beaches.

Prices start from around £280 per person for a hired tent for two weeks.

A package holiday in Turkey

This year, take a carefree holiday in Turkey, gateway to the Middle East and Asia. The sun shines endlessly in summer. Book a package holiday, get on a plane at Gatwick or Luton and in hours you are in Turkey.

Hotels are up-to-date, many with their own swimming pools. Most are within walking distance of the sea, with good water sports facilities. The package deal includes breakfast and evening meal and starts at £340 per person for two weeks. Traditional Turkish food is served. At night you can walk along the quiet waterfront or in the wooded hills. But if you want local colour, you can sit in an open-air bar and watch traditional Turkish dancing and listen to Turkish music.

From Gatwick to Turkey

6 Suppose the four friends decide to go to Turkey. Their holiday now falls into two parts – travelling, and actually staying in Turkey. Each part of the holiday helps to provide jobs. Their flight is from Gatwick to Izmir. Using an atlas, draw a map to show Gatwick and Izmir, and the distance between them.

7 With the help of Source C, list the jobs which the students are helping to create by travelling to Izmir.

8 Source D shows some aspects of a holiday in Turkey. In groups, answer the following:

a) What jobs are being created by tourism?

b) Are they likely to be done by Turkish people?

c) What sort of person do you think will work in tourism in Turkey? (Think about age, gender, education and so on.)

d) Do you think tourism in Turkey creates similar employment problems to those in Looe (pages 26-7)?

Checking in at Gatwick airport

Aboard a Boeing 757

The risks of tourism

In many parts of the world, countries are using tourism to create jobs and wealth. But tourism brings risks as well as opportunities to make money.

9 In your group, discuss what might be the effect on jobs in the UK and Turkey of each of the following:

a) Europeans spend more on holidays.

b) Fashions in holidays change.

c) Another Mediterranean country invests heavily in promoting its own tourism industry.

d) Turkey suffers political troubles.

e) Turkey joins the EEC.

Tourism has opened up a whole new range of job opportunities

To many poorer and economically developing countries, tourism seems a great opportunity to create wealth. Often, these countries have many resources – sun, sea, sand, interesting cultures, buildings and so on – which will attract tourists. As a result, they use these resources and create jobs.

At first, all goes smoothly, but there are losses as well as gains. The effect on the environment and the people is enormous, as is shown in Source A. Much of the extra money may go to foreign tour companies, rather than to local people and the government. In Turkey, as in other countries, not everyone agrees with encouraging large-scale tourism.

Many remote areas in Turkey are being transformed into tourist centres

1 With a partner, read Source B.
   a) For each speaker, put forward his view of the effects of tourism under three headings: economic, social and environmental.

b) Use your headings to sum up the key differences of opinion between the two speakers.

c) What values and attitudes do you think lie behind each of these two viewpoints?

The good and the bad side

It isn't a question of *should*. Turkey *must* develop its tourist industry. There is not much else we can develop. We have the resources tourists want. We must make use of our attractions.

Local people need work. Tourism provides jobs in hotels. There are other jobs too, like selling crafts and driving taxis. And of course building the hotels and apartments provides a great deal of employment. We should build different types of accommodation. It is good that the government encourages local businesses. Many villas and hotels are family-run and that must be good for the country. The government is encouraging tourism in some of the more remote areas. We also get improved facilities like airports and harbours and this provides extra employment. We can all use these facilities.

We have to continue to develop, otherwise tourists will go elsewhere and our people will lose out. Our economy will then be even worse.

I don't know why the government encourages the tourist industry. How does it benefit local people? Some of the hotels and apartments are owned by foreigners. Jobs offered are menial, low paid and aren't even all year round.

People leave farming to take temporary jobs. Tourists don't want our food – they want imported frozen food which is no help to our farmers. Most of the hotels and villas are in one part of the country. There are few jobs in the villas. You are bound to get arguments and pressure on land if you have tourist developments in one place. Hotels take up space. Beaches I used to know are full of rich tourists, sunbathing and water skiing. Local people don't get to use the facilities. Turkey is a beautiful country – we must look after it. We can't rely on tourism. What if the tourists stop coming as in 1986 after the Chernobyl nuclear scare?

What about the welfare of the local people? We don't want to be exploited by others. We are a law-abiding people, but I worry that these changes might make the crime rate go up. We are a religious people and followers of Islam. We don't want to see naked bodies on our beaches. Let's keep our traditional values.

Turkey: tourists by country of origin (thousands)					
Country	1983	1984	1985	1986	1987
France	88	103	150	144	169
West Germany	175	242	300	388	524
Greece	139	179	213	211	174
Iran	36	175	354	—	—
Italy	58	66	75	88	102
Syria	99	94	54	—	—
United Kingdom	84	90	125	154	267
USA	189	213	196	79	131
Yugoslavia	60	180	366	366	343
Total (inc. others)	1,507	2,117	2,615	2,391	2,800
Total receipts from foreign travel (£ million)	n.a.	900	1,790	1,560	2,790

Central Bank

Employment breakdown by types of work	Males	Females
Agriculture	5,155,000	5,950,000
Mining and quarrying	130,000	1,000
Manufacturing	1,670,000	300,000
Construction	760,000	5,000
Trade, restaurants and hotels	1,034,000	50,000
Transport, storage and communications	510,000	30,000
Services	2,320,000	400,000
Others	130,000	40,000
Total employed	11,710,000	6,810,000

I.L.O., Year Book of Labour Statistics

Exports from Turkey (£ million)			
Type of product	1983	1984	1985
Agricultural	1,130	1,040	1,030
Fishing	12	12	13
Forestry	9	15	8
Mining and quarrying	115	146	149
Industrial	2,224	3,137	3,650
Total	3,490	4,350	4,850

Central Bank

Social and economic effects

Source B on page 30 contains few hard facts. The information on this page gives you some more evidence about the effects of tourism.

2 Look at 'Source C and answer the following questions:
   a) How rapidly is tourism growing?
   b) Do most of the tourists come from wealthy countries?
   c) How much money did tourism make in 1987?

3 Study Source D. Does the Turkish economy already have a broad base across a range of industries?

4 a) What proportion of jobs depended directly on the tourist industry?
   b) What proportion of jobs might have depended partly on it in 1980?
   c) In 1980, over 80% of women were employed in agriculture. Do you think they would welcome tourism or not? Why?

Is the whole of Turkey affected by tourism?

5 Does Source E suggest that tourism affects all regions of Turkey? If not, is this a good or a bad thing?

6 Does Source E and the rest of the information on this page give the impression that tourism benefits local people?

7 a) From your answers, and from Source B, give three reasons supporting tourism in Turkey and three rejecting it.
   b) What is your own view?

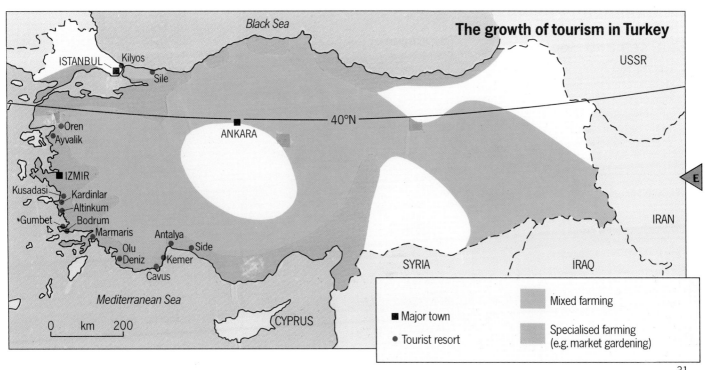

The growth of tourism in Turkey

Black Sea · ISTANBUL · Kilyos · Sile · Oren · Ayvalik · ANKARA · 40°N · USSR · IZMIR · Kusadasi · Kardinlar · Altinkum · Gumbet · Bodrum · Marmaris · Antalya · Side · Olu Deniz · Kemer · Cavus · Mediterranean Sea · 0 km 200 · CYPRUS · SYRIA · IRAQ · IRAN · E

■ Major town
● Tourist resort

Mixed farming
Specialised farming (e.g. market gardening)

Soviet holiday-makers relax at Sochi on the shores of the Black Sea

An interview with Fyodor Ivanovic

Q: Where do you come from?

FI: I work in Moscow. I'm an electrician in an engineering factory. I've come to Sochi for 24 days. I think it's a lovely place – nice climate, warm sea and attractive hills.

Q: Where are you staying?

FI: I'm at one of the sanatoria (health resorts) in the town. We Russians like health cures, sulphur treatments and mud baths, which we get at health resorts like this. Having a beach nearby is an added bonus.

Q: How did you get here?

FI: We're very lucky in this country. Most industrial workers are entitled to at least a fortnight's holiday. We pay social insurance. This gives us the opportunity to visit health resorts or rest homes. I'm a little different though – you could say I'm more privileged. My vacation has been mainly paid for by my trade union.

The holiday industry is a service sector industry. We have seen that it employs many people in countries like the UK and Turkey. This page and page 33 look at holidays in a communist country – the Soviet Union – and investigate how state-run holidays are organised.

Sun, sea and Sochi

1 a) The resort of Sochi has a great deal to offer the Soviet holiday-maker. Use Sources A and B to draw an annotated sketch showing the main natural and artificial environmental attractions.

b) Add further details from your atlas (for example, information about climate).

2 What does Source B tell you about the organisation of holidays in the Soviet Union? How does this differ from a UK holiday?

The growth of health resorts

3 a) Health resorts have been built in Sochi since the early 1900s. On a copy of Source C, work out the total number of jobs created by Sochi's health resorts between 1900 and 1975. (The first three columns have been done for you.)

b) Use your figures to draw a line graph to show the increase in jobs.

4 a) Many national and local events have affected the growth of health resorts and jobs. Using two different colours, one for national and the other for local events, add the following labels to your graph in the appropriate places:

Early 1900: First health resorts built in Sochi

1917 – Russian Revolution: all land owned by the State

1936 – first regional development plan for Sochi

1939–45 – 'Great Patriotic War'

1946 – airport built nearby

1960s – National Railway electrified

1966 – new regional development plan

Average working week USSR 1956 – 48 hours; average working week USSR since 1970 – 39 hours.

b) Suggest how these events have affected the building of health resorts and the creation of jobs.

Health resorts and jobs in Sochi

Year	1900–1910	1910–1920	1920–1930	1930–1940	1940–1950	1950–1960	1960–1970	1970–1975
Health resorts built	4	0	16	21	12	20	62	20
Number of jobs created	512	0	2048	2688	1536	2560	7963	2560
Cumulative number of jobs	512	512	2560					

Holidaying at Artek: morning line-up

A trip on a launch near Artek

D

The leisure industry: jobs and trends

Holiday types	Health resorts	Other resorts	Camps and lodges	Other tourist facilities	Children's camps
Managed by	Trade unions Central Council for Resort Management		Government agencies which finance them	Trade unions Central Council for Tourism	Trade unions
Number of institutions	2,345	1,170	5,446	954	10,000
Number using (millions per year)	4.5	5.2	2.6	16.6	6.0
Jobs provided – Zone 1 Zone 2 Zone 3 Zone 4	120,000 132,000 45,000 3,000	41,000 61,000 17,000 1,000	26,000 73,000 10,000 1,000	25,000 29,000 9,000 2,000	38,000 312,000 120,000 10,000
Total number of jobs	300,000 (100%)	120,000 (100%)	110,000 (100%)	65,000 (100%)	480,000 (100%)

E

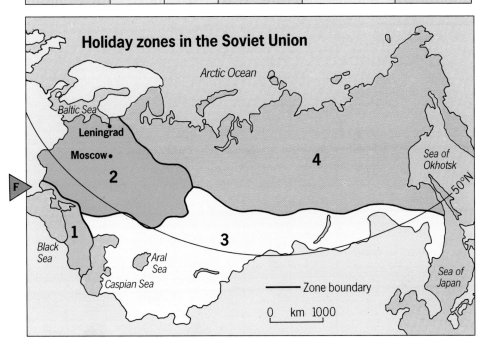

Holiday zones in the Soviet Union

Arctic Ocean

Baltic Sea

Leningrad

Moscow •

2

1

Black Sea

Aral Sea

Caspian Sea

3

4

Sea of Okhotsk

50°N

Sea of Japan

—— Zone boundary

0　km　1000

F

A choice of holidays

5 Holidays at health resorts are one popular type of recreation amongst several in the Soviet Union. Look at Source D. In groups discuss:
a) who is involved in the holiday.
b) how it seems to be organised.
c) what sort of place is shown.

6 The students shown in Source D were interviewed. They all valued the holiday they were on. Draw a cartoon which shows what they might think its advantages are.

7 a) Look at Source E. For each holiday type, draw a bar graph to show the number of institutions available. Next to this, draw another bar graph to show the numbers taking each holiday per year. Comment on what your graphs show.
b) Add details to your graphs of who organises and goes on each type of holiday.

Where are the holiday facilities?

8 a) Look at Source E. On a large copy of Source F, use the information from Source E to show the distribution of the recreation facilities of each zone of the Soviet Union. Use a shading method to show great or little representation.
b) Display your maps.

9 a) Using Source E, draw a map to show the number of jobs available in leisure in each zone. (Use proportional circles or other methods.)
b) Comment on what your map shows.
c) Use an atlas to suggest some reasons for the patterns your maps of leisure and jobs show.

10a) Look back over this page and page 32. Do you think the holidays described are attractive?
b) Would you like to take part in a state-organised holiday? Give reasons for your answer.

TOURIST BROCHURES: AN INVESTIGATION

Holiday photos

The travel industry employs people to advertise holidays. National tourist boards also advertise. The photos used affect the impression we have of places and can influence people's choice of holiday. By carefully studying photos in travel brochures we can get some idea of how advertising can give us a certain image of a place. For the exercise which follows you will need a holiday brochure.

1 Select one country in the brochure and make a large copy of Source B. Decide what information you think each picture is trying to put across.
2 Now study the illustration codes in Source B. Tick the box which you believe most applies to each picture. Some pictures will come into more than one category. For example, sunbathers on a palm-fringed beach would count as showing both re-creation and landscape. Give different weightings for different-size photos – the larger the photo, the greater its impact. Give four points to a double-page photo; three to a full-page photo; two to a half-page one and 1.5 to a quarter-page one. Award one point to any smaller photo. Mark your total scores in column X on your copy of Source B.
3 Now calculate the percentage that each code scores (i.e. each category score divided by the number of pages analysed).
4 Label one code the dominant or main image and another the secondary image.
5 Repeat the exercise for another country and compare the results.

Projecting images of abroad							
Picture codes	Picture 1 Weighted score	Picture 2 Weighted score	Picture 3 Weighted score	Column X Total score for brochure photos or one country	Percentage	Dominant image	Secondary image
Landscape							
Coastal (L/C)							
Mountain (L/M)							
Rural (L/R)							
Urban (L/U)							
Flora & fauna (L/FF)							
Culture							
History & Art (C/HA)							
Local people (C/LP)							
Local economy (C/LE)							
Recreation							
Good for participation (R/P)							
Good for observation (R/O)							
Services							
Picture to attract people (S/A) (open markets, shopping)							
Picture to reassure people (S/R) (comfortable rooms, restaurant)							

Hams Hall Power Station

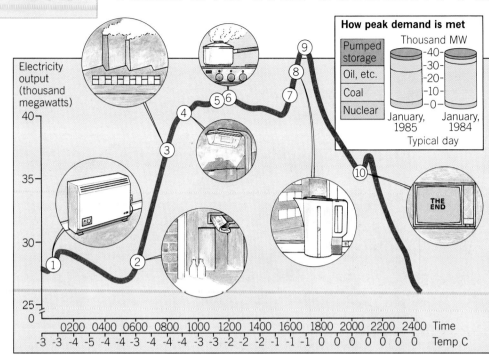

How peak demand is met

Electricity output (thousand megawatts)

Tuesday 8 January 1985: the toughest day in the life of the CEGB

1 Big switch-on of storage using Economy Seven off-peak tariffs. **2** The UK begins to wake up to one of the coldest mornings of winter. **3** Breakfast time overlaps with switch-on in factories and offices. **4** Overcast day means street lights stay on, postponing the usual morning decline in demand. **5** Highest-ever morning demand: 41,000 megawatts. **6** Mid-day peak as UK cooks its lunch. **7** Lighting-up time 4.31 (London). **8** Late afternoon surge. Factories and offices still working; people arriving home switch on kettles, heating etc. **9** Peak 'spot' demand at 5.01 p.m. is 45,046 megawatts - the highest ever recorded. **10** *The Italian Job* ends on BBC1 and *Fresh Fields* on ITV; several million people make a hot drink or go to the lavatory, creating a surge in demand from water pumping stations.

In the UK we take electricity for granted. But the electricity supply has to be organised and managed. There are alternatives to follow and choices to make. This Unit examines alternative ways of generating electricity and of organising the industry.

Demand and supply

How do you use electricity on a typical winter's day? Many other people have similar needs at the same time. Look at Source A:

1 Describe the pattern of electricity use on 8 January. What were the main factors influencing its use?

2 Draw a similar graph to show what the pattern of electricity use might be like on a hot summer's day. Explain the main points on your graph.

Our demand is met by the supply of electricity in power stations where heat is used to produce steam. This steam is used to turn turbines which are linked to generators producing electricity. Some electricity is produced directly from running water, which powers turbines in hydro-electric power stations.

3 How is peak demand for electricity met? Look at Source A. Rank the sources of electricity production for January 1985 in order of importance.

4 The electricity supply can be shown as a flow diagram. Study Source B. Copy the headings below and list the drawings which should go under each one.

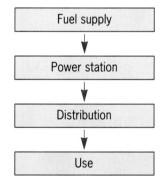

In the UK we take electricity for granted. But the electricity supply has to be organised and managed. There are alternatives to follow and choices to make. This Unit examines alternative ways of generating electricity and of organising the industry.

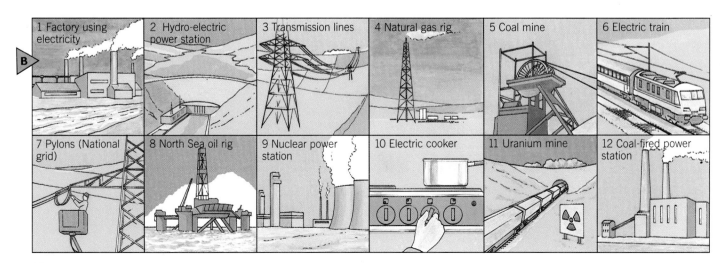

1 Factory using electricity
2 Hydro-electric power station
3 Transmission lines
4 Natural gas rig
5 Coal mine
6 Electric train
7 Pylons (National grid)
8 North Sea oil rig
9 Nuclear power station
10 Electric cooker
11 Uranium mine
12 Coal-fired power station

Policy decisions

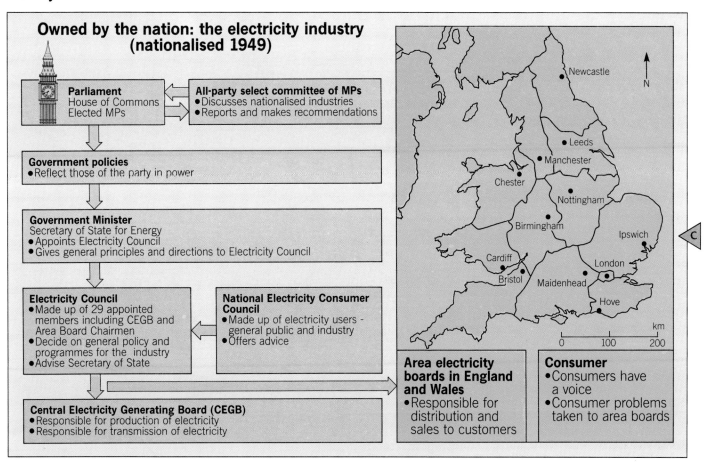

Owned by the nation: the electricity industry (nationalised 1949)

Parliament
House of Commons
Elected MPs

All-party select committee of MPs
- Discusses nationalised industries
- Reports and makes recommendations

Government policies
- Reflect those of the party in power

Government Minister
Secretary of State for Energy
- Appoints Electricity Council
- Gives general principles and directions to Electricity Council

Electricity Council
- Made up of 29 appointed members including CEGB and Area Board Chairmen
- Decide on general policy and programmes for the industry
- Advise Secretary of State

National Electricity Consumer Council
- Made up of electricity users - general public and industry
- Offers advice

Central Electricity Generating Board (CEGB)
- Responsible for production of electricity
- Responsible for transmission of electricity

Newcastle, Leeds, Manchester, Chester, Nottingham, Birmingham, Ipswich, Cardiff, London, Bristol, Maidenhead, Hove

km 0 100 200

Area electricity boards in England and Wales
- Responsible for distribution and sales to customers

Consumer
- Consumers have a voice
- Consumer problems taken to area boards

C

The electricity industry in the UK is a NATIONALISED industry.

5 Who owns this nationalised industry? Look at Source C.
a) Who decided that the industry should be nationalised in 1949?
b) A government decides to emphasise nuclear power. Who tells the Electricity Council to put this policy into practice?
c) A select committee might investigate the safety of power stations. How could this committee influence decisions?

6 The CEGB (Central Electricity Generating Board) and the area boards are responsible for the management of the electricity industry. Copy the table below. Tick the board responsible for each of the activities listed.
7 How is a large organisation responsible to the public? In groups, use Source C to consider the following cases.
a) Your parents' electricity bill is three times the amount they paid in the same quarter last year. They suspect a faulty meter. How can they get their bill reduced?

b) At a local meeting with her MP, Mrs Blower of Ratcliffe-on-Soar complained about the amount of smoke from the power station just outside her village. How can Mrs Blower get her complaint listened to?
c) An industrialist is worried about increasing electricity costs in his firm. How can he get his case considered?
8 What is a nationalised industry? Read the definition (Source D). What three main characteristics does a nationalised industry have?

Type of activity	CEGB	Area board
Selling an electric cooker		
Mending damaged transmission lines		
Collecting money from electricity bills		
Building an oil-fired power station		
Developing new technology for nuclear power		
Repairing cookers and fridges		
Paying power-station employees		
Buying fuel for power stations		
Installing an electric meter in a house		
Paying showroom employees		

The Structure of Industry, Stewart Hughes (Economist Books, 1988)

"The nationalised industries are those parts of the public sector (government owned organisations) that supply goods and services directly to customers in a similar fashion to any private firm. Such a definition excludes non profit-making spending such as that on defence, education, health and the major social services. Specifically, nationalised industries are defined to include only those public corporations whose assets are in public ownership, whose boards are appointed by a Secretary of State, and which are engaged in industrial or trading activities."

D

Sunday Times, 13 March 1988

A

“ Where does the coal come from? As you can see from the data (Source B) a lot is produced locally. Sources of fuel change from time to time, depending on price, availability, quality and so on. The CEGB tries to keep fuel costs down by using the latest computer technology to decide where to allocate fuels available.

All coal comes by road, because it's cheaper than rail. The amounts we use are fairly small. Routes are carefully planned to minimise traffic effect on local communities. ”

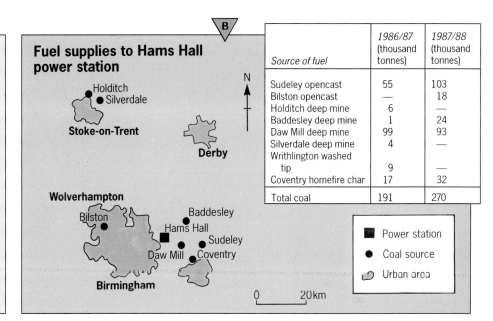

Fuel supplies to Hams Hall power station

Source of fuel	1986/87 (thousand tonnes)	1987/88 (thousand tonnes)
Sudeley opencast	55	103
Bilston opencast	—	18
Holditch deep mine	6	—
Baddesley deep mine	1	24
Daw Mill deep mine	99	93
Silverdale deep mine	4	—
Writhlington washed tip	9	—
Coventry homefire char	17	32
Total coal	191	270

- ■ Power station
- ● Coal source
- 🖐 Urban area

The CEGB as a nationalised industry is responsible for supplying electricity to England and Wales. (Electricity in Scotland is supplied by the Scottish Electricity Generating Board and in Northern Ireland by the Northern Ireland Electricity Generating Board.)

Whichever fuels are used, the CEGB must produce electricity reliably and efficiently. The managers of power stations have to make decisions about fuel supply. Some fuel sources are given in Source A, an interview with John Hamilton, the manager of the Hams Hall power station in Warwickshire (photo on p.35).

Coal

1 *Where does the coal come from?*
a) Use the information given in Source A and Source B to draw two large flow maps to show the sources of coal for Hams Hall power station in 1986/7 and 1987/8. Use a scale in proportion to the amount of coal supplied (e.g. 1 mm = 10,000 tonnes).
b) What are the main differences between the maps? Think about the number of sources for the coal and the amount coming from deep mines, OPENCAST PITS and other sources.
c) What reasons might there be for these differences?

C

Source of coal	Pithead price of coal (£ per tonne)	Sea transport costs (£ per tonne)	Unloading and land transport costs (£ per tonne)
UK	42	—	4
USA	30	3	10
Australia	26	3	10
Colombia	27	4	10

Source of coal	Cost of 1 tonne of coal at pithead	Cost of transporting 1 tonne of coal to UK	Cost of unloading/ moving 1 tonne of coal in UK	Total cost of 1 tonne of coal at power station	Total cost of coal for one year (Hams Hall needs 270,000 tonnes of coal each year.)
UK					
USA					
Australia					
Colombia					

2 *Where could the coal come from?* Hams Hall uses UK coal. Is it cheaper to use imported coal in UK power stations?
a) Copy and complete the table above using information from Source C.
b) On economic grounds, which coal would the manager of Hams Hall choose?

3 *Where should the coal come from?* In groups discuss whether each of the following would approve or disapprove of using imported coal in power stations: road haulage worker, electricity consumer, coalminer, power station manager, CEGB official, Secretary of State for Energy.

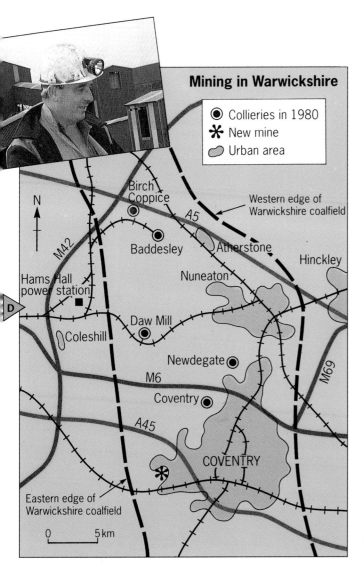

Mining in Warwickshire

Key:
- ◉ Collieries in 1980
- ✳ New mine
- ◖ Urban area

Map labels: N, M42, Birch Coppice, A5, Baddesley, Atherstone, Hinckley, Hams Hall power station, Nuneaton, Coleshill, Daw Mill, Newdegate, M6, Coventry, A45, COVENTRY, M69, Western edge of Warwickshire coalfield, Eastern edge of Warwickshire coalfield, 0 — 5 km

D

Warwickshire mining statistics

Output (thousands of tonnes)

Year	Birch Coppie	Baddesley	Daw Mill	Newdigate	Coventry
1971	438,500	649,100	741,500	376,300	725,700
1973	335,900	434,800	982,400	497,700	532,600
1975	541,500	490,500	1,108,000	376,100	447,500
1977	538,600	356,600	1,146,000	409,100	671,500
1979	529,000	549,100	1,202,200	272,600	355,700

Number of employees

Year					
1971	954	986	1,048	740	1,231
1973	922	967	1,052	697	1,114
1975	956	925	1,015	655	1,054
1977	975	992	1,063	755	1,148
1979	994	1,025	1,142	750	1,195

E

Output per shift (tonnes)

Year					
1971	2.09	2.87	3.22	2.32	2.57
1973	1.65	2.03	4.25	3.46	2.27
1975	2.52	2.41	4.96	2.66	1.98
1977	2.52	1.67	4.90	2.64	2.78
1979	2.36	2.49	4.79	1.77	1.42

Warwickshire mining: future trends

Year	Output (tonnes)	Average workforce	Output per shift (tonnes)	Number of pits
1980	2,950,000	5,280	2.56	5
1983	3,085,000	4,750	3.02	4
1987	3,160,000	4,050	3.74	3
1990s	?	?	?	?

F

The future of coal mining

The CEGB relies heavily on home-produced coal as fuel for its power stations. British Coal (which is nationalised like the CEGB) relies on power stations as a major market for its coal. Just as the CEGB decides about the coal source for its power stations, so British Coal has to decide where to invest in coal mining for efficient production.

The example of Warwickshire

Mining in Warwickshire has been concentrated in the area between Atherstone, Nuneaton, Coventry and Coleshill (Source D). In the 1950s there were about twelve collieries (mines or pits) working the coalfield. Many of these closed down in the 1960s and by 1970 there were only five mines left in Warwickshire. Decisions have to be made about the future of mining in the area.

4 It is 1980 and you are a Coal Board Official. Your job is to recommend closure of inefficient pits. Use the data about Warwickshire pits (Source E) to make your decisions.
a) How could you measure the efficiency of a coal mine?
b) Which of the five pits seem to be least efficient?
c) You decide to close two pits. Which two will you recommend for closure? Why?
d) What other information do you require before you make a final decision?
e) Present your recommendations in the form of a report to British Coal. Include a map to show the pattern of Warwickshire coal mining in the 1980s.

National Coal Board decisions have resulted in the closure of two Warwickshire pits since 1980. (These may not be the two that you recommended). But there are plans to invest in a new pit in Warwickshire (Source G).

NCB Plan for Pit worth £450 million at Hawkhurst Moor

The go-ahead has been given for a 2,000-job mine to produce 3 million tonnes annually. An NCB spokesman said the pit, just west of Coventry . . .

G

5 a) Draw graphs to show the statistics from the table (Source F). Project your graph to the year 2000.
b) Explain how the new development might affect mining in Warwickshire.

4.3 NUCLEAR POWER

Magnox reactors

The CEGB has a choice of fuels to use in its power stations. In the late 1950s it developed nuclear power stations that rely on a nuclear reaction from uranium fuel. The heat produced in the reaction is taken away by carbon dioxide gas and used to produce steam which drives TURBINES to make electricity. The uranium fuel is cased in a magnesium alloy (magnox) cover. Such stations need a large level site, with solid foundations. Large amounts of water are needed for cooling. Isolated locations are preferred. Early nuclear power stations were built at Wylfa, Sizewell, Bradwell, Dungeness, Oldbury, Berkeley and Hinkley Point.

Power station engineer Beryl Williams

❝ You can see a nuclear power station in the photograph (Source B). A lot of people welcomed it because the new technology brought jobs. Before it was built, the people of North Wales worked in the slate industry, in sheep farming and in the service jobs found in any village or small town. When the nuclear power station was opened, 70% of the 600 jobs created were for local people. Of course, some people didn't like a power station in a NATIONAL PARK, but the government wanted the first stations built away from large towns. ❞

(Source A) was involved with the new technology at Trawsfynydd nuclear power station (Source B).

Trawsfynydd nuclear power station

Closure: options for the workforce
- REDEPLOYMENT with the CEGB outside the area.
- Look for alternative employment outside the area.
- Stay in the area and look for other employment.
- Other options

manager, moved to area ten years ago

white-collar worker, locally born

manager, locally born

blue-collar worker, moved to area two years ago

1 Read Source A.
   a) Why was investment in nuclear power made at Trawsfynydd?
   b) What job opportunities existed before 1950?
   c) What job opportunities existed after 1950 and for whom?
   d) Who might have been against building the power station? Why?
   e) Using your atlas, draw a map to show the location of the early nuclear power stations in the UK.

2 New technology quickly becomes out of date, and this can cause power stations to be closed down. Use Source C to complete a copy of the table under it. Show how a nuclear power station can be decommissioned (dismantled).

3 The closure of early nuclear power stations will also affect people. Look at Source D. It shows four workers who have decisions to make. In pairs discuss:
   a) what you think each of them might decide.
   b) how they came to their decision.

Decommissioning a nuclear power station

Stage 1
- Remove fuel
- Build concrete shield to seal off reactors
- This may take 5 years employing half the present staff

Stage 2
- Dismantle all buildings except sealed reactors (this leaves two 30m concrete cubes)
- This gives 5–7 years of contract work

Stage 3
- Concrete structures left for up to 100 years, then removed

Stages	Time needed (years)	Procedures

CEGB pamphlet

The new pressurised-water reactor at Sizewell

Public reaction

The CEGB is investing in newer technology for the Sizewell B power station. People like Derek Frost (Source E) are in favour of Sizewell B.

F

Sizewell B and jobs

Nuclear power is now the major source of electricity in Europe. Over 93% of the plant and equipment for Sizewell B would be made by UK companies. On average, about 10,000 jobs would be created each year for seven years in UK industry and on site.

More than 1,200 of the construction jobs would be filled by people living locally or within daily travelling distance of Sizewell B. Once built, the station would provide jobs for 470 operating staff, mostly local, for about 35 years.

Jobs created by Sizewell B

Turbine generators: Larne, Leicester, Old Trafford, Rugby and Stafford.
Steam generators: Doncaster, Hatfield, Hereford, Livingston, London, Manchester, Renfrew, Sheffield and Wolverhampton, Christchurch.
Pressuriser: Derby and Gateshead.
Pressuriser forgings: Sheffield.
Reactor Coolant-pump motors: Norwich.
Construction: Leiston.

High-pressure pipework: Derby, Knutsford, London, Renfrew, Tipton and Birmingham.
Pumps for auxiliary systems: Glasgow and Alloa.

Adapted from a CEGB pamphlet

> **E**
>
> ❝ I work at Sizewell A as a physics engineer. It is an old Magnox power station, like Trawsfynydd. I started work there when it was first opened in 1966. It has already changed employment opportunities in this coastal area of rural Suffolk. The present plan is to build another power station, Sizewell B, on the same site. This will use the very latest pressurised water technology. It will use water at a high pressure (instead of carbon dioxide gas) to transfer heat from the reactor. ❞

4 Look at Source E and Source F and answer the following questions:
a) What job opportunities are being created by the new technology at Sizewell B?
b) Draw a map of the UK to show the areas which will gain. Are they local, national or international jobs?

However, many people do not want Sizewell B. A public inquiry in 1986, headed by Sir Frank Layfield, asked whether Sizewell B should be built.

5 Work in groups.
a) Discuss which statements from Source G might be used by people opposed to the power station.
b) Group the arguments according to whether the points they make are: economic; concerned with the environment and safety; social or political.
c) What other information would you need to state a full case against building a nuclear power station?
(d) Do you think Source H answers the arguments against building Sizewell B? If not, why not?

H

Layfield report: the outcome

'My conclusion is that Sizewell B is likely to be the lowest-cost choice for new generating capacity. The probability of a coal station having lower costs is remote . . . the cost advantages of nuclear stations compared with coal capacity would be reinforced by benefits from the achievement of greater fuel diversity.'
'On economic grounds alone the project should go ahead now. . . .'

Guardian, January 27th 1987

G

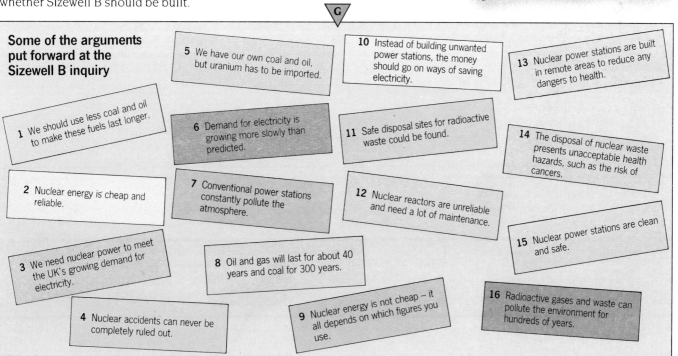

Some of the arguments put forward at the Sizewell B inquiry

1 We should use less coal and oil to make these fuels last longer.

2 Nuclear energy is cheap and reliable.

3 We need nuclear power to meet the UK's growing demand for electricity.

4 Nuclear accidents can never be completely ruled out.

5 We have our own coal and oil, but uranium has to be imported.

6 Demand for electricity is growing more slowly than predicted.

7 Conventional power stations constantly pollute the atmosphere.

8 Oil and gas will last for about 40 years and coal for 300 years.

9 Nuclear energy is not cheap – it all depends on which figures you use.

10 Instead of building unwanted power stations, the money should go on ways of saving electricity.

11 Safe disposal sites for radioactive waste could be found.

12 Nuclear reactors are unreliable and need a lot of maintenance.

13 Nuclear power stations are built in remote areas to reduce any dangers to health.

14 The disposal of nuclear waste presents unacceptable health hazards, such as the risk of cancers.

15 Nuclear power stations are clean and safe.

16 Radioactive gases and waste can pollute the environment for hundreds of years.

Elementary power

On these pages we look at the relationship between natural forces and UK energy.

1 You are a member of Friends of the Earth. Your group is producing a booklet about the variety of RENEWABLE ENERGY sources in the UK. As a geographer you have to draw a simple sketch map to show where these are found. All you have is an atlas and the information in Source A, B and C. Draw your map, showing as many types of renewable energy as possible.

Tomorrow's weather, there will be heavy rain in the west over the mountains. Sunny spells will occur in the south and east, but gale-force winds are expected later in the afternoon. That's all for tonight, but those of you living near the Severn estuary should watch out for the biggest bore (high wave) for a number of years.

> ... The problem is we have only thought of using coal and oil to generate electricity. But we are using these up fast, and they are not renewable. We have built high technology nuclear power stations to try to replace coal and oil. Instead, we ought to be looking at the country's renewable resources – solar energy, wind power, hydroelectric power and so on. We have got real choices. Some of these renewable resources can be economic.

Friends of the Earth pamphlet

Any atlas map and weather forecast show that in the UK we have an ideal environment for producing energy from sources other than coal, oil and nuclear power. We have a lot of land over 400 metres high. We have long rivers and broad estuaries. Many places have over four and a half hours of sunshine per day. In western parts of the country average wind speeds reach 60 km/h.

We have a variety of rocks. Geologists tell us that if we dig deep into certain rocks, such as granite, we can use the heat stored there. And because the UK is an island, with many estuaries just imagine the potential for tidal and wave power.

Should renewables be developed?

2 You work for the Department of Energy. You have listened to the arguments for using renewable energy sources. Your job is to gather information about these sources in order to assess the prospects of them being developed in the UK. Use the information in Source D on page 43. For each renewable energy source, list the possibilities and limitations of its development.

3 Estimate the cost of generating electricity from each source. Present your findings in a table like the one on the right.

Renewable sources of energy

Technology	Prospects in UK	Locations	Limitations on development	Estimated cost of electricity per kW hour	Rating 1–5
Large-scale hydroelectric power stations	Possible pumped storage schemes; suitable physical conditions; costs competitive with coal fired stations	North and West	Most suitable/ available sites used up; possible environmental objections	3–5 pence	

4 Rate each renewable resource on a 1–5 scale (5 = economically attractive; 1 = unpromising).

5 Would you recommend the Department of Energy to encourage renewable resources? If so, which three should be encouraged? Give your reasons.

Renewable energy resources

Hydro-electric power

Water under high pressure is used to drive a turbine which is linked to a generator to produce electricity. In many schemes, once the water has passed through the turbines, it is returned to the river system. Some schemes involve pumped storage.

Most large sites have been used up, but there is still plenty of scope for using small rivers to provide for houses and villages. Local authority rates for extraction of water are high, so not many sites have been developed.

The costs of generation are favourable and compare well with thermal power. (It costs approximately 3–5 pence per kWh.)

Tidal power

A dam built across a bay or estuary holds back the tide when sea level falls again. This water then drives the turbines and generates electricity as it returns to the lower tide level. Schemes to develop tidal power in the UK have been talked about since 1910, but none actually exist. The possibilities are shown on page 46. Studies have shown that the costs of electricity from this source could barely compete with coal or nuclear generated electricity. A tidal scheme would take seven years to build and a further two years before electricity was produced.

Costs of electricity could be from about 3 pence per kWh, depending on the estuary used.

Wind power

With aerogenerators like the one in the photograph, wind pushes the blades around and these are connected to a generator. In the UK, 23 medium and large scale machines run by private and public corporations exist. The generation costs are comparable with coal-produced electricity and there is a potential for 10% of present electricity generation from wind sources.

Costs per kWh: 2.5–7 pence.

Wind turbine, Orkney, Scotland

The Dinorwig pumped-storage scheme in North Wales

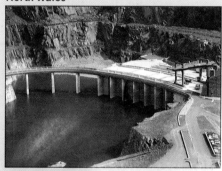

La Rance power station, France

Wave energy machine, Loch Ness, Scotland

House with domestic solar water heater, Israel

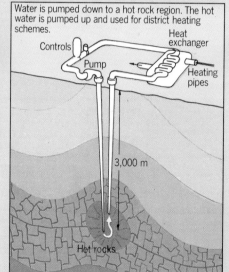

Water is pumped down to a hot rock region. The hot water is pumped up and used for district heating schemes.

Controls — Pump — Heat exchanger — Heating pipes — 3,000 m — Hot rocks

Wave power

Specially shaped hollow blocks of concrete rock with the waves and collect energy. Problems arise with the storm waves which might damage machinery, but these potential energy sources would be useful during peak winter demand for energy. Experimental plants exist on the island of Islay in the Inner Hebrides, but there are limits to where these stations could be developed.

Costs of electricity vary from 5 to 14 pence per kWh depending on site.

Solar power

To produce electricity, the sun's rays need to be concentrated as in the photo. If the amount of sunlight is sufficient it may be possible to have solar power stations. The cost of this technology is very high and would be much more expensive than coal produced electricity. There are four ways of storing the electricity and the UK has a mismatch between supply (summer) and demand (winter).

Costs of electricity vary from 8 to 64 pence, depending on site.

Geothermal power

There are few areas in the UK where sufficient heat is available for this type of electricity. Experiments have been carried out by boring into the granites of Cornwall.

Costs (estimated) of electricity would be between 3 and 6 pence per kWh.

4.5 NATIONALISATION OR PRIVATISATION?

Electricity – the future

The electricity industry is one of a number of nationalised industries in the UK. These are industries that the government owns and manages. Some politicians think these industries should be PRIVATISED (sold back to the private sector).

1 *How should industry be owned?* The table in Source A shows some UK industries which have been owned and organised in different ways.
a) When were these industries nationalised?
b) Which political party was in power at the time?
c) Which of these industries have been privatised?
d) Which political party was in power when privatisation took place?

2 People have many different views about nationalisation and privatisation. What is your view?
a) In pairs discuss the statements below (Source B).

A

Year	1945	1951	1964	1970	1974	1979
Party of government	Labour	Conservative	Labour	Con	Labour	Conservative

Industry	Nationalised	Privatised
British Airways	1946	1987
National Coal Board	1947	
British Rail	1948	1986
British Gas	1949	
Electricity	1949	1953
British Steel	1951	1988
	1967	
British Telecom	Run as a government dept until 1969	1984

b) Divide the statements into those which support nationalisation and those which favour privatisation.
c) Group the statements under the following headings: economic, social, political, and strategic. (Some statements will come under more than one heading.)
d) Rank the statements supporting nationalisation in order of how convincing they seem
e) Now do the same with the statements supporting privatisation.
f) Compare your rankings with other pairs.

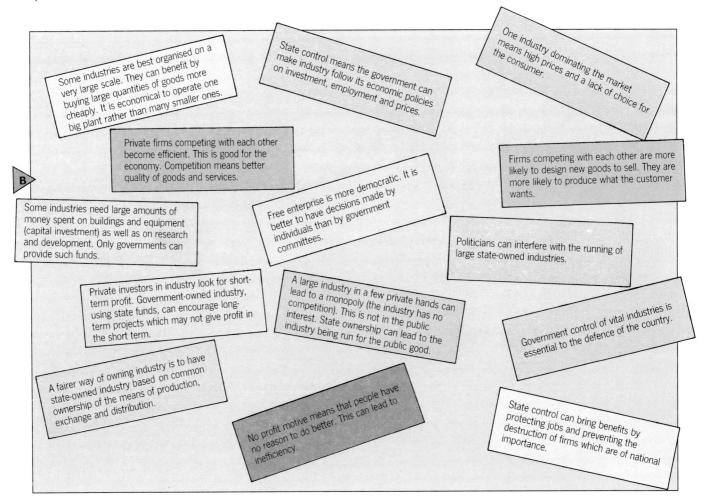

B

Some industries are best organised on a very large scale. They can benefit by buying large quantities of goods more cheaply. It is economical to operate one big plant rather than many smaller ones.

State control means the government can make industry follow its economic policies on investment, employment and prices.

One industry dominating the market means high prices and a lack of choice for the consumer.

Private firms competing with each other become efficient. This is good for the economy. Competition means better quality of goods and services.

Firms competing with each other are more likely to design new goods to sell. They are more likely to produce what the customer wants.

Some industries need large amounts of money spent on buildings and equipment (capital investment) as well as on research and development. Only governments can provide such funds.

Free enterprise is more democratic. It is better to have decisions made by individuals than by government committees.

Politicians can interfere with the running of large state-owned industries.

Private investors in industry look for short-term profit. Government-owned industry, using state funds, can encourage long-term projects which may not give profit in the short term.

A large industry in a few private hands can lead to a monopoly (the industry has no competition). This is not in the public interest. State ownership can lead to the industry being run for the public good.

Government control of vital industries is essential to the defence of the country.

A fairer way of owning industry is to have state-owned industry based on common ownership of the means of production, exchange and distribution.

No profit motive means that people have no reason to do better. This can lead to inefficiency.

State control can bring benefits by protecting jobs and preventing the destruction of firms which are of national importance.

How to privatise?

Plans are being drawn up to privatise the Central Electricity Generating Board.

3 In groups, study Source C which shows how the industry is organised.
  a) How many power stations does the CEGB operate?
  b) How much electricity do they produce?
  c) What percentage of electricity comes from non-nuclear sources?
  d) Which two area boards sold most electricity in 1987?
  e) Which two area boards sold least electricity in 1987?

Type of power station	Amount produced (millions of kilowatts per hour)	Number of stations
Coal-fired	30,537	37
Coal gas-fired	366	1
Coal oil-fired	4,504	3
Oil-fired	6,775	7
Nuclear	5,029	10
Gas turbine	1,442	11
Hydro	112	7
Pumped-storage	2,088	2
Auxiliary gas turbines	1,510	—
Total	52,363	78

C

Power to the people?

The present situation

Electricity production
The CEGB is a monopoly producer – the government gives it exclusive control for the production of electricity.

CEGB
78 power stations
9.6% nuclear

Electricity distribution
The CEGB owns the national grid, which distributes electricity to different parts of the country.

The twelve area boards distribute electricity to the consumer. They have to take their electricity from the CEGB.

Name of board	Sales (£ million)
East Midlands	950
South-Eastern	756
North-Eastern	623
South Wales	466
Southern	1077
South-West	552
Eastern	1210
London	912
North-Western	919
Yorkshire	961
Merseyside and North Wales	678
Midlands	980

Privatisation possibilities

Production
- Sell off part of the 78 power stations to a separate private electricity company.
- Set up two companies. Put all nuclear and some other stations under the control of one company. The rest of the power stations to go to another company.
- Sell off all coal-fired stations to one company, all nuclear stations to another company and oil-fired stations to a third.
- Sell off a balanced mixture of power stations – e.g. one coal-fired, one oil-fired and one nuclear.
- Sell off a balanced mixture of power stations to one company.

Distribution by grid
- Sell off the national grid to a separate independent company.
- Give the grid to the producing companies to control.
- Give the grid to the boards selling the electricity to control.

Distribution to consumers
- Scrap the existing boards. Create new boards to compete with each other to sell electricity to the consumer.
- Replace existing area boards by new distribution companies to serve the same regions as the area boards.
- Keep the existing area boards but let them choose to buy electricity from the cheapest available source.

D

4 a) In groups discuss the advantages and disadvantages of each option shown in Source D. Decide how your group would privatise the CEGB.

b) Present your group plan to the rest of the class.
c) Do you agree with the policy of privatisation?

5 Why not investigate? Read newspapers and watch current affairs programmes on television to find out more about the government's plans for privatising electricity.

TIDAL BARRAGES

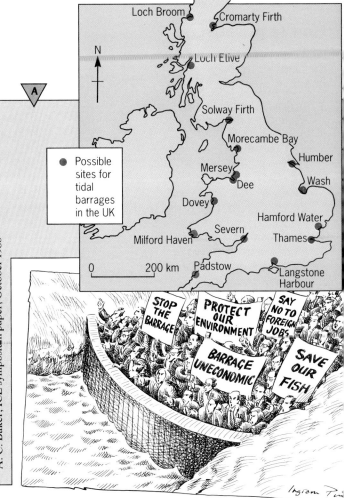

Comparative tidal scheme performance (Estimates)				
	Mean tidal range (metres)	Barrage length (metres)	Installed capacity (million watts)	Annual energy output (million kilowatt hours)	Cost of energy per kilowatt hour
Severn – Inner line	7.0	17,000	7,200	12,900	3.7
Severn – Outer line	6.0	20,000	12,000	19,700	4.3
Morecambe Bay	6.3	16,600	3,040	5,400	4.6
Solway Firth	5.5	30,000	5,580	10,050	4.9
Dee	5.95	9,500	800	1,250	6.4
Humber	4.1	8,300	1,200	2,010	7.0
Wash	4.45	19,600	2,760	4,690	7.2
Thames	4.2	9,000	1,120	1,370	8.3
Langstone Harbour	3.13	550	24	53	5.3
Padstow	4.75	550	28	55	4.2
Hamford Water	3.0	3,200	20	38	8.5
Loch Etive	1.95	350	28	55	11.7
Cromarty Firth	2.75	1,350	47	100	11.8
Dovey	2.90	1,300	20	45	7.2
Loch Broom	3.15	500	29	42	13.9
Milford Haven	4.5	1,150	96	180	10.0
Mersey	6.45	1,750	620	1,320	3.6

A. C. Baker, ICE symposium paper, October 1986

- Possible sites for tidal barrages in the UK

Loch Broom · Cromarty Firth · Loch Etive · Solway Firth · Morecambe Bay · Humber · Mersey · Dee · Wash · Dovey · Hamford Water · Severn · Thames · Milford Haven · Padstow · Langstone Harbour

N

0   200 km

This Unit has shown that electricity can be generated from a variety of sources, both renewable and non-renewable. Pages 42–3 showed that tidal power is one form of renewable energy which might be used in the UK.

A barrage is built across an estuary and the daily tidal movements drive turbines to give electricity. It may be best if there is a large tidal range (difference between high and low tide) and a long barrage so that a greater area can be used to make electricity. At present 17 sites are under consideration for barrage construction in the UK.

I The CEGB wants your advice about where to build a barrage. The map and table 1 in Source A give you the information you need.
a) Make a copy of the table on the right so you can add your information to it.
b) Using an atlas, find out about the estuaries which are possible sites. Comment on their size and characteristics. One example has been done for you and is shown on the right.

2 Rank the schemes in order, considering each of the following:
a) tidal range. (Assume the larger the tidal range the better the prospects for the scheme.)
b) barrage length. (Assume the longer the barrage the better.)
c) installed capacity (size of station). (The larger the installed capacity the better.)
d) energy output. (The larger the yearly output, the better.)
e) the cost of electricity produced. (The lower the cost the better.)
3 Total your ranks for each scheme. (Some schemes may have the same ranking for some factors, e.g. installed capacity at Padstow and

Loch Etive. Your next scheme would then be two places down.) On the evidence from the tables, answer the following questions:
a) Where would you build your barrage? Give reasons for your choice. You may decide to give more weight to one set of information.
b) What other *economic* information would you wish to know before you came to a final decision?
4 You want more information before you decide whether to build the barrage or not. Use the cartoon as a starting point and list what this other information would be.

Scheme	Details from atlas (counties involved, relief size)	Rank of mean tidal range	Rank of barrage length	Rank of size (installed capacity)	Rank of yearly output	Rank of cost	Total rank
Solway Firth	NW England–Cumbria–SW Scotland–Dumfries–Galloway. Broad estuary. Flat land between mountain area.	[6]	[1]	[3]	[3]	[6]	[19]

An aerial view of the Bournville factory in Birmingham

Manufacturing means making things in factories of all different kinds. Some are small sheds with just one owner and an assistant. In contrast, there are huge buildings, like those in the photograph on page 47, which employ thousands of workers.

This Unit raises three key issues:
- how and why companies organise and locate their factories in certain places.
- the effects these decisions have on people's jobs and lives.
- the influence people can have upon the decisions.

The example of Cadbury's

The photograph on page 47 shows the Bournville factory owned by Cadbury's in Birmingham. Cadbury's has existed for over 100 years, providing many jobs directly and in other companies linked to Cadbury's.

1 a) Describe what the photograph tells you about the location of the factory.
b) Use Source A to draw a graph of job trends at Bournville.

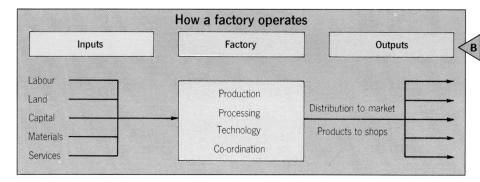

How a factory operates

| Inputs | Factory | Outputs | B |

Labour
Land
Capital
Materials
Services

Production
Processing
Technology
Co-ordination

Distribution to market
Products to shops

c) Describe briefly what the graph tells you.
2 A factory must be organised efficiently if it is to make a profit. Put simply, *sales – costs = profit*. With a partner, use Source B to suggest how *inputs* and *organisation* in the factory may have to change if the market (demand for outputs) changes.

How to organise
Many large firms like Cadbury's run a number of factories in different places. Decisions are made which affect all the factories. Cadbury's decided on a system in which each factory specialises in certain products.

3 Using Source C, list the products of each factory in the confectionery division. In what ways do the factories depend on each other?
4 a) Decisions affect job opportunities. Use Source D to draw a graph of national job trends at Cadbury's. Compare this graph with the one you drew for Source A.
b) What percentage of the jobs were based at Bournville between 1879 and 1912? What percentage are based there now? (Use Sources A and D.)

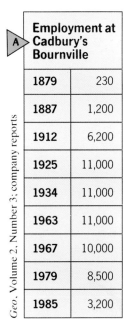

A	Employment at Cadbury's Bournville	
	1879	230
	1887	1,200
	1912	6,200
	1925	11,000
	1934	11,000
	1963	11,000
	1967	10,000
	1979	8,500
	1985	3,200

Geo, Volume 2, Number 3; company reports

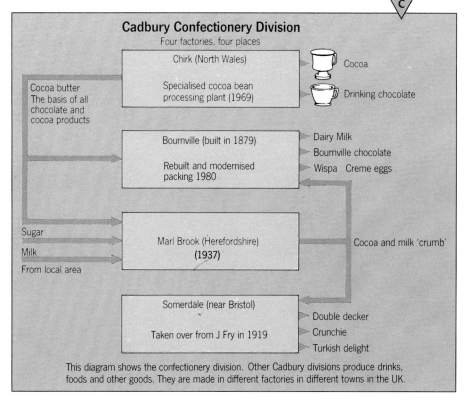

Cadbury Confectionery Division
Four factories, four places

Cocoa butter
The basis of all chocolate and cocoa products

Chirk (North Wales)
Specialised cocoa bean processing plant (1969)
→ Cocoa
→ Drinking chocolate

Bournville (built in 1879)
Rebuilt and modernised packing 1980
→ Dairy Milk
→ Bournville chocolate
→ Wispa   Creme eggs

Sugar
Milk
From local area

Marl Brook (Herefordshire) (1937)
Cocoa and milk 'crumb'

Somerdale (near Bristol)
Taken over from J Fry in 1919
→ Double decker
→ Crunchie
→ Turkish delight

This diagram shows the confectionery division. Other Cadbury divisions produce drinks, foods and other goods. They are made in different factories in different towns in the UK.

D	Employment at Cadbury's UK	
	1879	230
	1887	1,200
	1912	6,200
	1925	14,000
	1934	14,000
	1950	15,000
	1963	16,000
	1967	25,000
	1979	29,000
	1983	22,000
	1985	19,000
	1987	13,000

Geo, Volume 2, Number 3; company reports

Chocolate – and more

Today Cadbury's, like many other famous firms, has become a member of a group of companies called a CORPORATION. In 1919 it merged with Fry's, the chocolate maker, and in 1964 with Schweppes. This corporate organisation produces a wide range of products including chocolates, drinking chocolate, marmalade and soft drinks. Each type of product is organised by a division – as in the confectionery division (Source C).

5 Work in small groups. Imagine it is 1972 and you are part of a high-level planning team at the head office of Cadbury Schweppes. You are discussing future plans for the corporation as a whole. Look at Source E and do the following:
a) Discuss how each idea might lead to increased efficiency. Rank the ideas.
b) Discuss the likely consequences of each one.
c) Suggest which are the best ideas.
d) What information would you need to have in order to assess each idea fully?

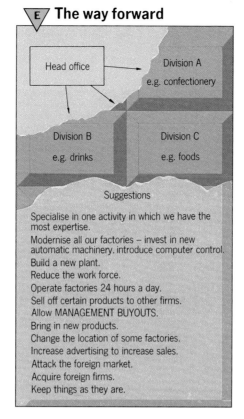

The way forward

Head office → Division A e.g. confectionery

Division B e.g. drinks

Division C e.g. foods

Suggestions

Specialise in one activity in which we have the most expertise.
Modernise all our factories – invest in new automatic machinery. introduce computer control.
Build a new plant.
Reduce the work force.
Operate factories 24 hours a day.
Sell off certain products to other firms.
Allow MANAGEMENT BUYOUTS.
Bring in new products.
Change the location of some factories.
Increase advertising to increase sales.
Attack the foreign market.
Acquire foreign firms.
Keep things as they are.

Redistributing jobs

Cadbury Schweppes put into practice many of the suggestions in Source E. One result was a change in the number of people employed in their factories.

6 Look at Source F and answer the following questions:
a) Which three places lost most jobs?
b) How many jobs disappeared?
c) How does the distribution of Cadbury Schweppes employment in 1972 compare with 1984?
7 In small groups use the information on this page and page 48 to discuss the main advantages and disadvantages of a corporation for:
a) the firm itself.
b) the managers.
c) the workforce.
d) customers.
8 Draw up a table to summarise your views.

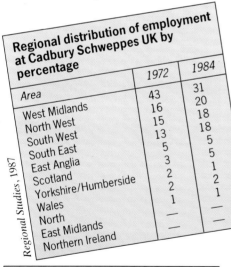

Regional distribution of employment at Cadbury Schweppes UK by percentage

Area	1972	1984
West Midlands	43	31
North West	16	20
South West	15	18
South East	13	18
East Anglia	5	5
Scotland	3	5
Yorkshire/Humberside	2	1
Wales	2	2
North	1	1
East Midlands	–	–
Northern Ireland	–	–

Regional Studies, 1987

"Large corporations like Cadbury Schweppes have many economic advantages. They can plan production on a large scale, and produce goods in the most efficient places. Large scale production means that each item is cheaper to produce. Corporations can be flexible and switch production between factories. They can choose when to open or close a factory. They can spend money on advertising to create a market for their products and can compete better with other firms. They can do market research and introduce new products. Their plan is called a CORPORATE STRATEGY."

Debbie Green, business analyst

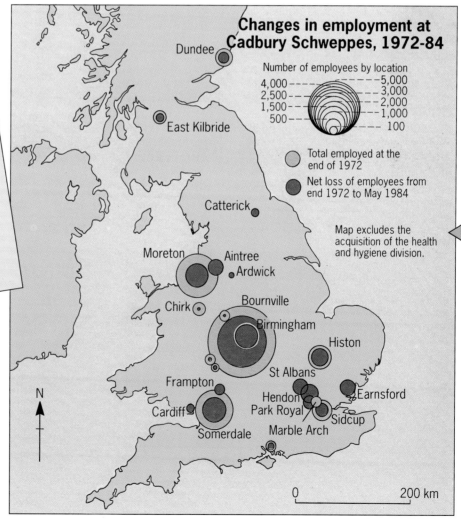

Changes in employment at Cadbury Schweppes, 1972-84

Number of employees by location
4,000 – 5,000
2,500 – 3,000
1,500 – 2,000
500 – 1,000
– 100

Total employed at the end of 1972

Net loss of employees from end 1972 to May 1984

Map excludes the acquisition of the health and hygiene division.

Dundee
East Kilbride
Catterick
Moreton
Aintree
Ardwick
Chirk
Bournville
Birmingham
Histon
St Albans
Frampton
Hendon
Earnsford
Cardiff
Park Royal
Sidcup
Marble Arch
Somerdale

N

0   200 km

The growth of a multinational

Cadbury Schweppes has made cutbacks which have led to job losses in the UK. However, as a corporation, the company has continued to grow. It invests in factories overseas, and therefore affects employment opportunities in other countries. It has become a MULTINATIONAL company.

1 Look at Source A. Cadbury Schweppes makes two types of products. What are they? Give examples of each.
2 Study Source B. Using an atlas, locate the countries with Cadbury Schweppes factories. Comment on the location pattern of the factories.
3 Look at Source C and answer the following questions:
   a) How many people did Cadbury Schweppes employ worldwide in 1987?
   b) Draw a bar chart to show the percentage employed in different parts of the world.
   c) Now draw a graph to show employment in the UK from 1979 to 1987 and in the rest of the world (everywhere except the UK) during the same period.
   d) Use your bar chart and graph to describe employment trends at Cadbury Schweppes.

Some well-known products of Cadbury Schweppes

The overall picture

4 You have been asked to prepare the draft of the company report for the Chairman. Working in pairs, use Source D to prepare your report. Include details of the following:
   a) Total sales in 1987 with a breakdown of where these have occurred.
   b) Total profit in 1987 and the most profitable areas.
   c) How sales and profits have changed between 1983 and 1987.
   d) Future trends in sales and profits. (Use recent trends to forecast what you think will happen.)

Employment			
Year	1979	1983	1987
UK	29,000	22,000	13,000
Rest of Europe	3,000	5,000	5,000
Latin America	2,000	3,000	3,000
Rest of World	7,000	7,000	8,000

Cadbury Schweppes: where the factories are		
Area	Number of factories	Countries
North America	8	Canada, USA
Latin America	1	Mexico
Europe	26	UK, Eire, W. Germany, Austria, France, Spain
Africa	12	Ghana, Nigeria, Kenya, Zambia, Zimbabwe, S. Africa
Asia	4	India, Malaysia, Singapore, Indonesia
Australasia	9	Australia, New Zealand

Profit figures £ million

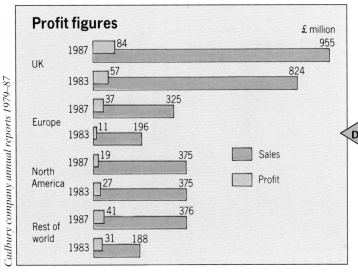

Cadbury company annual reports 1979–87

Cadbury Schweppes in India

5 Carefully study Source E. Why do you think the Indian Government limited foreign ownership of companies in 1978?

6 In groups discuss whether the following have benefited from the Hindustan Cocoa Products Company a part of the Cadbury's group.
   a) Indian farmers.
   b) Indian workers.
   c) the government.
   d) Cadbury Schweppes.

7 Using Sources E and F to help you, draw up a list of the advantages and disadvantages of multinational companies. What is your view of multinationals?

The story behind Hindustan Cocoa Products

Hindustan Cocoa Products Ltd is a factory in Bombay, and is owned by Cadbury Schweppes. Has the factory brought benefits to the local people? We tried to find this out by asking the people affected how they felt...

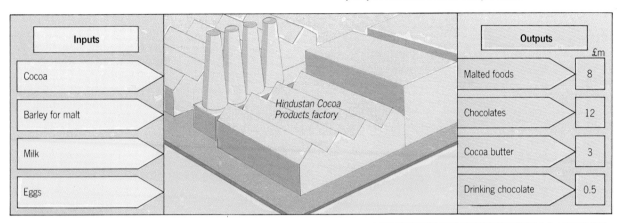

Inputs	Outputs	£m
Cocoa	Malted foods	8
Barley for malt	Chocolates	12
Milk	Cocoa butter	3
Eggs	Drinking chocolate	0.5

Hindustan Cocoa Products factory

E

Government officer

'After we became an independent country in 1947, Cadbury started manufacturing chocolates from imported cocoa. We did not encourage this – we taxed such items and allowed only 1000 tonnes of cocoa to be imported every year. In 1978 we passed a law limiting foreign ownership of a company to 40% of its shares. This meant that Indians bought shares in the newly named Hindustan Cocoa Products Ltd, a part of the Cadbury group. Now all the staff and all but one of its directors are Indian.'

Indian farmer

'The Hindustan Cocoa Products factory has helped me to grow cocoa on my smallholding of 4 ha. They have given me free seedlings and buy the harvested crop from me.

'I can grow cocoa between my other crops, so I can still produce enough food for my family. Field workers from the factory have helped me to store and market my cocoa. There are about 6000 people like me producing cocoa.'

Indian farmworker

'I work on the Hindustan Cocoa Products dairy farm at Induri, between Bombay and Poona. Milk from our 800 cattle provides for the factory. Other farmers produce barley and eggs for the factory.'

Financial advisor

'Hindustan Cocoa Products sells £24 million worth of cocoa products in India. The overall profit is around £600,000. It pays £750,000 in tax to the Indian government and £300,000 to its Indian shareholders. The government allows Cadbury to take only a small amount out of the country. Most of the profits are put back into Hindustan Cocoa Products.'

Sally West, foreign aid worker

" This newspaper article seems too good to be true. Who decides the price the farmers get for their cocoa beans? Do the farmers now have a choice of what they grow? Is the system fair to the farmer? What happens to farmers in a year of poor harvests? How much does the farm worker earn? What are his working conditions like?

In other countries where the governments are not so strong, foreign firms are allowed to take most of the profits out of the country. Skilled foreign workers get the better jobs. Local firms making similar products are forced out of business. Some firms use a lot of machinery and need few workers. In difficult economic times, firms may pull out of the country. Some companies may have bad effects on local politics and culture.

Anyway, what use are chocolates to the millions of poor people in India? "

F

The rest of this Unit investigates three key questions about changes in UK manufacturing industry:

- Which industries have grown?
- What effect have government policies had?
- Has investment come from local sources or from overseas?

1 In small groups, think about your local city or area and make lists showing:

a) which factories (if any) have recently closed down.

b) which manufacturing industries seem to be declining.

c) which new manufacturing industries have recently been set up.

d) why the changes in manufacturing industry have taken place.

The example of Dundee

For over a hundred years, Dundee was known as the city of jute, jam and journalism. Jute was imported from India to make sacks, ropes and carpet backing. James Keiller and Sons made jams and marmalades. The firm of DC Thomson published a range of magazines and comics including *The Dandy* and *The Beano*.

After the Second World War, the local jute-using industry went into decline although the other established industries still continue to exist.

New firms and new industries have brought different employment to the city in the post-war years.

2 **a)** Look at Source A. What type of products does each firm make?

b) When did each firm come to Dundee?

c) Which firm employs the largest number of people?

d) What type of employment does each one offer?

3 **a)** Draw a pie-graph to illustrate the figures in Source B. You will first need to work out the percentage of workers in different types of manufacturing industries.

b) Comment on what your pie-graph shows.

c) How important do you think instrument and electrical engineering are for employment opportunities in Dundee?

New industries in Dundee

Firm	Origin	When came to Dundee	Products	Numbers employed
Timex	USA	1946	Watches, electronic equipment (including microcomputers)	600–700
Veeder Root	USA	1950	Electronic equipment – e.g. tachographs to record hours and speed of a journey	300–400
National Cash Registers (NCR)	USA	1946	Self-service automatic bank machines	1,000–2,000
Ferranti	UK	1953	Electronic equipment (including devices for the automatic telephone exchange)	600–700

A

Statistical portrait of Dundee, 1988

Population	183,000
Numbers employed	87,000
Jobs in manufacturing	21,000

Types of manufacturing

Mechanical engineering	1,813
Investment engineering	3,733
Electrical engineering	2,141
Textiles	2,535
Paper, printing and publishing	3,610
Food and drink	1,336
Other manufacturing	5,832

B

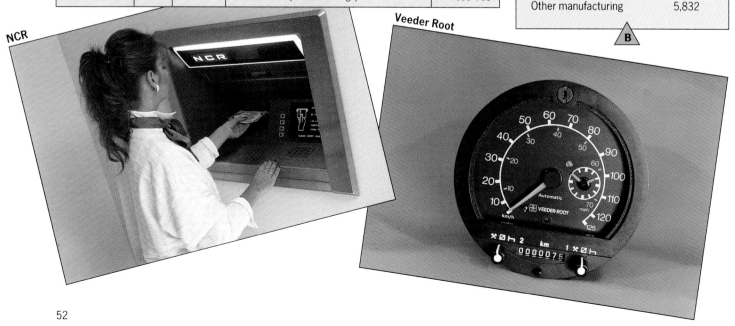

NCR

Veeder Root

The electronics industry in Central Scotland

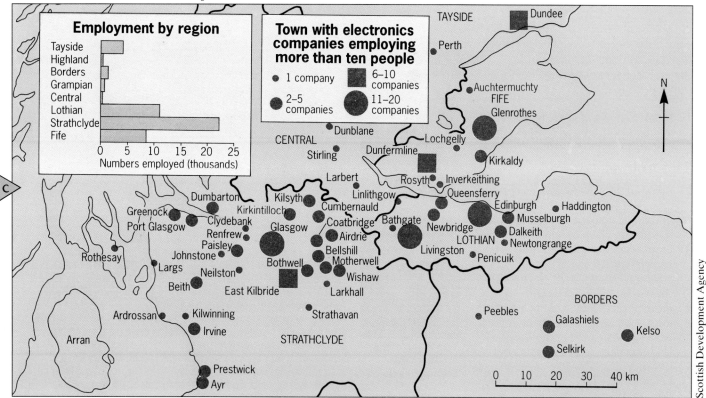

Employment by region

Tayside
Highland
Borders
Grampian
Central
Lothian
Strathclyde
Fife

Numbers employed (thousands)
0   5   10   15   20   25

Town with electronics companies employing more than ten people

- 1 company
- 2–5 companies
- 6–10 companies
- 11–20 companies

Scottish Development Agency

0   10   20   30   40 km

4 **a)** Place a piece of tracing paper over Source C.
b) On this draw a grid of squares 10km by 10km.
c) Shade in those squares which have more than four electronics companies.
d) Mark and label the seven most important towns for electronics.
e) Draw a boundary line to show the maximum extent of the electronics industry in Central Scotland. This is the area often referred to as *Silicon Glen*. Label this on your map.

5 Use the graph in Source C to calculate the number of people in Scotland who work in the electronics industry.

Foreign investment in Scotland

6 In Scotland, 10% of all factories are owned by foreign companies. Look at Source D.
a) What percentage of the jobs provided by foreign firms come from US-owned factories?
b) What percentage come from factories owned by EEC based firms?

7 Some people think foreign owned plants are good for Scotland. Others disagree. Working in pairs, imagine one of you represents a foreign company and the other a group of Scottish workers.
a) On your own, sort Source E out into two lists, one to show the advantages to you of foreign owned factories, the other to show the drawbacks.
b) Now compare your list with your partner. Which statements are given as advantages by *both* of you? Which statements are given as advantages by one of you and as drawbacks by the other?
c) Do you think foreign owned plants are good for Scotland? (Look again at the information on these pages.)

Place of origin of foreign firms in Scotland and the percentage of jobs they provide

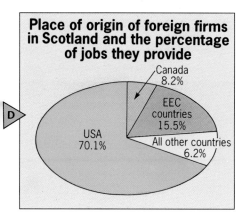

Canada 8.2%
EEC countries 15.5%
USA 70.1%
All other countries 6.2%

Some advantages and disadvantages of foreign-owned companies

- Money (capital) is invested.
- Profits are sent back to the home country.
- The factories provide jobs.
- Many of the jobs are unskilled.
- Most of the jobs are for women.
- The work is low paid.
- Foreign companies bring in new technology.
- Research and development is done in the home country.
- Many foreign factories are large.
- Workers have to belong to a single union.
- The products are mainly exported.
- The firm imports components from the home country. The factory then assembles these in Scotland.
- Decisions are made at the Head Office outside Scotland.
- Overseas plants are the first to close when the firm is in difficulties.
- The firms use local suppliers and services and so create more jobs.
- Their working conditions in modern factories are good.

Alec Dawson, who is American, is General Manager of Veeder Root in Dundee (Source A).

1 From Source A, give six reasons why Veeder Root came to Scotland.

The unions

2 Some US firms who have recently come to Scotland want a non-unionised workforce. What reasons for this are given in Source B?

3 From Source B and your own knowledge, list the major advantages a union brings to both the workforce and the company.

4 From Source C, try to work out what questions were asked about unions. Now suggest some of the worries US firms had. You can do this by drawing up a table like the one below Source C.

5 Why are US companies in a particularly strong position when bargaining with trade unions in Central Scotland?

Government aid

Alec Dawson's firm came to Scotland for good reasons. One thing not mentioned by him is that many firms are helped by the British government. Since the Second World War, the government has given grants to firms which move to areas with high unemployment and/or declining industry.

6 Imagine you are trying to encourage firms to move to an area with economic problems. The choices you have are shown in Source D.
a) In groups, discuss what each of the policies would involve.
b) Rank them in order of possible effectiveness.
c) Compare your rankings with other groups.

Alec Dawson of Veeder Root

Tom Bryan of the Amalgamated Engineering Union

We came to Dundee because the labour is good. There were plenty of skilled people and the quality of work was high. I've negotiated a single union agreement with the Amalgamated Engineering Union, like many other industrialists here.

    The education in the area is of a high standard. There are close links between industry, and Dundee University and the colleges of technology and further education. Now that the UK is part of the EEC, there is a big market for us.

    The local council is pretty go ahead, too. **A**

Alec is part of a US multinational which has been here for a long time. We have negotiated successful single union agreements with this firm and with National Cash Registers (NCR) in Dundee. But our problem is with those US firms which have come more recently. They don't want trade unions in their factories. From IBM in Greenock to Hewlett Packard in Edinburgh, there is a chain of fairly large non-unionised industries stretching across Central Scotland. These US firms think unions would slow down the rapid changes necessary in the modern, hi-tech electronics industry.

    We know unions can bring benefits to both workers and the company. Look at what the survey shows (Source C). We want to get the best for our workers in health, safety, working conditions and pay. **B**

The workforce and the unions: results of a survey

- Of US plants in Scotland, 92 per cent reported having a better or similar industrial relations record compared with other plants in the company in other countries.
- The vast majority of plants find the Scottish workforce to be flexible, co-operative and keen on training programmes.
- Almost half of the plants consider productivity levels to be good or very good.
- Almost half the plants of those surveyed negotiated with the workforce to improve productivity. Only one agreement did not work out.
- Nearly four fifths of the plants thought the operating atmosphere in Scotland was favourable to future expansion; 58 per cent had firm plans to expand over the next five years.

Silicon Glen, A. Hargreaves

Industrial relations in Scotland	
Employers' worries	*Survey results*
Many Scottish plants will have a bad strike record.	92% of US plants in Scotland have a better or similar industrial relations record compared with plants elsewhere.

- Give grants to firms.
- Give loans to firms.
- Plan and build industrial estates (areas for factories).
- Retrain the workforce.
- Give firms a subsidy for each person they employ.

- Introduce tax allowances.
- Build factories for firms to move to.
- Provide reliable water supplies, sewerage and roads (INFRASTRUCTURE).
- Restrict development in prosperous areas so that firms are more likely to locate in areas with economic problems. **D**

7 a) Look at Source E. On an outline map of the UK, locate and name the government-assisted areas in 1984.
b) Label the city of Dundee.
c) What percentage of factory investment costs did a grant cover from 1984 to 1988?

The attraction of Central Scotland

Many US firms decided to locate in Central Scotland for a variety of reasons. A researcher interviewed US managers of high technology branch plants. The results are shown in Source F.

8 a) Copy the table below. For each high technology firm (A–H) use Source F to tick the reasons for its location.
b) Why did US firms locate in Scotland? What seem to be the most important reasons?
c) Have the reasons for locating in Scotland changed in recent years?

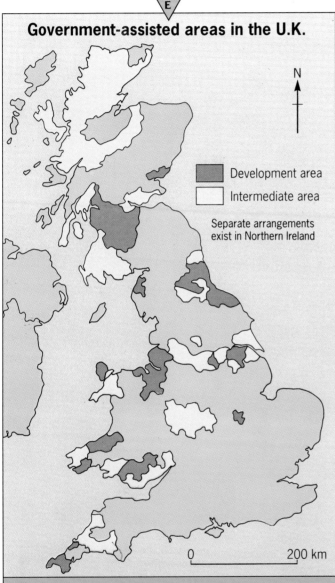

E

Government-assisted areas in the U.K.

N

■ Development area
□ Intermediate area

Separate arrangements exist in Northern Ireland

0   200 km

Government financial aid

Standard grants as % of factory investment	Special development areas	Development areas	Intermediate areas
Pre-1980	22%	20%	20%
1980–1984	22%	15%	Selective assistance only
1984–1988	Status ended	15%	Selective assistance only

Location factors	A	B	C	D
Available labour	✓			
Skilled labour				
Attitude of workforce				
Education of workforce				
Cost of labour				
Financial assistance	✓			
Communications				
Nearness to market				
Low investment cost	✓			
Other reasons				

US high technology firms in Scotland

Decade of arrival	Firm	Reasons for locating in Scotland
1940s	A	Financial assistance and labour were available; low investment costs.
	B	Scottish Industrial Estate Corporation offered new factories and there was a pool of skilled labour.
1950s	C	A new factory was available and was near to major market; firm liked attitude of workforce.
	D	Skilled labour and financial assistance were available. There were profit opportunities and firm had experience of Scotland from existing Scottish factory.
1960s	E	Local financial assistance programmes and low cost labour were available. The Forth Road Bridge provided an excellent communications network.
	F	Financial assistance was given from Scottish agencies; universities providing research skills were nearby.
1970s	G	Easy location of North Sea oilfields and port facilities a great advantage.
	H	Central Belt of Scotland had a long history of high technology investment. Language and nearness to European markets were bonuses.

F

A

The photograph shows Dundee and four parts of the Enterprise Zone. Enterprise Zones have been set up to attract industry to areas with severe economic problems and high unemployment. A firm locating in the Enterprise Zone pays no property taxes until 1994 and gets 100% tax allowances for money spent on industrial and commercial buildings. Sites are immediately available and it is easier to get planning permission for buildings than elsewhere, as less paperwork is involved.

Dundee: city centre waterfront looking towards airport

What is an Enterprise Zone?

Some areas like Dundee have been given development area status but still suffer from severe economic problems. The government has acted by giving further help. In 1980 an ENTERPRISE ZONE was created within Dundee. This page and page 57 look at Enterprise Zones and examine why they are set up, why they appeal to firms and their advantages and disadvantages.

1 Using Source A, give six characteristics of an Enterprise Zone.

2 Using Source A and Source B (the photo and the map), draw a labelled sketch to show the following:
   a) the Enterprise Zone sites.
   b) the city centre.
   c) the road and rail bridges.
   d) major places of education.
   e) other public services.
   f) existing industrial opportunities.
3 Imagine four firms wish to build in the Dundee Enterprise Zone. Using the map in Source A, select the most appropriate sites for the following:
   a) an electronics firm.
   b) a firm making dental equipment.
   c) a firm building hotels.
   d) an agricultural research firm.
   Give reasons for your choice.

Developing a site
The Central Waterfront site consists of 12 ha and is due to be made into a multi-million pound shopping, leisure and heritage centre. It is situated between the road and rail bridges.

4 a) Using Source A, draw a sketch map of this area.
   b) Suggest how it could be developed. Add notes to your sketch.
5 What evidence is there to show how successful this Enterprise Zone has been?

Some people say that Enterprise Zones have a negative side. Some of the disadvantages they name are:

- Industries causing pollution may be attracted to the area because fewer planning controls exist.
- More shopping and other non-manufacturing industries are set up.
- The new jobs do not make up for those lost in manufacturing decline.
- Each new job created costs £16,500.
- Investment is reduced in other equally needy areas.
- Non-local firms are attracted.

6 There are also major benefits. From the material on these pages list the major advantages of Enterprise Zones.

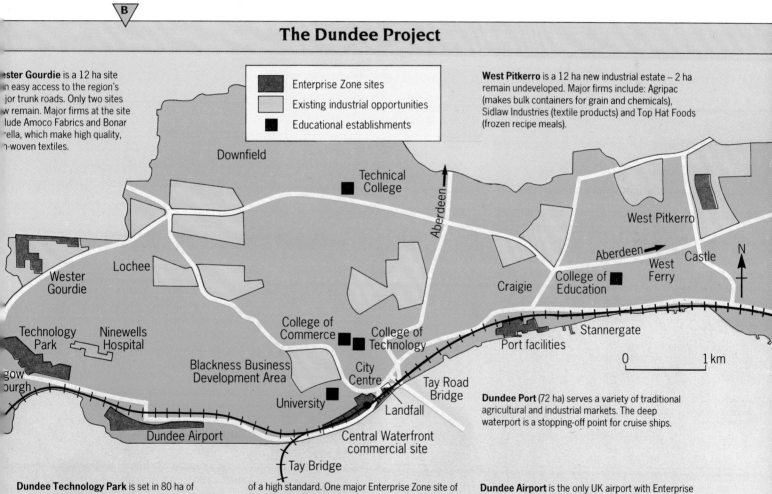

The Dundee Project

Wester Gourdie is a 12 ha site with easy access to the region's major trunk roads. Only two sites now remain. Major firms at the site include Amoco Fabrics and Bonar Brella, which make high quality, non-woven textiles.

West Pitkerro is a 12 ha new industrial estate – 2 ha remain undeveloped. Major firms include: Agripac (makes bulk containers for grain and chemicals), Sidlaw Industries (textile products) and Top Hat Foods (frozen recipe meals).

Legend:
- Enterprise Zone sites
- Existing industrial opportunities
- Educational establishments

Map labels: Downfield, Technical College, Aberdeen, West Pitkerro, Aberdeen, West Ferry, Castle, N, Lochee, Craigie, College of Education, Wester Gourdie, Technology Park, Ninewells Hospital, College of Commerce, College of Technology, Port facilities, Stannergate, 0 1 km, Blackness Business Development Area, City Centre, Tay Road Bridge, Glasgow Edinburgh, University, Landfall, Dundee Airport, Central Waterfront commercial site, Tay Bridge

Dundee Port (72 ha) serves a variety of traditional agricultural and industrial markets. The deep waterport is a stopping-off point for cruise ships.

Dundee Technology Park is set in 80 ha of parkland, half of which have Enterprise Zone status. It commands scenic views of the famous River Tay, yet is only minutes from Dundee city centre. Dundee University and Ninewells Hospital (one of Europe's leading teaching hospitals) are close at hand, as is Dundee Airport.

The Technology Park was designed to promote technology-related research, development and manufacturing. The building and landscape design are

of a high standard. One major Enterprise Zone site of 8 ha remains. Consultancy, research and software firms have taken sites. For example, WI Gore, a firm making cables, have invested £30 million. Twyford seeds development is a BIOTECHNOLOGY firm in a joint venture with Plant Genetics, Inc. of California. The Company is setting up laboratories and greenhouses to produce and market improved agricultural seed products. The technology park is near to the Scottish Crop Research Institute.

Dundee Airport is the only UK airport with Enterprise Zone status. The 12 ha site has opportunities for light aircraft manufacture, and other aviation-related industries. Small sites for general industrial use are also available. The airport is less than five minutes from the city centre and Technology Park.

LOCATION – A COMPANY INVESTIGATES

Edinburgh or Dundee?

Labtech is a successful company and wants to expand. It decides to locate a new 1000-square-metre factory in the UK. It will cost £75 per square metre to build. The company decides it needs a ½ ha site to allow for expansion in the future. It could choose a site in Edinburgh, which is not in a development area (see page 57), or it could choose a site in Dundee, which is in a development area.

1 Look at Source A. On a copy of the data calculate which would be the cheaper location.
2 Labtech decided to locate in Dundee. How much money a year did they save by doing so?
3 Labtech would gain further financial advantages if they chose to move to the Dundee Enterprise Zone. On a copy of Source B, calculate the annual repayment costs for the Dundee Enterprise Zone.
4 What do your calculations and the information from pages 56–7 tell you about the advantages of locating in an Enterprise Zone?

The calculation for Dundee

Cost of development

- 1000m² of building at £75 per m²   = ☐
- ½ ha of land at £70,000 per ha   = ☐

Total development costs   = ☐

Grants available

- Regional Development Grant £15,000   = ☐

Net development costs   = ☐

Loan repayments

The firm has borrowed money to finance the net development costs. It pays back at 13% per year
Annual repayment costs   = ☐

Tax allowance

By locating in a development area the firm claims a tax allowance of £3,500 per year

Annual repayment costs after tax allowance   = ☐

The calculation for Edinburgh

Cost of development

- 1000m² of building at £75 per m²   = ☐
- ½ ha of land at 75,000 per ha   = ☐

Total development costs   = ☐

Loan repayments

The firm has borrowed money to finance the development costs shown above. It pays back at 13% per year.

Annual repayment costs   = ☐

Changes

The government's regional development policy is changing and developing. For example, in January 1988 it announced some new measures:

- Automatic regional development grants will be ended.
- Small and medium sized businesses (those employing less than 500 people) will receive two thirds of the cost of employing consultants for advice.
- Small companies in development areas will be eligible for an investment grant of 15% (maximum £15,000) and an innovation grant of 50% (maximum £25,000).
- Spending is to stay at £550 million per year.

Local investigation

The amount of help available for industry constantly changes and varies from place to place. Find out about grants and help available in your area from:

- Local government and other local sources.
- National government.
- International sources such as the EEC.

The calculation for the Dundee Enterprise Zone

a) Total costs of development for Dundee (as before)	=	☐
b) Less Regional Development Grant (as before)	=	☐
c) Larger tax allowance	=	87,500
d) Total deductions (**b**) + **c**))	=	☐
e) Net cost of development (**a**) − **d**))	=	☐
f) Annual repayments (at 13% per year)	=	☐
g) In addition, the factory does not have to pay local authority rates (except water rates) until 1994	=	5,265
h) Annual repayment costs (after all savings)	=	☐

Data based on Dundee Project material, Nethergate, Dundee

WORK, DECISIONS AND EMPLOYMENT: FARMING

An auction of Suffolk rams in Taunton, Somerset

FARMING – FOR PLEASURE OR PROFIT?

Robert Boyes

Moorbarns Farm, Leicestershire

Robert Boyes owns a mixed farm in South Leicestershire. He took it over from his father in 1980.

'My father would say farming is a way of life. He cares for the land and the undulating fields. He knows the soil can produce good cereals and grass. He enjoys looking after the animals.

But farming has changed. For me, farming is a business like any other business. I invest capital. I've put up new buildings and bought a new milking parlour and corn drier. I've bought a lot of machinery. We work hard – my wife and myself and our children, together with the two full-time workers we employ. We work the land to get the highest yields. That's why we use the highest quality seed, chemical fertilisers and the best animals.

The weather can still upset our plans. But I plan to make a profit. I need to make a profit to live. Remember, I reinvest for next year. My livelihood depends on organising the farm efficiently to make a profit.'

A

1 Using Source A and Source C answer the following questions:
a) What animals does Robert raise?
b) What is the workforce on the farm? (How many people work on it?)
c) What capital is tied up in Robert's farm?
d) Robert also has to pay regular costs for running the farm, such as wages. Give some more examples of these OVERHEADS.

To be a successful farmer, Robert adds *human inputs* (labour) and *economic inputs* (capital) to *land* to make a profit:

2 Using the map (Source B) answer the following questions:
a) How many fields are there?
b) What is the total area of the farm?
c) What is the average size of a field?
d) What crops are grown? Which crop covers the largest area?
3 Robert works a farming SYSTEM. He buys INPUTS which are used on the farm to produce OUTPUTS which are sold.
a) Robert's main inputs are labour and capital. Look at Source C. What are his main outputs? Give examples of their selling price.
b) Explain what Robert has to do to make a profit.

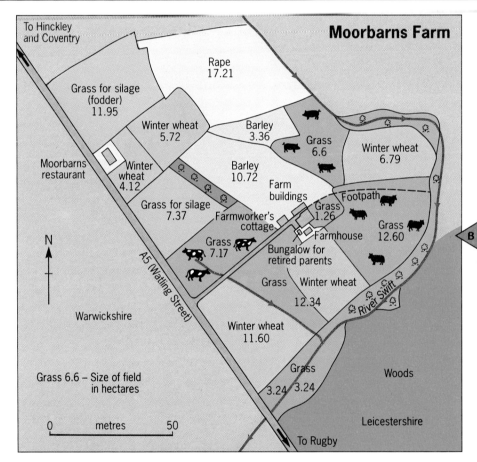

Moorbarns Farm

To Hinckley and Coventry

Rape 17.21

Grass for silage (fodder) 11.95

Winter wheat 5.72

Barley 3.36

Grass 6.6

Winter wheat 6.79

Moorbarns restaurant

Winter wheat 4.12

Barley 10.72

Farm buildings

Footpath

Grass 1.26

Grass 12.60

Grass for silage 7.37

Farmworker's cottage

Farmhouse

N

Grass 7.17

Bungalow for retired parents

Grass

Winter wheat 12.34

Warwickshire

A5 (Watling Street)

Winter wheat 11.60

River Swift

Grass 6.6 – Size of field in hectares

Grass 3.24 3.24

Woods

Leicestershire

0   metres   50

To Rugby

B

What the farm produces

- Beef cattle (24–30 months) sold to wholesale meat markets at £450–£680.
- Lambs sold at £40 each (old ewes and surplus cows are also sold).
- Milk sold at guaranteed price (18p per litre) to the Milk Marketing Board.

• *Cereals*	*Yield per ha*	*Income per ha*	*Expenditure per ha*
Wheat	6.5 tonnes	£728	£637
Barley	4.7 tonnes	£531	£489

C

Cash questions

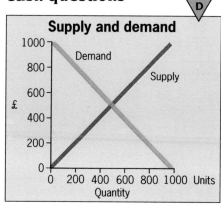

Supply and demand

Graph showing Demand and Supply lines crossing, with £ (0–1000) on the y-axis and Quantity (Units, 0–1000) on the x-axis.

4 Robert responds to guaranteed prices, premiums and grants paid to him by the government. He also responds to the MARKET PRICE. Imagine Robert has asked you to advise him about what is likely to happen in certain situations. Using the graph (Source D) to help you, complete the sentences.

a) Assuming costs remain constant, when the price of a crop is high, Robert will make more money from selling it. The amount he is likely to produce and supply will therefore be (HIGH/LOW).

b) When the price of a crop is low, the amount produced and supplied will probably be (HIGH/LOW).

c) When you are trying to decide whether or not to buy something, the price is going to influence you. So when the price of a crop is high, Robert should expect the amount bought and demanded by the consumers to be (HIGH/LOW).

d) When the price of a crop is low, Robert should assume that the amount bought and demanded by the consumers will be (HIGH/LOW).

e) The market price will be where supply and demand are balanced. What is the market price shown in this example on the graph?

Where does the money go?

Robert is one UK farmer amongst 199,000 full-time, 92,000 part-time and 325,000 salaried managers who are also making economic decisions on their different farms.

As Source E shows, there are four types of farm. The owner of a *livestock* farm depends on the rearing of animals – such as cattle, sheep and pigs – to make a profit. The livelihood of an *arable* farmer comes from cultivating and selling crops. Some farmers, like Robert, rear animals *and* grow crops – this is called *mixed farming*. The fourth type, *horticultural* farming, is when the farmer makes a living by growing and selling fruit, vegetables and plants.

5 Look at Source E, which shows total inputs and total outputs for the whole of UK farming.
a) What are the five greatest costs for UK farmers?

b) What are the five greatest outputs of UK farmers?

6 How might inputs and outputs vary according to the type of farm? Make an enlarged copy of Source F and complete it.

7 Having worked through this page and page 60 do you agree with Robert Boyes (Source A) that 'farming is a business like any other business'? If not, why not?

Types of farming

Input costs (£ million)	
Livestock feeds £2601	26%
Labour £1998	20%
Depreciation £1418	14%
Miscellaneous costs £1104	11%
Fertilisers and lime £967	10%
Machinery £557	6%
Fuel and oil £534	5%
Seed £295	3%
Farm maintenance £265	3%
Livestock £187	2%

Map key:
- Livestock
- mixed
- arable
- horticulture

0 km 200

Value of total output (£ million)	
Milk and milk products £2393	20%
Cereals £2310	20%
Cattle and calves £1919	16%
Horticultural crops and fruit £1240	11%
Pigs £973	8%
Poultry £703	6%
Sheep and Lambs £590	5%
Eggs £530	5%
Potatoes £303	3%
Oilseed rape £244	2%
Other sales £236	2%
Sugar beet £233	2%
Wool £43	3%

Inputs and outputs on a farm

Type of farm	Location of farm type	Inputs needed	Outputs produced
Arable farm			
Livestock farm			
Mixed farm			
Horticulture			

Money

Exercise 3 on page 60 shows the farm as a system. Farmers today are trying to make the whole system more efficient. To do this they are investing large sums of money, and farms are becoming *capital-intensive*. Source A shows what is happening.

Work with a partner.

1 Discuss the cycle shown in Source A and write a brief description of what the farmer hopes will happen.

2 Can you see any dangers for the farmer who enters this cycle?

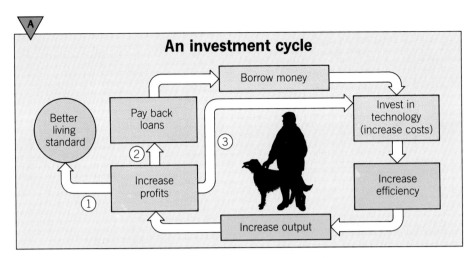

A

An investment cycle

Borrow money → Invest in technology (increase costs) → Increase efficiency → Increase output → Increase profits → Pay back loans → Borrow money

Better living standard

B

A 1930s farm

- Small fields, many hedges and trees. Natural ponds

- Traditional farmyard and buildings. Tied cottages.

- A lot of farmworkers. Some use of electricity. Use of mains water.

- Machinery, such as ploughs and binders, usually drawn by horses.

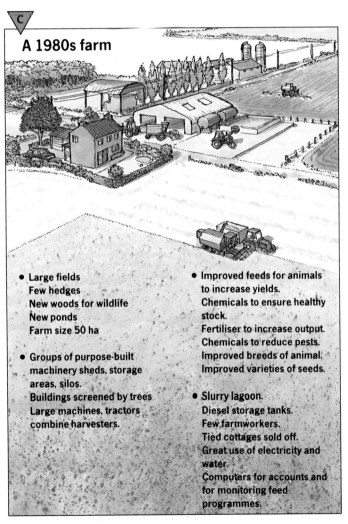

C

A 1980s farm

- Large fields
  Few hedges
  New woods for wildlife
  New ponds
  Farm size 50 ha

- Groups of purpose-built machinery sheds, storage areas, silos.
  Buildings screened by trees
  Large machines, tractors combine harvesters.

- Improved feeds for animals to increase yields.
  Chemicals to ensure healthy stock.
  Fertiliser to increase output.
  Chemicals to reduce pests.
  Improved breeds of animal.
  Improved varieties of seeds.

- Slurry lagoon.
  Diesel storage tanks.
  Few farmworkers.
  Tied cottages sold off.
  Great use of electricity and water.
  Computers for accounts and for monitoring feed programmes.

Technology

3 Farmers have invested in technology to increase efficiency. This has changed farms and farming.

a) Draw a sketch of the 1980s UK farm in Source C.
b) Add labels to show the technology and changes which have occurred from 1930 to 1980.

4 a) In what ways do these technological changes make farming more efficient?
b) How does each change alter the nature of work on the farm? What problems may result?

What changes?

5 Use Source D.
   a) Which sizes of holdings have decreased in number since 1975? Suggest reasons for this.
   b) Which size of holding shows the greatest decrease? Is this a good thing?
   c) Why have only a few holdings increased in size?
   d) What will the figures be for sizes of holdings in 1995 assuming the same rate of change?

6 Look at Source E. Draw graphs to show the changes in numbers of people in UK agriculture between 1975 and 1985 and to 1995. Assume the same rates of change between 1985 and 1995. (You don't need to do any calculation, just continue the lines on the graph.)

Farm size D

Crops and grass area (ha)	Number of holdings 1975 (thousands)	1985
1 – 19.9	120	95
20 – 49.9	73	64
50 – 99.9	42	41
100 and over	29	31

Labour E

Number of persons engaged in UK agriculture (thousands)

	1975	1983	1985
Full-time regular workers	222	168	157
Regular part-time workers	80	61	61
Seasonal or casual	73	96	99
Salaried managers	7	8	8
Farmers, partners, directors	280	290	291
Total	662	623	616

Capital: the example of fertiliser

Susan Fletcher, one of 10% of UK female farmers

F

Susan Fletcher inherited her farm five years ago. She has a choice. On a 10 ha field like the one in the photograph (Source F) she has to decide whether to grow potatoes or wheat. She has the information in the table (Source G), which is data from a UK government farm which carries out research. She makes her choice by calculating the profit or loss for growing wheat or potatoes and using NPK fertiliser or not using fertiliser. (NPK fertiliser is made from ammonium nitrate, ammonium phosphate and potassium chloride.)

7 a) Complete a copy of Source G to work out what she decided.
   b) Comment on your findings.
   c) This is an economic decision. Are there any other considerations Susan needs to think about?

8 In pairs, discuss what changes may occur on farms in the future. Show your ideas in a drawing similar to Source B and Source C.

G

Production costs for wheat and potatoes

Type of crop	1 Cost (£ per ha)	2 Cost for whole field (£)	3 Yield (tonnes per ha)	4 Total yield from field (tonnes)	5 Market price (£ per tonne)	6 Revenue (£) column 4 × column 5	7 Profit/loss (£) column 6 minus column 2
Wheat – not using fertiliser	479	4,790	1.69		112		
Wheat – using fertiliser	575	5,750	6.60		112		
Potatoes – not using fertiliser	1,468	14,680	8.47		101		
Potatoes – using fertiliser	1,564	15,640	38.57		101		

Over the past 20 years, much of the UK countryside has been transformed by the introduction of a new crop – oilseed rape.

I Look at Source A, which shows a mixed farming area of the Midlands.
a) What different types of farming are there?

b) How can you tell it was taken in Midland England?
c) What time of year was the photo taken?

A The countryside in transition

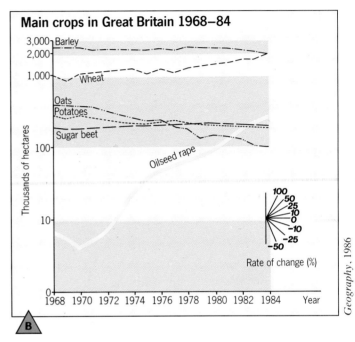

Main crops in Great Britain 1968–84

Thousands of hectares

Barley, Wheat, Oats, Potatoes, Sugar beet, Oilseed rape

Rate of change (%)

1968 1970 1972 1974 1976 1978 1980 1982 1984 Year

Geography, 1986

B

A revolution in agriculture

2 Many UK farmers have decided to grow oilseed rape. Using Source B answer the following questions:
a) Approximately how much was sown in 1970 and how much in 1984?
b) Estimate what the percentage change has been.

3 Using Source C and your atlas:
a) Mark the top ten counties growing oilseed rape by area.
b) List the top ten counties growing oilseed as a percentage of total tillage (land cultivated).
c) Which measure of the importance of oilseed rape is the better one? Why?
d) On a map of the UK, show your top ten rankings. Use an atlas to suggest why these areas have more oilseed rape than others.
e) How many oilseed rape crushing mills are there in the UK? Add these to your maps. Draw the areas from which each mill might take this crop.
f) What might the oil be used for?

C

Oilseed rape as a percentage of total tillage
12.0
7.6
4.5
%
2.25
1.0
0

The distribution of oilseed rape in Great Britain

Glasgow △

Oilseed rape by area
34,000
20,000
10,000
5,000
1,000

Hull
Liverpool
Selby

Crushing mill capacity (tonnes)
325,000
100,000
50,000

Erith

N

0 40 80 km

Geography, 1986

Advantages for a farmer

Oilseed rape is a valuable break crop in my rotation. It can prepare the ground for winter cereals because it is harvested between July and August. The long roots help to get air into the soil.

I don't need any special equipment for oilseed rape because I can use my cereal equipment.

I like this crop because it yields high prices and I know I can sell it to make margarine.

It can help my cash flow, as oilseed rape is an earlier crop than potatoes and sugar beet which I used to grow.

Robert Boyes

4 Using Robert's comments (Source D), answer the following questions:
a) What financial advantages does Robert see in growing oilseed rape?
b) What benefits to the farm does it bring which other crops do not?

Oilseed rape 1973–86		
Year	Yield (tonnes per ha)	Average market price (£ per tonne)
1973	0.4	75
1980	0.6	230
1984	0.6	275
1986	3.2	252

5 A farmer plants a 5 ha field with oilseed rape in 1973. Look at Source E and provide answers to the following:
a) How much would he have produced?
b) How much income would he receive?
c) What would similar figures be for 1984?
d) Is this income all profit? Give details.

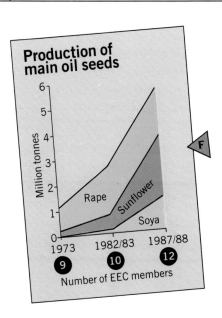

Production of main oil seeds

EEC farmers profit from oil seed rape

Farmers are growing more oil seed rape as the European Common Agricultural Policy (CAP) continues to offer good prices. Officials are worried that the EEC is not self-sufficient in vegetable oils. So they have welcomed oil seed rape, the only oil seed that grows profitably in Europe's temperate climate.

Since the UK joined the EEC in 1973, farmers have been quick to take advantage of the support prices offered. Oil seed rape is today 20% more profitable than growing barley and oats. In 1986 the farmer got £252 per tonne, and he or she does not have to buy expensive new equipment.

Rape is also a useful break crop, improving the soil in a rotation. With new varieties being developed, more rape seed is being used as animal fodder. The consumer gains, as the use of rape seed oil for margarine has meant cheaper prices in the shops. UK farmers now produce 30% of the country's edible oil seeds – the yellow fields are here to stay!

6 With a partner, use Source G to make a list of reasons why more oilseed rape is being grown (see Source F). Suggest ways you could group these reasons.

Wheat and milk – two successes?

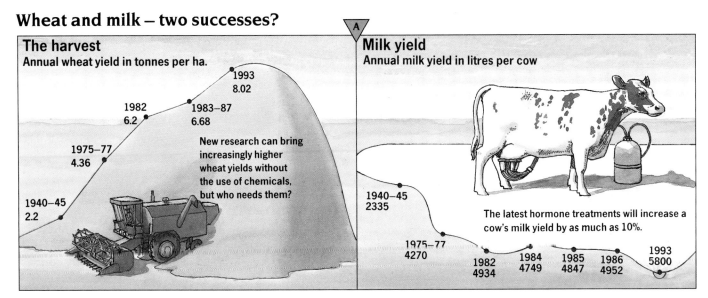

The harvest
Annual wheat yield in tonnes per ha.

1993
8.02

1982
6.2

1983–87
6.68

New research can bring increasingly higher wheat yields without the use of chemicals, but who needs them?

1975–77
4.36

1940–45
2.2

Milk yield
Annual milk yield in litres per cow

The latest hormone treatments will increase a cow's milk yield by as much as 10%.

1940–45
2335

1975–77
4270

1982
4934

1984
4749

1985
4847

1986
4952

1993
5800

A

Farmers decide to grow certain crops and raise certain animals. The UK government has helped them to produce more food. When the UK joined the EEC, the Common Agricultural Policy (CAP) encouraged farmers to produce even more. This policy has helped farmers and consumers. It has allowed the export of food to other countries. But does this story of increased food production have any drawbacks?

I **a)** Look at Source A. The figures are accurate but misleading. Draw two line graphs to show the increase in wheat and milk yields between 1945 and 1986/7.
b) Add notes to your graph to explain this increase (refer back to pages 62–3).
c) Why is it predicted that the increase will continue?
d) How do your graphs compare?
e) Have wheat and milk been a success story?

The CAP

Within the EEC, farmers have been protected and helped by governments. This has been done through the CAP, particularly through its pricing policy. Within the EEC each year a TARGET PRICE is fixed for a crop like oilseed rape. This is the highest price at which oilseed rape is traded within the EEC (£313 per tonne in Source B).

Then an INTERVENTION PRICE is fixed at 8% below the target price. When the price falls to this level, the crop is bought by the EEC. In the world market the WORLD PRICE for the produce is often lower (oilseed rape is about £155 per tonne). Anyone from outside the EEC wishing to sell their produce to any EEC country is faced with a tariff wall. They must pay a LEVY so that the imported produce is raised to the THRESHOLD PRICE (approximately £300 in this case).

2 Copy the diagram (Source B). Label the different prices. Using your diagram, try to explain to a partner how the CAP pricing policy works.

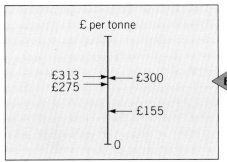

£ per tonne

£313
£275

£300

£155

0

B

1986: EEC expenditure on agriculture was 22,000 ECUs (European currency units). This is 65% of all EEC spending.

Does a pricing policy work?

The European pricing policy has had the results shown in these headlines.

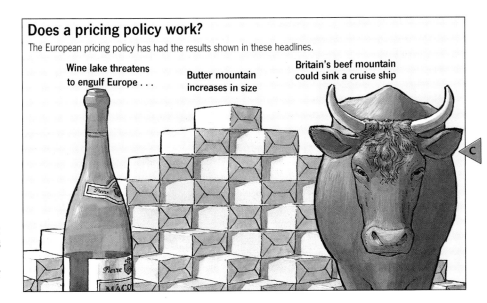

Wine lake threatens to engulf Europe . . .

Butter mountain increases in size

Britain's beef mountain could sink a cruise ship

C

An investigation into the EEC pricing policy

3 Accurately copy Source D. Use it to answer these questions.

a) If supply and demand were operating on their own, what would be the market price and number of units produced ((1) on the diagram)?

b) At this free market world price shown (2), how much would be demanded, and how much produced by the EEC?

c) At this free market world price level (2), would EEC farmers produce or not?

d) The EEC fixes target and intervention prices above world prices. At this intervention price (3), how much would be demanded and how much would be produced?

e) Would this intervention price encourage EEC farmers to produce?

f) In this example, what is the result of the EEC setting intervention prices?

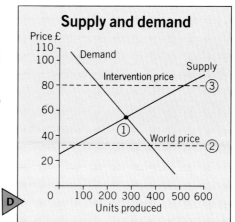

D Supply and demand

4 Source E shows what has happened to one product. What is the problem shown here? Use what you have learned to explain how this has come about.

5 The EEC can sell its surplus on the world market or use the produce for animal feed, industrial inputs or food aid. With a partner:

a) Discuss the merits of each.

b) Rank them in your own order of priority.

6 You have knowledge about the difference between world prices and the price paid to EEC farmers for a product. Source F shows that there is a tariff wall around the EEC.

a) Name the 12 countries which make up the EEC.

b) Why has the EEC put a tariff wall around its borders?

7 Using all the information on these two pages, decide whether EEC food production increase is a success story or not.

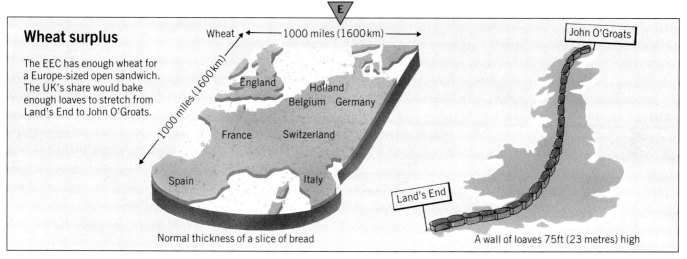

E Wheat surplus

The EEC has enough wheat for a Europe-sized open sandwich. The UK's share would bake enough loaves to stretch from Land's End to John O'Groats.

Normal thickness of a slice of bread

A wall of loaves 75ft (23 metres) high

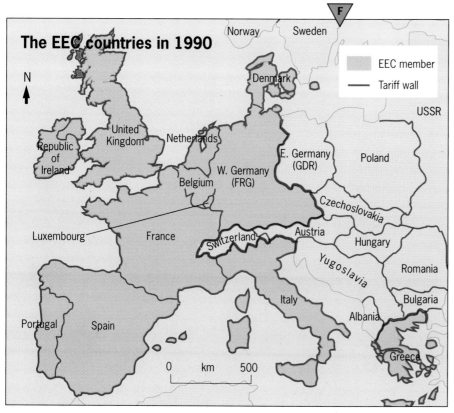

F The EEC countries in 1990

EEC member

Tariff wall

IMPROVING EFFICIENCY

The EEC and various other bodies have increased food production in Europe. They have also tried to improve farming efficiency, particularly in isolated areas. These policies have encouraged farmers to make their plots of land larger and to rearrange the land layout of their farms. But it has not been easy, and many schemes have taken years to be completed.

Problems in Galicia

One area which has been beset with problems is that of Galicia, an isolated region in north-west Spain (Source A). How could this agricultural landscape be made more efficient? What are the difficulties? Read on to find out.

A

BAY OF BISCAY

Corunna

Santiago de Compostela

GALICIA

Cantabrian Mountains

Gijon

Oviedo

Santander

San Sebastian

Vitoria

Pamplona

Pyrenees

Logroño

Miño

Leon

Burgos

Lima

Valladolid

Saragossa

Duero

Oporto

SPAIN

Salamanca

PORTUGAL

Madrid

ATLANTIC OCEAN

N

0   100 km

What is the farming landscape like?

1   Look at Source B. Galicia appears a fertile area.

a) Draw a labelled sketch of the photo showing evidence of this.

b) Actually, it is a poor area. This is the result of land being constantly divided amongst families for over 200 years, so that holdings have become smaller and smaller. Add notes to your sketch to show evidence of this.

Galicia in north-west Spain: an area of woodland, maize, potatoes and grassland

B

San Juan and San Julian de Laino are in Dodro parish, in the province of La Coruna in Galicia.

Location	25km south south-west of Santiago de Compostela	
Area	720 ha	
Farm sizes	less than 1 ha	453
	1 ha–2 ha	144
	2 ha–3 ha	52
	3 ha–5 ha	36
	over 5 ha	9
	Total	694
Ownership	Total number of plots 22,897 Average size 315m² Average number of plots per owner 17.4	

No owners could be traced for 503 plots (8.05 ha); the remaining 22,359 plots were owned by 1,286 people. Of these, 207 were absentee owners, of which 115 lived either in North or South America, 5 lived in Europe (outside Spain), 29 lived outside Galicia but in Spain and 58 lived in Galicia but not in the area of Dodro.

How do people hold land?

2 Señor Bustelo and Señor Castro held land in this area (Source C and Source D). Compare their holdings by completing the table below.

	Señor Bustelo	Señor Castro
Number of plots		
Total size of holding		
Average size of plots		
Pattern of plots		

What can be done to make farming more efficient?

3 You are a member of a government team working in the parish of Dodro in the province of La Coruna. With the results of an aerial survey, you have drawn the map (Source D). You are to write a report suggesting

Land ownership in San Juan and San Julian de Laino

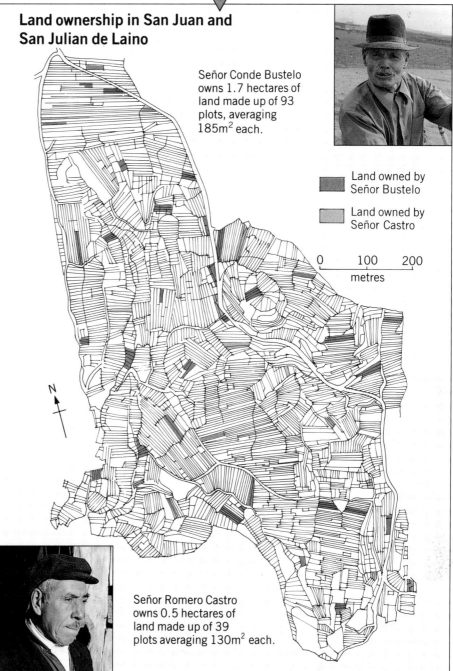

Señor Conde Bustelo owns 1.7 hectares of land made up of 93 plots, averaging 185m² each.

■ Land owned by Señor Bustelo
□ Land owned by Señor Castro

0   100   200
metres

Señor Romero Castro owns 0.5 hectares of land made up of 39 plots averaging 130m² each.

Erdkunde, 1985

how the farming pattern in the parish could be made more efficient. Use Sources B, C and D to

a) describe the size and pattern of plots.

b) give details of the size of farms and their ownership.

4 a) Illustrate your description with a variety of graphs.

b) Why might this pattern be inefficient?

5 a) Now recommend changes to the pattern of plots, fields and ownership to increase efficiency.

b) Illustrate your report. You could

do this by drawing a map to show Señor Bustelo's and Señor Castro's holdings after the changes you suggest.

What are the difficulties?

6 The land needed to be reorganised and reallocated. But it took ten years for the process to be completed. From the evidence and your own knowledge, discuss in pairs why land reorganisation is often difficult.

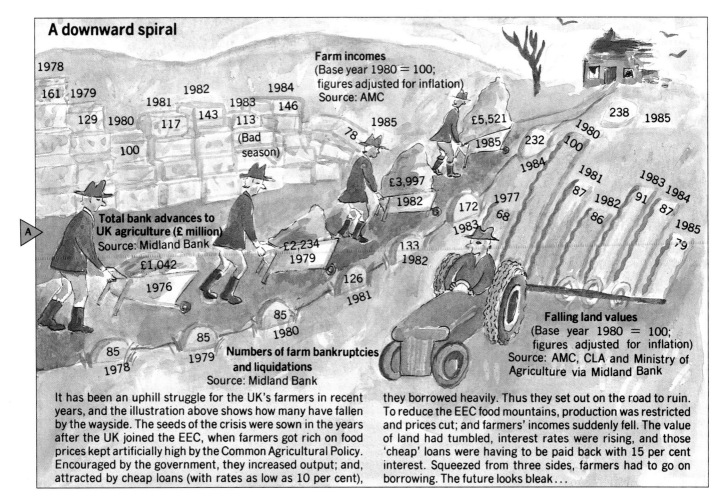

A downward spiral

Farm incomes
(Base year 1980 = 100;
figures adjusted for inflation)
Source: AMC

1978
161 1979
1980 129
100
1981 117
1982 143
1983 113
(Bad season)
1984 146
1985 78

£5,521 1985
£3,997 1982
£2,234 1979
£1,042 1976

Total bank advances to UK agriculture (£ million)
Source: Midland Bank

172 1977
68 1983
133 1982
126 1981
85 1980
85 1979
85 1978

Numbers of farm bankruptcies and liquidations
Source: Midland Bank

238 1985
232 1985
1980 100
1984
1981 87
1982 86
1983 91
1984 87
1985 79

Falling land values
(Base year 1980 = 100;
figures adjusted for inflation)
Source: AMC, CLA and Ministry of Agriculture via Midland Bank

It has been an uphill struggle for the UK's farmers in recent years, and the illustration above shows how many have fallen by the wayside. The seeds of the crisis were sown in the years after the UK joined the EEC, when farmers got rich on food prices kept artificially high by the Common Agricultural Policy. Encouraged by the government, they increased output; and, attracted by cheap loans (with rates as low as 10 per cent), they borrowed heavily. Thus they set out on the road to ruin. To reduce the EEC food mountains, production was restricted and prices cut; and farmers' incomes suddenly fell. The value of land had tumbled, interest rates were rising, and those 'cheap' loans were having to be paid back with 15 per cent interest. Squeezed from three sides, farmers had to go on borrowing. The future looks bleak . . .

The activities on this page give you the basis for a piece of coursework. In it you can investigate questions such as:
● What recent problems face UK farmers?
● How have farmers tackled these problems?
● What possible alternative solutions are there?

The fortunes of UK farmers may be on a downward spiral. With a partner:
a) Work out what Source A tells you about this. Single out a particular aspect of it, such as farm incomes, and try to explain what this part of the cartoon is attempting to show.
b) Use the text below the cartoon. Draw a flow diagram to show how and why farmers have had financial problems since 1973.

Change on the farm
2 You may be able to arrange a visit to a farm through your teacher or as part of a field trip. Before you go, draw up a list of questions to ask the farmer. You may want to find out about the effects of government policies on the farm, or about any future changes the farmer is planning.

Alternatives
3 Farmers have produced surpluses (see pages 66–7). As a result the government is encouraging land to be taken out of farm production. How might farmers use the land taken out of agricultural production? You could investigate forestry, tourism or other methods by looking at publications such as *Countryside Commission News* and *National Parks Today* in your library.

What about the farmworkers?
Farming is changing. If farmers are on the road to ruin, then so are farmworkers (see Source B). Their employment depends on decisions made by the farmers.

4 Find out about the quality of life of the UK farmworker. Your class could write to the Farmworkers' Union, now part of the Transport and General Workers' Union (TGWU).

> 66 I would not advise anyone to take a job in farming. I am a farmworker. We have to be skilled to use the machines yet we only get paid £135 a week. A worker in industry gets £170 a week. The machines are putting more and more of us out of a job. In 1950 there were 850,000 of us – now there are fewer than 130,000. I can't see a future in it. 99

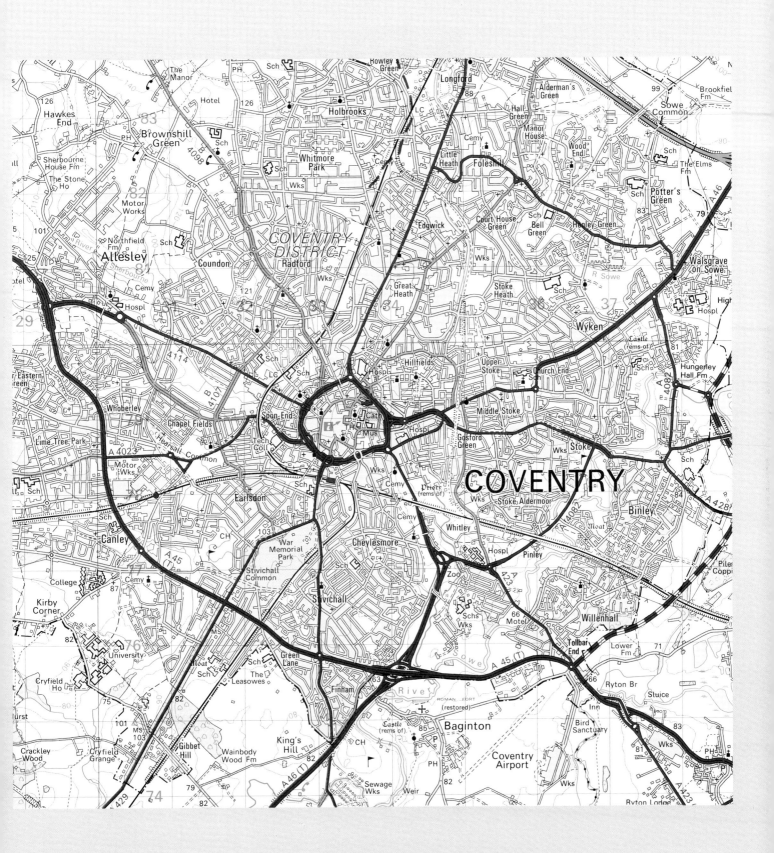

Coventry and surrounding areas

© Crown copyright reserved

Fishing near Whitby, Yorkshire

Welder repairing a ship, Hull

Working in an office with computers, London

When you leave school or college, you will look for a job. You may need to leave your home town to find employment. Jobs available vary from place to place. This Unit looks at employment opportunities in two areas of the UK. It discusses the reasons why these opportunities vary across the country and examines the changes taking place.

1 In groups discuss the types of work shown in Source A. Think about the following:
a) What is being done?
b) Where is it being done and by whom?
c) What skills are needed?
d) Are there any limitations on where the work could be done?

Regional trends

2 **a)** Divide into groups of between four and six people. Make a list of the types of job each group member would most like to do. Using Source B, decide which employment groups the jobs are in and which region you live in.

Types of employment: a regional breakdown	Employees (thousands) in all industries (nos 0–9), 1987	Agriculture, forestry, fishing (0)	Energy and water supply (1)	Metals, minerals and chemicals (2)	Metal goods, engineering and vehicles industries (3)	Other manufacturing (4)	Construction (5)	Distribution, hotels and catering, repairs (6)	Transport and communication (7)	Banking, finance and business services (8)	Public admin. and other services (9)
Area		(0)	(1)	(2)	(3)	(4)	(5)	(6)	(7)	(8)	(9)
		%	%	%	%	%	%	%	%	%	%
North	1,090	1	5	5	10	9	5	19	5	7	34
Yorkshire and Humberside	1,802	1	4	5	8	12	5	22	6	8	29
East Midlands	1,528	2	4	4	12	17	4	19	5	6	27
East Anglia	795	4	1	4	10	12	5	20	8	9	27
South East	7,448	1	1	2	9	7	4	21	8	15	32
South West	1,592	3	2	3	11	9	4	23	5	10	31
West Midlands	2,051	1	2	6	19	9	5	18	4	9	27
North West	2,262	1	2	4	11	12	5	22	5	9	29
England (total)	18,568	1	2	4	11	10	4	21	6	11	30
Wales	863	2	4	7	8	9	5	20	5	7	33
Scotland	1,886	2	2	2	10	9	7	20	6	9	33
Northern Ireland	485	4	2	2	6	12	6	16	4	6	42
United Kingdom (total)	21,802	1	2	3	10	10	5	21	6	11	31

Regional Trends (23), 1988

Joanna Dunham
- lives in the Green Lane area of Coventry, in a semi-detached house which she and her husband own.
- works as the manageress of a large department store in Coventry city centre.
- moved to Coventry from Leicester when the opportunity to become store manageress arose.

Michael Wallace
- lives in the Great Heath area of Coventry in an old terraced house.
- doesn't have a job at the moment but used to work in an engineering works in the Edgwick area before it closed down.
- has spent all his life in Coventry.

C

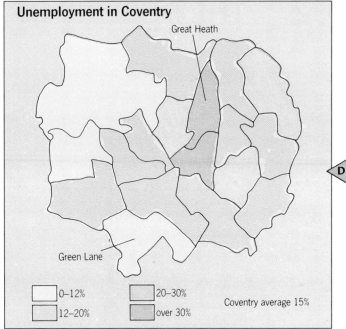

Unemployment in Coventry

Great Heath

Green Lane

D

☐	0–12%	☐	20–30%
☐	12–20%	☐	over 30%

Coventry average 15%

Unemployment rates (%) for 1989

Scotland – 9.7	West Midlands – 6.5
North – 10.2	South West – 4.8
North West – 9.0	East Anglia – 3.4
Yorks & Humberside – 7.7	South East – 4.0
East Midlands – 5.7	Northern Ireland – 15.7
Wales – 8.4	UK average – 6.5

E

b) Make a list of the employment groups in order of importance for your region.

c) Compare this list with the first list you made. Do the jobs you want to do come high up in the ranking list or not?

d) Are there any jobs it might be difficult to do in your region?

e) If you had to move to find the work you want, which two regions would give you the best chance of finding this work? Do the same two regions occur for all the job choices in the group?

3 a) Divide the UK economic regions among the members of your group. Using Source B, produce a set of graphs (bar-graphs, pie charts and/or maps) to show employment patterns in each region. Your group should first decide on a common scale and colour.

b) Prepare a brief group statement on what you think the main characteristics of employment are in each region.

c) What differences are there between the regions? Are there any similarities?

Keeping a job

Finding a job to suit you is difficult enough. Some people might not be able to get a job when they leave school. But even if you do get a job, keeping it can be difficult. To what extent are your chances of finding permanent employment determined by where you live?

Patterns of unemployment

4 Joanna Dunham and Michael Wallace both live in Coventry, part of the West Midlands. Study Source C, and using the Ordnance Survey map on page 71, locate the areas where Joanna and Michael live. Describe each area.

5 a) Use Source D to decide how typical their employment situation is of their areas.

b) Suggest reasons for their different employment prospects.

c) Why do you think Joanna and Michael live where they do?

6 Unemployment varies from region to region. Use Source E to plot the above and below-average unemployment figures on a map of the UK.

Unemployment

New technology		
Mineral resources exhausted		
Firms re-organising and cutting back (rationalisation)		
Foreign competition		
Lack of money for investment		
High costs of production		
Product less in demand		
New methods of production		
Seasonal change		
Political decisions		
Development of rival products		

F

7 Which two regions offer the best employment opportunities? In which two areas are people most likely to be unemployed?

8 *Investigation*: for your local area or region, show how some or all of the reasons given in Source F might have led to unemployment.

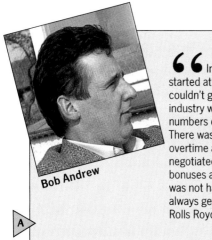

A

> **66** In the early 1970s, when I started at the Triumph car works we couldn't go wrong. The vehicle industry was in full swing and record numbers of cars were being sold. There was steady work, lots of overtime and the unions had negotiated good deals on wages, bonuses and working conditions. If I was not happy at Triumph I could always get similar work at Jaguar or Rolls Royce. **99**

Bob Andrew

Car factories in Coventry

Grid reference	Former works use	Works use now
300818	Jaguar	Jaguar
332822	Car bodies for taxis	Car bodies for taxis
332808	Daimler works	Jaguar
353810	Morris engine works	Demolished
321795	Alvis cars	Armoured vehicles
305784	Standard Triumph	Unipart spares
306779	Coventry radiators	Coventry radiators
338783	Armstrong Siddeley	Rolls Royce
352779	Humber engines	Peugeot-Talbot
348762	Hillman cars	Jaguar design centre
376747	Hillman	Peugeot-Talbot

D

Most people want and need to work. But in many places it is not easy to find a job. Everywhere industry is changing and so are the opportunities for work. In some places the number of jobs is declining; in others it is growing.

The vehicle industry

In Coventry, job opportunities have changed. Until about 1970 it was a thriving industrial town. There was work in car manufacturing. Then the UK car industry declined and jobs became scarce (Source A).

1 Look at Source B.
  a) What work is being done?
  b) Who is doing the work?
  c) What levels of skill do you think are needed to do the job?

2 Using Source C, work out the total numbers employed in primary, secondary and tertiary occupations in Coventry in 1971. Draw a bar graph or pie graph to show these figures.
3 **a)** List the secondary industries shown in Source C in order of importance.
  b) How many of these occupations are linked with the vehicle industry? What sort of links might there be with it?
  c) How important was the vehicle industry to Coventry in 1971?
4 Using Source D and the map on page 71, draw a sketch map to show the distribution of some of the car factories in Coventry.

C

Employment in Coventry 1971

Employment groups	Number
Primary	
Agriculture, forestry, fishing	423
Mining and quarrying	1,476
Secondary	
Food, drink and tobacco	1,623
Coal and petroleum products	129
Chemicals and allied industries	133
Metal manufacture	1,022
Mechanical engineering	21,303
Electrical engineering	19,162
Vehicles	70,171
Other metal goods	6,919
Textiles	5,828
Clothing and footwear and leather goods	236
Bricks, pottery, glass and cement	760
Timber, furniture etc.	1,142
Paper, printing, publishing	1,475
Other Manufacturing Industries	1,176
Tertiary	
Construction	5,973
Gas, electricity, water	1,424
Transport and communication	4,223
Distributive trades	11,723
Insurance, banking, finance	2,785
Professional and scientific services	18,354
Miscellaneous services	10,315
Public administration, defence	4,730
Total	192,505

The Triumph car works at Coventry in 1971

B

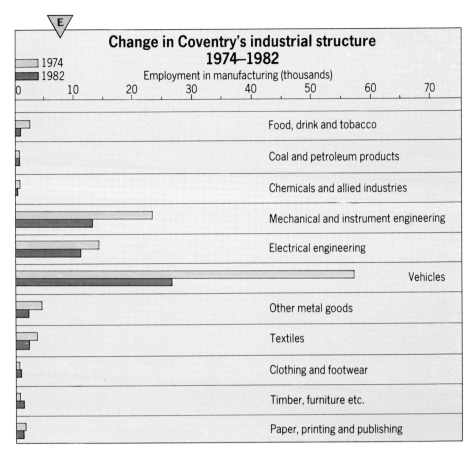

Change in Coventry's industrial structure 1974–1982

■ 1974
■ 1982

Employment in manufacturing (thousands)

0   10   20   30   40   50   60   70

Food, drink and tobacco

Coal and petroleum products

Chemicals and allied industries

Mechanical and instrument engineering

Electrical engineering

Vehicles

Other metal goods

Textiles

Clothing and footwear

Timber, furniture etc.

Paper, printing and publishing

The effect of decline

Things are a lot different now! I don't work in the car factory any more. I lost my job there a long while ago. At the time, there were a lot of problems in the car industry: competition from imported cars ... not making the right cars at the right price ... making too many different types of cars ... poor industrial relations. ... All I know is that the company cut back on staff and invested more in machinery. Even with my skills I haven't been able to get another job in a car factory.

The effect of all these changes is rather depressing. Factories have changed what they make. Some have closed down altogether. With unemployment well above the national average of 6.5%, the future isn't very bright. It certainly won't be like the old days at Triumph.

The scale of decline

5 Using Source E complete a copy of the table below to show industrial change in Coventry from 1974 to 1982.
  a) List the top five manufacturing industries in 1974 and 1982.
  b) Work out the number of employees in each industry in each year.
  c) Calculate the changes between 1974 and 1982.

d) Are there any manufacturing industries where employment has increased?

6 **a)** Look at Source F. What problems did the car industry face in the late 1970s?
  b) How did these problems affect workers in the car industry?

7 Using Source G, describe what has happened to:
  a) each type of employment in Coventry.
  b) total employment.

8 You are the industrial correspondent of the *Coventry Evening Telegraph*. You have been asked to write a front-page article about industrial change in Coventry. Use the information from this page and page 74 to write your article. Include at least two illustrations (maps, graphs or similar) and make up a suitable headline. If you have access to a word processor, use it to present your article as a newspaper story.

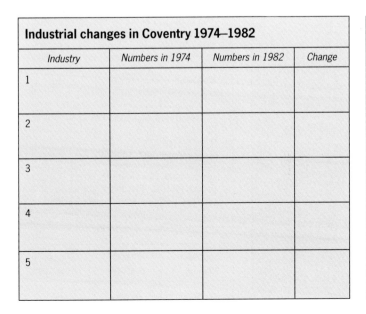

Industrial changes in Coventry 1974–1982

Industry	Numbers in 1974	Numbers in 1982	Change
1			
2			
3			
4			
5			

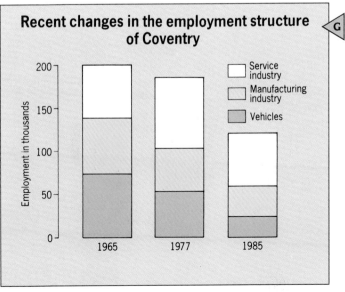

Recent changes in the employment structure of Coventry

Employment in thousands

200
150
100
50
0

1965   1977   1985

☐ Service industry
☐ Manufacturing industry
☐ Vehicles

A

Stopping the decline

Coventry is making a great attempt to combat the decline in industry by attracting new businesses. The town is competing with many other areas, so it is essential that publicity is good. Coventry offers businesses a range of financial incentives, although since 1988 the government has cut back on some of its regional funding.

1 Look at Source A and in small groups discuss the following:
   a) How does the advertisement attempt to attract new businesses to Coventry? How effective do you think it is?
   b) What other information do you think a business person might want to know about Coventry?

Financial assistance

2 Use Source B to complete the table below it. Which source of assistance do you think would be most effective? Say why.
3 Other regions are also competing for new businesses. They often put advertisements in national newspapers.
   a) Collect examples of promotional material from different regions.
   b) Analyse how they attempt to attract businesses to their area.
4 The advertisements aim to emphasise such points as the attractions of the place, people, services offered and quality of life. Using one example from those you have found, examine how each of these points is brought to the attention of the reader. Is it by map, photograph, slogan, text, use of colour, layout or overall effect?
5 Design your own advertisement to attract new businesses to your area.

B

Financial Assistance

Firms moving to Coventry may get help with their investment costs from several sources:

● European Coal and Steel Community. The loans can be up to 50% of costs with a maximum of £10,000 per new job. The rate of interest is approximately 4% below commercial rates and there is a four year repayment holiday.
● British Coal Enterprise. Loans at commercial rates of interest, but with discretionary interest rate subsidies and/or repayment holidays. The loans can be up to 25% of total project costs or £5,000 per job created.
● Coventry City Council. The Council provides discretionary Business Expansion Loans for manufacturing service industry firms. The loans are up to 50% of costs, with a maximum of £100,000.

Source of finance	What is available	Special provisions

The science park

One of the main attractions of Coventry is the science park at Warwick University. It is one of 38 science parks in the country, but is likely to become one of the most important ones in the future.

6 **a)** Using the map on page 71 and Source C, give the grid references of the following: Westwood, University of Warwick; central campus, University of Warwick; Cannon Park shopping centre.
b) Source C was taken from a helicopter. In which direction was the camera pointing?
c) Draw a sketch map to show the location of the Warwick University science park. Add notes to show why this is a good site.

Warwick University science park

C

University of Warwick Central Campus

Science Park

Cannon Park Shopping Centre

University of Warwick Westwood

D

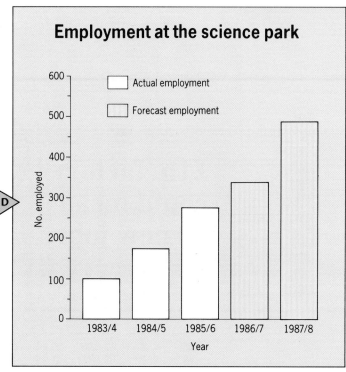

Employment at the science park

☐ Actual employment
▨ Forecast employment

No. employed

600
500
400
300
200
100
0

1983/4 1984/5 1985/6 1986/7 1987/8
Year

E

Some employers at the Science Park

Animal embryo transfer and genetic engineering

International Embryos

COMPUTERVISION

Computer and communication systems for industrial applications.

Invention and development of new products for manufacturers.

EXOTECH
INNOVATIVE PRODUCTS FOR MANUFACTURERS

sinclair /Vehicles

Development and marketing of electric vehicles.

7 **a)** At the end of 1986 there were 32 companies operating from the science park. They were housed in 14 buildings. Assume that the park is now complete. From Source C, draw a large outline of the site of the science park. On your outline, show where you would locate the buildings within the area. (Don't forget to include roads and car parks.)
b) Show how you would landscape the area – e.g. with small lakes, trees and so on. (Science parks pay great attention to providing attractive landscaping.)

8 **a)** Use Sources D and E to describe the types of businesses found at the science park from 1983 to 1988.
b) Suggest why this location is an advantage for these businesses.

Who benefits?

9 **a)** Describe the type of person who is most likely to work in the science park. Think about factors such as age, sex, skill level, qualifications and experience.
b) Who is *not* likely to benefit from the new jobs at the science park?
c) How do you think the growth of the kind of jobs provided by the

science park will affect Coventry's employment structure? (Look again at the traditional jobs shown in Source E on page 75.)

10 Science parks, industrial estates and business parks all try to keep business together in particular locations. Why should they try and do this? For a local example investigate:
● where it is situated.
● the number and types of firms.
● its layout.
● its particular advantages and disadvantages.

Adrian Cobley is a planner. He has lived all his life in East Anglia.

'There have been lots of changes around here. That new industrial estate is built on land that used to be farmed. I remember when there were good crops of wheat and potatoes there. The town has changed too. It has grown. A lot of people have moved here from the South East. There are lots of new industries too. That helps to make up for the lost farming jobs.'

Mildenhall Industrial Estate

Growth and prosperity

We have seen how Coventry has declined industrially and how it is making attempts to halt this decline. Other regions have been going from strength to strength. They seem to have an air of prosperity. On these pages we focus on why some regions have been so successful in attracting people and industry.

1 From Source A, make a list of the changes which have taken place in East Anglia over the last few years.

2 Look at Source B. What sort of industry might be found on the Mildenhall Industrial Estate?

Where to locate?

3 A group of geography students were asked why firms might be attracted to places like Mildenhall in East Anglia. The suggestions they made are given in Source C.
a) Rank the reasons in order of importance.
b) Collect the rankings for your class. In groups discuss what conclusions you can draw from these rankings.
c) What other factors not mentioned in Source C do you think industrialists might need to think about in deciding on a location? Make a table to show your findings.

4 Your class list may or may not paint an accurate picture of how industrialists decide on a location.
a) Read Source D and on a copy of Source C tick the ones which seem to apply to the firm of Spong.
b) What other reasons are mentioned in the case study? Add these to your list.

Reasons for location	
Close to market	
Close to raw materials	
Links with local industry	
Suitable labour available	
Land available	
Premises available	
Pleasant surroundings	
Personal reasons	
Central location for distribution	
Room to expand	
Availability of housing	

£1m factory could mean 70 new jobs

A new £1 million factory is to be built in Mildenhall, with up to 70 new jobs created over the next 15 months.

This is part of a growth plan by the retail display manufacturers, Spong Retail Systems.

Spong has decided to centralise all its retail activities in Mildenhall from where it plans to grow into an international concern by the early 1990s.

At Mildenhall, Spong currently has a 2,323 sq. m factory employing 90 production workers and another 35 in administration and sales.

Under the new scheme, it plans to build another 2,787 sq. m extension which is expected to employ about 150 at the April opening, rising to about 190 at the end of 1989.

Mr Banks explained: 'We intend to become one of the major suppliers of retail display systems in the UK and after we have reached the right level we hope to extend into Europe and North America.'

Mr Banks said the firm would need more people after 1989, but he expected the workforce to level out at about 200.

Newmarket Weekly News 15 September 1988

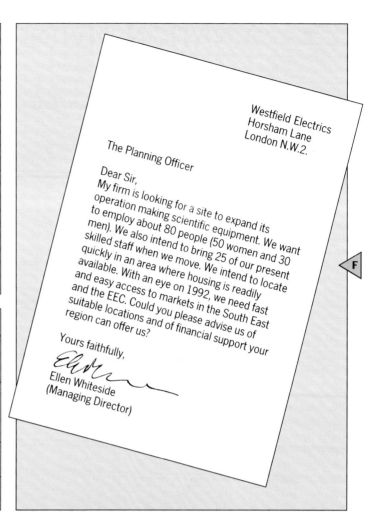

Adrian: I often get letters from firms like Westfield Electrics. They want information to help them make a sensible locational decision.

Interviewer: What do you say to them?

AC: I try to encourage them to locate in East Anglia. I say that there are many growing towns in our area. They offer attractive locations. They can offer accommodation to key workers. This is important to firms which are moving out of London.

Interviewer: But don't industrialists complain about East Anglia's isolation?

AC: Perhaps that was true a long time ago. But the government invested in better roads. You have only to think of the M11 and the A45, now dual carriageways. And we have the big attraction of Felixstowe, one of the fastest growing ports in the country, one of our outlets to Europe. We expect it to grow even more after 1992, when Europe becomes one market.

Westfield Electrics
Horsham Lane
London N.W.2.

The Planning Officer

Dear Sir,
My firm is looking for a site to expand its operation making scientific equipment. We want to employ about 80 people (50 women and 30 men). We also intend to bring 25 of our present skilled staff when we move. We intend to locate quickly in an area where housing is readily available. With an eye on 1992, we need fast and easy access to markets in the South East and the EEC. Could you please advise us of suitable locations and of financial support your region can offer us?

Yours faithfully,

Ellen Whiteside
(Managing Director)

Location Analysis Sheet

Company Name Company Type Size			Requirements		
Towns where sites are available	Population	Distance from London (km)	Distance from port (km)	Expansion scheme or not?	Major trunk road?
Peterborough	110,000	150	King's Lynn 55	Yes	Yes: A1/A47
King's Lynn					

The move from London

Many manufacturing firms have moved to East Anglia. Between 1955 and 1985, jobs in manufacturing in the region increased by 75%.

5 Read Source E and Source F. Now imagine you are Adrian Cobley and you have to reply to the letter from Ellen Whiteside (Source F) to advise on suitable locations for her firm. You first need to be familiar with the characteristics of the firm. In pairs:
a) Write the information about the company on to a copy of the location analysis sheet.
b) Using Source G, complete the sheet for the following towns: Kings Lynn, Great Yarmouth, Thetford, Mildenhall, Bury St Edmunds, Newmarket, Cambridge, St Neots, Huntingdon, Haverhill, Sudbury and Ipswich.
6 Write a letter to Ellen Whiteside. Give your recommendations and outline the reasons for your choices.

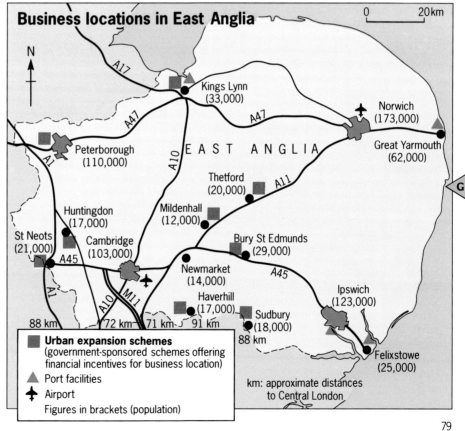

Business locations in East Anglia

Urban expansion schemes (government-sponsored schemes offering financial incentives for business location)
Port facilities
Airport
Figures in brackets (population)

km: approximate distances to Central London

7.5 A NATION DIVIDED?

A

'I can earn good money, but in this area it's impossible for people like me to buy a house of their own. A two-bedroomed cottage here went for £100,000. I haven't got money like that, but there are plenty of people who have, so it's not going to get any better. And yet there's such a wait for the council, you need to be some kind of a special case to get a place from them.'

The North-South divide

N

THE NORTH

Stockton-on-Tees

Wallingford

0   100 km

THE SOUTH

'I've not had a job since I left school two years ago, although I did YTS for a year. Youth unemployment here is very high. We are told to move to where the jobs are, but that is difficult. Where would we live, even if we found a job? At my age it would be too expensive to buy a house. Rented property isn't cheap either.'

The West Midlands and East Anglia are both trying to attract new industry, but at the moment these regions have different employment potential. Wealth, employment and the quality of life also differ throughout the UK. Many people think that the UK has become two nations with a North–South divide. What is the evidence to support such a view?

North and South

1 Tracey Rose and Andy Smith have different views on life in the UK. One of them lives in Stockton-on-Tees, the other in Wallingford in Oxford-shire. Study Source A and answer the following questions:
   a) Which person lives in the North and which in the South?
   b) Where does the North–South divide occur in the map?
   c) What is the main problem for Tracey and Andy?
2 You can compare economic circumstances to find out whether a significant North–South divide exists. Using Source B, show how wealth varies around the country. Draw an ISOPLETH MAP of average weekly household incomes. (Isopleths are lines showing equal values, so choose your values carefully, for example £180, £200, and so on.)

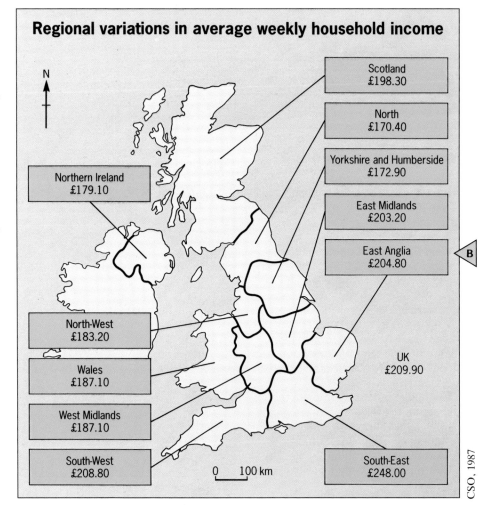

Regional variations in average weekly household income

N

Scotland £198.30

North £170.40

Yorkshire and Humberside £172.90

East Midlands £203.20

East Anglia £204.80

B

Northern Ireland £179.10

North-West £183.20

Wales £187.10

West Midlands £187.10

South-West £208.80

UK £209.90

South-East £248.00

0   100 km

CSO, 1987

3 Turn to Source E on page 75. Draw a CHOROPLETH MAP to show how unemployment varies around the country.

4 Do the maps you have drawn suggest the existence of a North–South divide? Give your reasons.

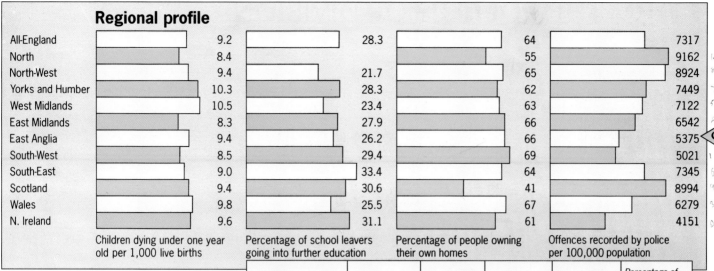

Regional profile

Region	Children dying under one year old per 1,000 live births	Percentage of school leavers going into further education	Percentage of people owning their own homes	Offences recorded by police per 100,000 population
All-England	9.2	28.3	64	7317
North	8.4		55	9162
North-West	9.4	21.7	65	8924
Yorks and Humber	10.3	28.3	62	7449
West Midlands	10.5	23.4	63	7122
East Midlands	8.3	27.9	66	6542
East Anglia	9.4	26.2	66	5375
South-West	8.5	29.4	69	5021
South-East	9.0	33.4	64	7345
Scotland	9.4	30.6	41	8994
Wales	9.8	25.5	67	6279
N. Ireland	9.6	31.1	61	4151

C

Industry and employment

Different regions have different industries and employment prospects. Some jobs pay higher wages than others. Is there a difference in occupational structure between North and South?

5 Look back to Source B on page 72. Complete a copy of the table on the right to show the over-representation of occupations in the different regions. To do this, compare the average figure for the U.K. with the figure for the region. If the percentage figure for the region is higher than the figure for the UK, then the occupation is over-represented in that region. Scotland has been done for you.

6 How does this information help to explain the divisions you have seen in wealth and employment prospects?

The quality of life

Economic factors show clear differences between regions in the UK. But such factors give an incomplete picture of what it is like to live in different regions. We can use social factors to get a fuller picture of material wealth in different regions.

7 a) Carefully study Source C. Using the table on the right, rank each region in the UK from best (1) to worst (11). (You must decide which end of the scale for each graph is good or bad.) A low figure for unemployment will therefore get a low score but a low figure for households with a telephone will get a high score.

Regional figures	Unemployment rate	GROSS DOMESTIC PRODUCT per head (£)	Average house prices (£)	Percentage of households with telephone	Percentage of workforce holding a degree or equivalent
South East	4.0	5,155	84,000	75.6	11.9
South West	4.8	4,147	69,000	65.6	7.7
East Anglia	3.4	4,204	69,000	68.2	7.3
West Midlands	6.5	3,814	60,000	63.9	6.5
East Midlands	5.7	4,104	56,000	61.1	6.5
Yorks and Humberside	7.7	3,958	47,000	60.6	6.4
North	10.2	3,880	43,000	52.9	5.9
North West	9.0	4,073	49,000	65.8	7.4
Scotland	9.7	4,173	46,000	69.4	8.4
Wales	8.4	3,627	50,000	58.5	5.9
Northern Ireland	15.7	3,156	33,000	45.5	6.1

Regions in your definition of the North	Occupations over-represented
Scotland	Agriculture Energy and water supply Construction Public administration and other services

Where would you like to live?

	Scotland	Wales	
Average weekly income			
Unemployment			
Percentage of school leavers in F.E.			
Children dying under one year old			
Notifiable offences			
Percentage owner occupiers			
GDP per head			
Average home prices			
Percentage of households with telephone			
Percentage of workforce with degree or equivalent			
Total			

b) Add up the scores for each region. Now rank the regions in order of best places to live as far as wealth is concerned. (Remember that the *lowest* score gives the best quality of life.)

c) Comment on your findings.

8 a) What other factors do you think should be considered to give a fairer picture of each region?

b) Where would you most like to live? Say why.

9 Where does this investigation show the North–South divide to be?

7 THE POLITICS OF DIVISION

A

B

Voting behaviour by region at the 1987 General Election

Region	% of votes cast			Seats		
	Con	Lab.	All	Con.	Lab.	All
Greater London	46.5	31.5	21.3	58	23	3
South East	55.6	16.8	27.3	107	1	0
East Anglia	52.1	21.7	25.8	19	1	0
South West	50.6	15.9	33.1	44	1	3
West Midlands	45.5	33.3	20.8	36	22	0
East Midlands	48.6	30.0	21.0	31	11	0
North West	38.0	41.2	20.6	34	36	3
Yorkshire & Humberside	37.4	40.6	21.7	21	33	0
North	32.3	46.4	21.0	8	27	1
Wales*	29.5	45.1	17.9	8	24	3
Scotland†	24.0	42.4	19.2	10	50	9

*excluding Plaid Cymru (Welsh Nationalists)
†excluding Scottish National Party

Jenkins, 1987

An investigation

1 Look at Source A. Where does the cartoonist show the North–South divide to be?

2 Trace the outline of the UK from Source C. Use Source B to draw a map to show voting behaviour by region at the 1987 General Election. Choose a colour for each party and shade each region according to which party got most votes there. Compare your map with that in the cartoon. Does the cartoon give a fair picture?

3 Put your tracing over Source C and compare the pattern it shows with your map of voting behaviour by region.

Explaining voting patterns

4 **a)** Try to explain the regional pattern of voting behaviour. You may think that there is a relationship between wealth and voting behaviour, or between unemployment and voting behaviour.

b) In groups, brainstorm other possible relationships which might help to explain these voting patterns.

5 Using data from this Unit, particularly Source E on page 73 and Source C on page 81, test your suggestions by drawing scatter graphs. Comment on your findings.

C

Voting behaviour by constituency in the 1987 General Election

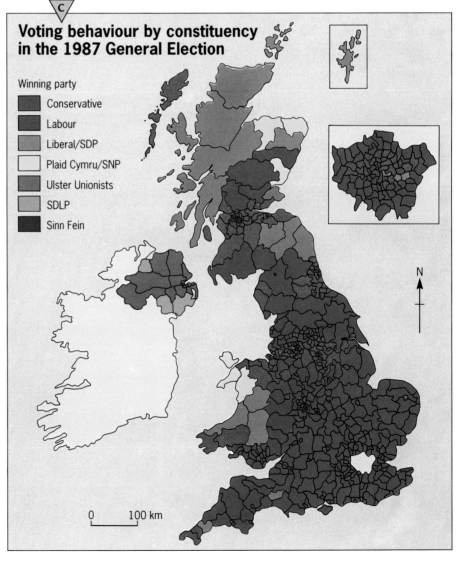

Winning party
- Conservative
- Labour
- Liberal/SDP
- Plaid Cymru/SNP
- Ulster Unionists
- SDLP
- Sinn Fein

N

0   100 km

A CAPITALIST ECONOMY: JAPAN

Sunday afternoon in the city

The capitalist economy

1 The photograph on page 83 is of the centre of a major city in one of the world's richest countries. In pairs discuss the following:

a) What major types of work might be going on in this city?

b) What is the environment like?

c) What economic, social and other characteristics do you think a society needs before it can create this type of environment?

Such an environment is found in many modern cities. The photograph on page 83 shows a concentration of wealth and activity characteristic of rich countries. These countries are run on an economic system known as CAPITALISM.

Capitalism can be described as an economic system which uses **capital** in the production of **goods** and **services** for sale in order to make a profit ... it is a system in which capital is **privately owned** ... not owned by the government. Private ownership is an essential feature of the economic system called capitalism.

... it is also a social system in that it consists of different sections of the population (we call them **social classes**) distinguished by their ownership or non-ownership of capital. Those who own capital have greater **power** than those who do not. Capitalism implies certain kinds of freedom.

Capitalism, Donaldson and Pollins, Hamish Hamilton (adapted)

What is capitalism?

2 Look at Source A. Helena Gregoriov comes from the Soviet Union and is visiting a school in the UK. She is studying economic geography and you have been asked to explain capitalism to her. In pairs, try to explain what each of the words in heavy type in Source A mean.

3 Capitalism is about producing goods or services for profit. These products are bought by people – the CONSUMERS. The words below refer to production and consumption.

> ... Capital is invested ...
> ... who decide what they want and need ...
> ... to produce goods and services ...
> ... who buys at a price ...
> ... in factories ...
> ... which are sold at a profit ...
> ... in raw materials ...
> ... Workers use their labour ...
> ... in technology and equipment ...
> ... to consumers ...

a) Use these words to write a paragraph describing production and consumption in a capitalist system.

b) Present your ideas about the capitalist system in simple diagrams. Draw one diagram to show production for a profit (refer to Source B) and another to show who has the power to make decisions.

An economy is a capitalist one:

● Where most of the capital (money and property) is owned by *private* companies and by individuals.

● Where making a profit is the main aim of economic activity.

● Where the competitive market (called the MARKET MECHANISM) rather than the government determines economic decisions.

4 How much freedom do you think a capitalist system offers to:

a) the businessman?

b) the worker?

c) the consumer?

The command economy

Many countries work a capitalist system, but some are run on a system where the State plays a more important part. Such a system is called a COMMAND ECONOMY.

5 Using Sources A, B and C, outline the main differences between a capitalist and a command economy. Think about who makes important decisions, who owns the capital and what the system is aiming at.

Change

Helena Gregoriov takes a traditional view of her country's economy. But things are changing. With GLASNOST (openness) and PERESTROIKA (restructuring) more attention is being paid in the Soviet Union to the ideas of profit, cost, efficiency and incentives. All these are ideas associated with capitalism.

The mixed economy

It is also important to realise that a capitalist system often includes much government ownership and involvement. In many parts of the world it may be more accurate to speak of countries with a MIXED ECONOMY.

6 a) What does Source D tell you about the economic systems of the countries shown?
b) Source D does not have a scale. How might you measure an economy so that you could place a country on the diagram more accurately?
7 Work in pairs. Choose two 'unclassified' countries from Source B. Discuss where you would position them on Source D. Use reference books to help you.

Helena Gregoriov, Soviet student

One of our basic communist ideas is that capitalism is unjust. It is unfair because capital is privately owned by a few rich people or groups. When the communist party took political power in the Soviet Union in 1917, it took away capital from private hands and took it into government ownership.

We are against the idea of leaving important economic decisions to rich individuals purely out to make a profit for themselves. We prefer decisions to be made by a central planning body. That way, things can be co-ordinated. However, some people feel that the bureaucracy of centrally-planned economies hinders progress and that the lack of a profit motive leads to less efficient production systems.

C

Central planning in the Soviet Union

Decisions made by Communist Party

Central Planning Commission (Gosplan) | Ministries and State organisations

Republic and regional planning commissions

Managers of individual enterprises

(This diagram is much simplified)

The next Units study work and employment within different economic systems.

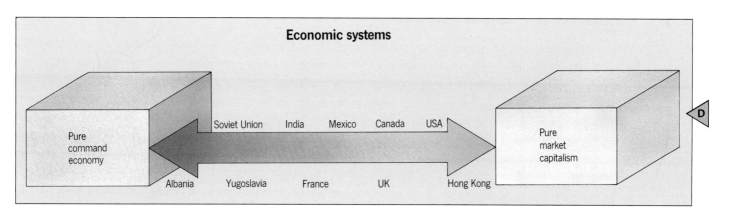

Economic systems

Pure command economy

Soviet Union · India · Mexico · Canada · USA

Albania · Yugoslavia · France · UK · Hong Kong

Pure market capitalism

D

WORKING AND LIVING IN CAPITALIST JAPAN

Japan is one of the richest countries in the world. It has an advanced capitalist economy. Capital is invested by individuals and firms to make a profit. The rest of this Unit examines the Japanese economy. It looks at the work created and discusses the quality of life. It also asks whether Japan fits into a simple definition of capitalism.

The microchip

Japan has invested a great deal of capital in manufacturing industry. Today it is a leading competitor in the advanced high technology industry. Japan makes half the world's microchips, which are essential for advanced modern industry.

1 **a)** Japanese firms are investing in microchip factories on the island of Kyushu. Some of the advantages of the island are given on the right. Using Source A, Source B and an atlas, discuss in pairs what evidence there is for each advantage. What benefits might each offer to a microchip firm?
b) Are there any advantages for which you cannot find any evidence?

2 **a)** Look at Source B. Five major Japanese firms making microchips have chosen the north east corner of the island of Kyushu – the Oita region – as the area to build a new factory. Each firm wants to find the best site. In pairs choose *one* of the firms from the following: Sony; Japan Texas Instruments; Toshiba; Aiwa; Nippon Electrical Company. Your firm has the capital to build a large factory. (It will need 70,000m² of land and will employ 2,000 people.) The ten available sites are shown in Source B.
b) Decide which is the best site for your firm. You will need to list the factors which are important to your decision. (Source C suggests some and you can add others). On a copy of Source C score each site on a 1–5 scale (5 = excellent; 1 = poor).
c) Decide whether all the factors are of equal importance. You may need to weight the factors. Total the score for each site. The site with the highest score will be the best one. List your five best sites in rank order.

3 If all the firms came into the area at the same time searching for the best site, they might all choose the same one. What influences do you think would decide which firm gained the most popular site?

Amakusa, Kumamoto Prefecture, Kyushu A

- Kyushu is a large agricultural area.
- Kyushu has only a few small, scattered concentrations of industry.
- It is away from congested Tokyo.
- There is a lot of cheap, high quality female labour.
- The government offers incentives.
- Kyushu has good road and rail transport.
- Kyushu has clean water and good environmental conditions.
- The environment is attractive.
- It has large airports originally built for the tourist trade.
- There is much cheap land available.

B The Oita region of Kyushu island

0   20km

Nakatsu
IYO GULF
▲ Airport
Hiji Kitsuki
Beppu
Oita

N

1000–1500
500–1000
200–500
0–200 metres
†† Railway
— Principal road   ✳ Possible factory site
▬▬ Motorway   North Oita
(under construction)   Technopolis

Factors influencing the location of industry

	Access to transport	Large area of flat land	Labour from nearby	Location in technopolis	Other factors	Total
1						
2						
3						

C

The 'technopolis programme' is sponsored by the Ministry of International Trade and Industry. Oita technopolis is one of 19 places in Japan where knowledge intensive industry is to be promoted.

The NEC factory at Oita

Q: Does the firm treat you well?

TT: In Japan, we have strong loyalty to the firm. We are involved in some decision making. Most of the big firms have good social and leisure amenities for the workers.

Q: What about the future?

TT: AUTOMATION is becoming a worry. The management argue that robots cut costs and improve quality. It's true they take over the monotonous and repetitive jobs. But the number of women employed is going down. Ten years ago we made up 80% of the workforce; now it's 61%. The proportion will continue to fall.

Working with the microchip

4 Look at Source D and answer the following questions:

a) What advantages does work in the microchip industry offer people like Toshiko Tanaka? What disadvantages do you think exist?

b) Microchip firms in Kyushu are having difficulties in filling job vacancies. Suggest reasons for this.

5 Look at Source E. Draw a sketch to show the characteristics of the factory and its environment. Add the following labels to your sketch (you can put in others of your own): 70,000m² site, single storey building, 2,000 employees, controlled environment inside factory, cheap land (in Tokyo land is five times more expensive), large amount of money invested.

Business links

The NEC factory at Oita relies on other firms in the area for equipment. It sells some of its products to firms nearby. All these linked firms provide job opportunities.

6 Study Source F. In pairs, discuss the advantages to firms of being located close together.

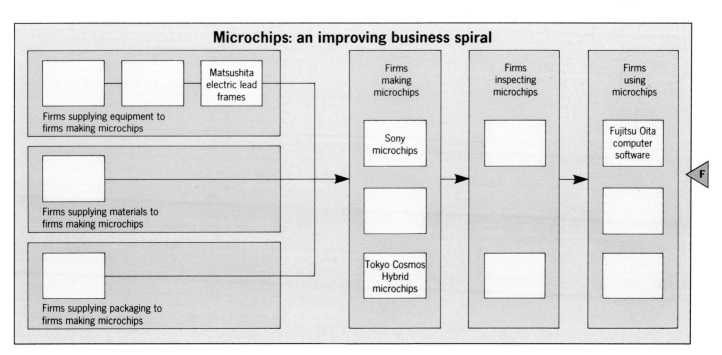

Microchips: an improving business spiral

Firms supplying equipment to firms making microchips — Matsushita electric lead frames

Firms supplying materials to firms making microchips

Firms supplying packaging to firms making microchips

Firms making microchips — Sony microchips — Tokyo Cosmos Hybrid microchips

Firms inspecting microchips

Firms using microchips — Fujitsu Oita computer software

MICROCHIPS: LOCATION AND INVESTMENT

Kyushu is the most important region in Japan for making microchips. It is also the world's third largest area for microchip manufacture after the Central Valley of California and the Dallas region of Texas. But there are many microchip firms in other parts of Japan.

Microchip production (millions of units)											
Year	1975	1976	1977	1978	1979	1980	1981	1982	1983	1984	1985
Japan	329	666	803	1,176	1,777	2,660	3,495	4,381	6,229	9,516	13,412
Kyushu	95	250	302	486	690	937	1,240	1,638	2,460	3,974	6,000

A

How many microchips?

1 a) Look at Source A. Using the same axis, draw two line graphs to show microchip production in Kyushu and in Japan from 1975 to 1985 in million units.
b) What proportion of production was made by firms located in Kyushu in 1975, 1980 and 1985?

Capital has been invested in the many factories shown in Source B. Some factories manufacture unpackaged chips (preliminary processing). Others fit the microchips into plastic or ceramic packages, and attach lead wires to allow external connection. This is known as *finishing*. There are also factor-

ies which undertake both preliminary processing and finishing. This is known as *integrated production*. Some plants are involved in development and design, including the production of experimental chips.

2 Using Source B, complete the table below by filling in the number and type of factories in each region.
3 a) Which of the three areas in Source B has the most factories?
b) Which type of factory is dominant in each area?
c) Which type has the largest number?

d) A Kyushu businessman was quoted as saying: 'This is not silicon island, but silicon colony'. What do you think he meant by this?
e) What evidence is there for this view in your table?

The world picture
4 a) Look at Source C. Rank the world microchip companies by order of 1988 sales.
b) How many Japanese firms are in the world top ten? Name them.
c) Rank the world microchip companies by growth from 1987 to 1988. Are the Japanese firms world leaders in terms of growth?

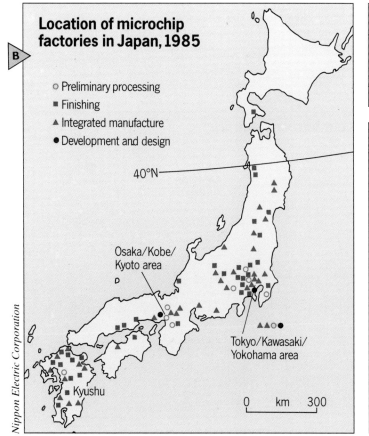

B

Location of microchip factories in Japan, 1985

○ Preliminary processing
■ Finishing
▲ Integrated manufacture
● Development and design

40°N

Osaka/Kobe/Kyoto area

Tokyo/Kawasaki/Yokohama area

Kyushu

0   km   300

Nippon Electric Corporation

Region	Preliminary processing	Finishing	Integrated	Development and design	Total
1					
2					
3					
Total					

Microchip companies worldwide						C
Country	Company	1987 rank	1988 sales (£ million)	1988 rank	1987–88 % growth	
Japan	NEC	1	2,577		30	
Japan	Toshiba	2	2,269		23	
Japan	Hitachi	3	2,052		32	
US	Motorola	4	1,827		24	
US	Texas Instruments	5	1,651		24	
Netherlands	Philips	6	1,241		25	
US	Intez	7	1,373		50	
Japan	Matsushita	8	1,157		16	
Japan	Fujitsu	9	1,250		47	
Japan	Mitsubishi	10	1,173		44	

Financial Times, 7 December 1988

Changing investment

Japanese business people aim to invest in profit-making activities. Read Source D to find out how their investment decisions have changed over the years.

5 a) Make a copy of Source E. On it, mark the 1959 figures for investment in industry from Source F. Use a red pen to join up the points to give a four-sided graph.
b) Now do the same with a black pen for the 1974 and 1985 figures.

6 What changes have taken place in Japanese industry over the past thirty years? Using Sources E and F, give examples of 'sunset' and 'sunrise' industries.

7 Study Source G. In pairs, using the information on this page, discuss how far you think Japan is a capitalist country. (You may find it useful to look back to Source B on page 84.) Do you think the Japanese economy is in any way different from a simple capitalist model?

Akiro Kurosawa explains the effect of changing investment decisions on Japanese industry

'In the 1960s and early 1970s Japan grew economically. It manufactured consumer goods such as motor vehicles and electrical goods. Industries like iron and steel grew up which relied directly on imported raw materials and fuels.

Since 1975 there has been a rapid growth in high tech industries such as micro-electronics and optical fibres.

You could say that this is the land of the rising sun. Sunset industries have been scaled down and sunrise industries have been encouraged. What this changing industrial structure shows is that we run a capitalist economy. Our industrialists use capital to invest in profit making activities. But it is not that simple. Many people say we have a guided MARKET ECONOMY.'

E

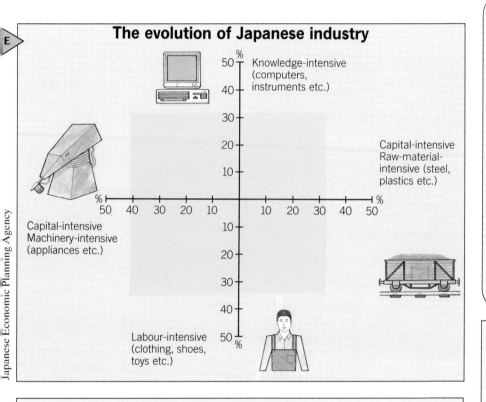

The evolution of Japanese industry

Japanese Economic Planning Agency

Sunset and sunrise industries

Type of industry	Examples	1959	1974	1985
Unskilled, labour intensive industries	Clothing Shoes Toys	52	14	13
Medium capital and labour intensive industries	Light machinery Appliances Motor cars	24	34	26
Medium capital and raw material intensive industries	Steel Plastics Fibres	13	33	23
Knowledge intensive industries	Computers Instruments Heavy machinery	11	19	38

F

From: *Global Shift*, Dickens (Harper and Row)

Japan helps its industries through ...

ploughing back profits
Private industry in Japan invests 30% of its sales revenue in new equipment, compared with the USA which invests 18%.

helping firms grow at home and abroad
Japan has large trading organisations which provide a variety of services for large and small businesses.

borrowing capital for investment
Japanese banks are amongst the largest in the world. Nine of the world's top 25 banks are Japanese.

government aid
Since 1949 the Ministry of International Trade and Industry has guided the Japanese economy. It has, for example:
● given priorities to industrial development
● protected firms from foreign competition.

G

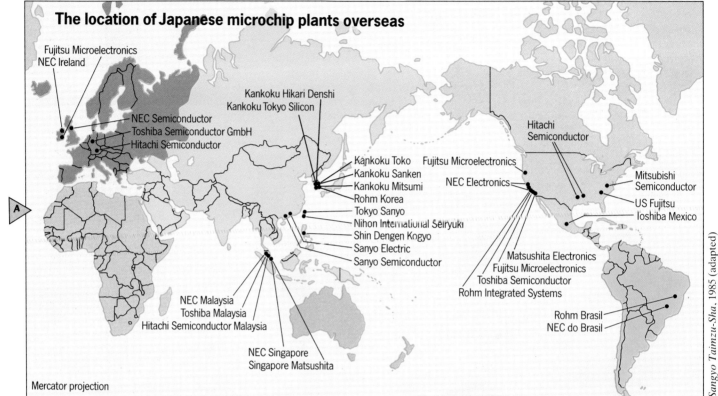

The location of Japanese microchip plants overseas

Mercator projection

Sangyo Taimzu-Sha, 1985 (adapted)

Japanese firms invest abroad as well as at home. Both the banks and the Ministry of International Trade and Industry encourage overseas investment. The firms take advantage either of local supplies of cheap labour (as in the case of South East Asia) or use locations in order to exploit major markets. This page and page 91 examine where Japanese firms invest, why certain locations are chosen and who benefits.

1 **a)** Look at Source A. In pairs, choose one of the multinationals and with the help of an atlas, list its locations around the world.
   b) Compare your company pattern with that of other pairs.
   c) Comment on the similarities and differences between the patterns.
2 Study Source B. Using an atlas, draw a sketch map to show the location of NEC in Scotland. Add notes to your map to describe what the plant makes.

NEC microchip in Scotland

Scotland is home to the biggest single investment by a Japanese electronics company in the UK, the £130 million *Livingston* plant in West Lothian, owned by NEC.

The plant, opened in 1983, uses high technology to manufacture large-scale integrated circuits. In 1987 Livingston employed 297 people. A massive 95 per cent of the plant's production is exported. The largest market is West Germany.

From: EAIJ pamphlet (adapted)

Comparisons in manufacturing hourly wages (£) in 1985

B

USA	5.90	Belgium	3.10
Canada	5.20	Italy	3.00
Japan	3.70	UK	2.95
Sweden	3.50	Ireland	2.70
West Germany	3.40	New Zealand	2.60
Netherlands	3.10	France	2.60

From: The Financial Times, December 1988

3 Several reasons have been forward to explain why NEC decided to locate in Livingston. These include:
   ● availability of suitable labour.
   ● local and national government assistance (see pages 54–7).
   ● access to European markets.
   ● an appropriate environment.
   Using Source B, which of the above reasons do you think best explains the company's decision?

The UK picture

The NEC factory (Source C) is one among many Japanese microchip firms that have invested in Scotland. There are also many Japanese electronics firms in England and Wales involved in both manufacturing and distribution. Different views exist about whether such large scale foreign investment is a good thing.

An aerial view of the NEC plant at Livingston

Japanese firms in the UK

Region	No. of firms	No. of jobs created	Products	% Regional unemployment
Wales	8	5,248	TV sets, video equipment, typewriters, microwave ovens	8.4
Scotland	2	397	Microchips, printers	9.7
North	1	422	Video equipment, hi-fi equipment	10.2
South West	1	1,491	TV sets, video recorders, microwave ovens	4.8
West Midlands	3	666	Videotapes, floppy discs, computer printers, photocopiers	6.5
East Midlands	1	30	Computer printers	5.7
East Anglia	1	510	TV sets, video recorders, hi-fi equipment	3.4
South East	21	5,040	TV sets, video equipment, hi-fi equipment, office electrical equipment, air conditioners, mobile telephones, personal computers, microwave ovens, pianos and speakers	4.0

4 Imagine you work in an advertising agency. You have been approached by a public relations representative from the Japanese electronics industry. She asks you to produce a publicity pamphlet about the advantages of Japanese electronics investment in the UK. Source D shows the main points she wants included and Source E gives facts which back up these points. Using Sources D and E, produce a small pamphlet with sketches, maps and graphs to show the positive side of Japanese investment.

Japanese electronics firms have brought many benefits since they started coming to the UK in 1971. Directly, we have created nearly 4,000 jobs. Indirectly, many thousands more are created among suppliers and dealers.

Manufacturing firms in particular have gone to development areas and new towns where there is high unemployment. The distributors have mainly gone to the South East.

In 1987, Japanese investment in the UK was £560 million. This investment has brought new technology to the UK and new management styles. It has increased the range of goods. It has added to consumer choice and helped the UK balance of payments, through exporting mostly to EEC countries.

We sponsor many different sports and events. We have good industrial relations, with either single or non-union plants. Both staff turnover and absenteeism are low.

There are many expansion plans in the pipeline. For example NEC have announced plans to locate their European manufacturing base for home electronics and business equipment at Telford. This will create 900 new jobs.

Disadvantages

5 Some people dislike foreign multi-national investment. (Refer to page 53.) They believe there are draw-backs from such investment to:
- the workers.
- other companies.
- the economy.

In groups list the questions you would ask the public relations repre-sentative which would point to these drawbacks.

THE QUALITY OF LIFE IN JAPAN

Kabuki-cho, Shinjuku, Tokyo

A

beautiful
chaotic
rich
interesting
noisy
old
drab
business-orientated
impersonal
friendly
unfamiliar
scenic
man-made
claustrophobic

Shinsaibashi, Osaka

B

The economy of Japan is an advanced capitalist one. Many jobs exist in industry. There is also much work in the TERTIARY SECTOR of the economy – 56% of people work in the service industry. Cities like Tokyo and Osaka have many service job opportunities. But what is the quality of life like in cities like these?

Living and working in the cities

1 With a partner, look at Source A. List the types of service jobs you think are shown in each photo.
2 Think about the list of words in Source A. Score each photo on a 1–5 rating, for example for its beauty (5) or its lack of beauty (1).
3 What are the similarities and differences between Tokyo and Osaka? In what ways do you think there are differences from cities in the UK?
4 How would you sum up the quality of life in Japanese cities like Tokyo and Osaka?

Tokyo and Osaka

Takiro Oshima is a Japanese businessman. He has been offered work in both Tokyo and Osaka and wants to find out which city is more attractive. His business magazine provides the relevant data about the two cities (Source B).

5 For each city draw up a table like the one on the right showing indicators of attractiveness. Put a cross on the

Measuring quality of life

Indicators	Tokyo	Osaka	London	Edinburgh
1 1987 population (thousands)	11,830	8,670	6,767	460
2 Population change (%) 1967–87	+9	+30	−10	+1
3 Area (sq km)	2,164	1,868	1,577	259
4 Distance to sea (km)	0	0	55	0
5 Temperature (highest average monthly daytime) (°C)	26	28	22	14
6 Temperature (lowest average monthly daytime (°C)	5	6	2	2
7 Annual rainfall (min)	1460	1400	595	673
8 Pollution	High	High	Average	Low
9 Rent of one-bedroom flat (per month, in £)	£1,670	£1,230	£1,120	£225
10 Parking	Poor	Average	Poor	Good
11 Distance city centre to airport (km)	66	20	24	11
12 Hotel (one night B & B first class hotel in £)	£135	£115	£170	£80
13 Concert hall	Yes	Yes	Yes	Yes
14 Opera House	No	No	Yes	No
15 Unemployment (%)	2.3	3.4	6.6	9.8

London and Edinburgh have been added to help as a comparison

grid for each indicator in the appropriate column. Join your crosses to form an attractiveness profile. Compare the profile for Tokyo with that of Osaka. Where do you think Takiro Oshima should decide to live and work?

Indicator	1	2	3	4
Favourable				
Little to choose				
Unfavourable				

Rural areas

There are several ways of measuring the quality of life. A photograph provides evidence of the quality of an environment.

6 a) Study Source C. List the features which make up the landscape shown – e.g. river, trees. rice field, houses, small road.
b) Group these features into broad categories, such as natural characteristics, vegetation, farmed land, settlement and so on.
c) Now list your features on a scoring sheet like the one below. Score each feature according to its contribution to the attractiveness of the environment. Use the scoring system shown below.
d) Total your scores for each broad category and give your total score for the landscape. How highly have you rated its attractiveness?

Kagoshima in south-eastern Kyushu

Category	Feature	Score
Natural characteristic	River	+2

Scoring system
+2 Major contribution
+1 Some contribution
0 Neutral
−1 Negative feature
−2 Very negative feature

But there is more to quality of life than just an attractive environment. Other indicators are:
● existence of job opportunities in farming, industry and services.
● low cost of living.
● good access to transport and communication.

7 Taking the indicators above into account as well as environmental ones, carry out a quality of life survey for the rural area of Kyushu (see page 86). Use the same method to do this as for question 6.
8 What conclusions do you come to about the quality of life in rural Japan?

Regional inequalities

The amount people are paid for their work varies between regions in Japan. These differences can be shown by measuring the per capita income in each area.

9 Study Source D. From it, draw a CHOROPLETH MAP to show variations in per capita income in Japan in 1982. How does income vary in Japan?

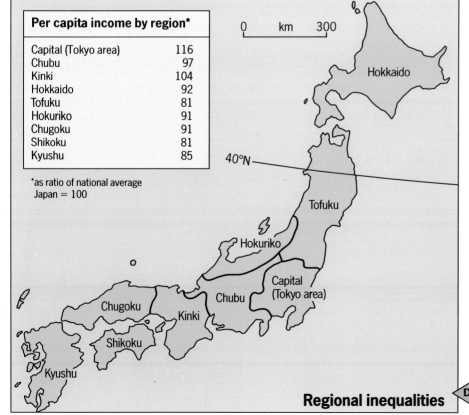

Per capita income by region*	
Capital (Tokyo area)	116
Chubu	97
Kinki	104
Hokkaido	92
Tofuku	81
Hokuriko	91
Chugoku	91
Shikoku	81
Kyushu	85

*as ratio of national average
Japan = 100

Regional inequalities

JAPAN: MYTHS VERSUS REALITY

A selection of students and adults were asked what characteristics they associated with the Japanese way of life. Their answers are shown in Source A. But how well-founded are these popular beliefs?

B

Performing the traditional tea ceremony

A

Japan is a country of workaholics. They hardly ever take holidays.

They earn a lot of money.

The Japanese are a violent people.

The Japanese are healthy and have a long life

They earn a lot but their money buys less. Their cost of living is high.

They have a high suicide rate.

Japan is a crowded country.

An investigation

● You have been asked by the *Economist* magazine to write an article which investigates Western myths about Japan. The Editor wants you to use Source B as a starting point for it. Write the article, using statistics from Source C to argue your case.

The Editor has also given you space for two photographs. Write a note to the picture researcher outlining what they should show.

Richer, harder, poorer 1987

	Net hourly earnings ($)	Working hours per year	Holiday entitlements per year, days	Net domestic purchasing power	Average apartment rents, monthly
Tokyo	10.70	2,013	16.1	100	1,430
New York	9.00	1,867	13.0	200	1,150
London	8.00	1,754	24.1	154	860
Paris	6.60	1,730	28.2	135	750
Frankfurt	9.00	1,723	29.5	225	540

Differing ills

Deaths per 100,000 people, 1985

	Heart disease	Strokes	Lung cancer	Stomach cancer	Suicide
Japan	45.0	123.6	25.0	42.9	19.6
USA	229.8	62.8	52.0	6.1	12.2
UK	243.3	104.3	57.7	16.0	8.5
France	74.4	79.8	31.7	11.6	21.3
Germany	167.0	104.5	34.6	18.8	18.6

Less-mean streets

Crimes per 100,000 people, 1986

C

	Murder	Rape	Robbery	Larceny/ Theft
Japan	1.4	1.4	1.6	1,130.2
USA	8.6	37.5	225.1	4,862.6
UK	4.3	10.4	60.1	5,796.9
France	4.4	5.3	91.8	3,692.7
W. Germany	4.5	9.2	46.8	4,455.7

World Health Organisation, JETRO and Union Bank of Switzerland

A collective farm settlement in Nara, near Moscow

Some countries such as the USA have a capitalist system. Some, like Japan, are run on a guided capitalist economy. The Soviet Union (The Union of Soviet Socialist Republics) works on a different economic system. It operates a *command* economy. This Unit investigates how work is organised in a command economy, how efficient such an economy is and what the future is likely to hold.

Farming in the Soviet Union

1 A crucial difference between capitalist and command economies lies in land ownership. Study Source A and the photo on page 95. List the main features of a collective farm. In what ways does a collective farm differ from a farm in the UK?

Many people – around 24 million – work on the land in the Soviet Union. But farming is often regarded as inefficient and badly-organised.

Igor Trubloff, a worker on a collective farm, explains how farming is organised in the Soviet Union.
"Land is owned by the State. It belongs to the people. A collective farm (called a KOLKHOZ) leases the land rent-free from the State. Collectives were set up between 1928 and 1932, often against the will of the peasants and by force. Smaller farms were joined together. Today around 26,000 collectives exist. A typical collective in the Soviet Union consists of 6,700 ha and 550 households. It cultivates 3,700 ha of grassland and has 1,800 cattle, 1,175 sheep and 1,100 pigs. It will also have 60 tractors and 20 combine harvesters. Collective farmers are also allowed to work on small private plots of 0.5 ha. These provide extra food for families. In all, 50 million private plots of land exist. The output from these plots makes up a third of the milk, vegetables and eggs eaten in the Soviet Union. Workers on collective farms get free holidays, and access to hospitals and schools as well as subsidised visits to the theatre and cinema."

A

2 Look at Source B and answer the following questions:
a) How many people work on the farm?
b) How many days work does each household put into cultivating their private land and how much into kolkhoz (collective) land?
3 **a)** On the kolkhoz land, how many days work per household are given to working on land that produces: food for human consumption; animal food including grass; industrial crops?
b) Are there any significant differences between the way the land is cultivated nearest the settlement and the way it is cultivated further away?
4 Compare the amount of work given to, the amount of land given to, and the output from private land with that of kolkhoz land. What does this tell you about the efficiency of kolkhoz farming compared with private farming?

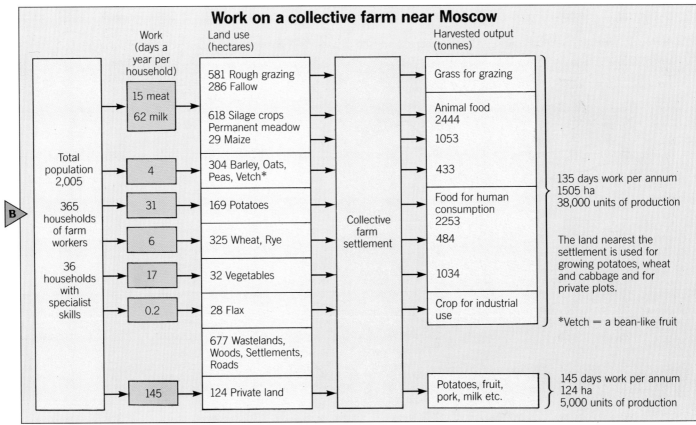

Work on a collective farm near Moscow

	Work (days a year per household)	Land use (hectares)		Harvested output (tonnes)
		581 Rough grazing 286 Fallow	→	Grass for grazing
	15 meat / 62 milk	618 Silage crops Permanent meadow 29 Maize	→	Animal food 2444 / 1053
Total population 2,005	4	304 Barley, Oats, Peas, Vetch*	→	433
365 households of farm workers	31	169 Potatoes	→	Food for human consumption 2253
	6	325 Wheat, Rye	→	484
36 households with specialist skills	17	32 Vegetables	→	1034
	0.2	28 Flax	→	Crop for industrial use
		677 Wastelands, Woods, Settlements, Roads		
	145	124 Private land	→	Potatoes, fruit, pork, milk etc.

Collective farm settlement

135 days work per annum
1505 ha
38,000 units of production

The land nearest the settlement is used for growing potatoes, wheat and cabbage and for private plots.

*Vetch = a bean-like fruit

145 days work per annum
124 ha
5,000 units of production

B

The ecology of agricultural systems, T Bayliss-Smith, Cambridge University Press (adapted)

Decision-making on the kolkhoz

5 Kolkhoz farming is carefully organised by the government. Use Source C to fill in details of this planning on a copy of the diagram below.

```
The State plans
      ↓
The kolkhoz decides
      ↓
The people work
      ↓
The kolkhoz produces
      ↓
The kolkhoz sells
```

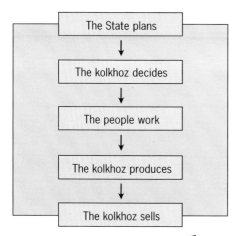

Igor Trubloff

C Our work is planned. The Ministry of Agriculture sets us production targets which we have to meet every year. We work in teams like a co-operative. We are paid by the number of days we work. Our income varies according to the skill of the work we do as well as the quality of the harvest. We elect a managing committee to organise the farming. It makes decisions about buying machinery, planting fields, the type of crop rotation to use and allocating work to each team.

The Ministry of Agriculture buys what we produce at fixed prices. If we produce more than the quota we can either sell this to the State at a higher price or sell to collective farm markets in the town. We workers make the day to day decisions, but this is not the case in all Soviet farms. Some of the big State farms are run like factories.

Other types of farm

The *sovkhoz* or STATE farm is more recent than the kolkhoz. These farms have often been set up to pioneer new farming methods (Source D). There are 21,000 in the Soviet Union and they take up 67% of the agricultural area. Each farm averages 20,000 ha and is tilled by 550 workers. One example of such a farm is that of Krasnopresnensk in the region of Kustanay.

6 How does a state farm compare with a collective farm? Use Source E and Source A to complete a copy of the table below.

Type of farm	Sovkhoz	Kolkhoz
Date set up		
Size of farm		
Machinery invested in		
Markets for produce		
State planning		
Farm organisation		
Labour (workers)		
Social amenities		
Problems		

Ploughing up new areas for cultivation at the Zavety Lenina State farm

The State farm: a case study

Krasnopresnensk sovkhoz is in Kazakhstan in the south of the Soviet Union. It was set up in 1954 in a virtually uninhabited area. Settlers were brought in from Moscow and other settlements. They started life in tents.

The farm consists of 50,000 ha, 80 per cent of which is used for arable farming, particularly growing wheat. It is a modern and well-equipped farm with 174 tractors and 126 grain harvesters. The combines can harvest wheat in the huge fields at a rate of 700 metric tonnes per day. The farm employs 900 workers and has 40 specialists. A third of the workers are mechanics. The farm is situated in steppe country, with a difficult climate and problems with soil erosion. Trees were planted to act as shelter belts and 5,500 livestock were introduced when the farm was set up. There are plans to increase wheat production by using improved seeds and more fertiliser.

The farm is under full government control. It works to the Ministry target plan and sells to the State purchasing agency. All the produce is State property. The farm is run like a factory. Workers are paid a wage according to the level of their skills. Many State farms specialise in one type of agriculture.

Workers are allowed small private plots of land. They gain social benefits such as State housing. There are six schools, a kindergarten, a boarding school, a hospital and a sports hall. The workers also have access to a palace of culture, eleven shops, a dining hall and a laundry.

Farming – the need for change

1 Read Source A. How does Igor Trubloff account for inefficiency in farming? Which reason does he see as the most important?

2 You have been asked to advise on how Soviet farming could be made more efficient. Source B gives some suggestions about how this might be done. In pairs, discuss the advantages and disadvantages of each proposal. List them in order of priority.

B
- Take all land into State ownership
- Sell land to farmers to work individually
- Rent land to farmers to work individually
- Educate and train farmers
- Allow free marketing
- Invest more in marketing and fertilisers
- Have more central planning and control of farming
- Sell land to farmers to work in teams
- Rent land to farmers to work as teams
- Free farmers from central planning
- Improve roads and other infrastructures

A

"We Soviet farmers know that farming is inefficient. We have a difficult climate in many areas but we've also had problems with government planning. The poor roads mean that a lot of produce gets wasted. As much as 50 per cent of the potato harvest is lost between the field and the market place. Grain storage is inadequate. There are constant shortages of spare parts and fuel for our old farm machinery. A lot of money has been invested in agriculture – around 15 per cent of the State's budget – but we still don't produce enough grain for our own needs. Because of this we have to import it. Soviet farmers are poor. But perhaps the real problems are to do with how farming is planned. We need to make changes."

Old combine harvesters in Kazakstan

Gorbachev and perestroika

Since 1985 when he came to power, the General Secretary of the Soviet Union, Mikhail Gorbachev has tried to carry out important changes. He is aiming to restructure many parts of the Soviet economy (a process called PERESTROIKA). He is also reforming agriculture.

3 Source C analyses the changes Gorbachev proposes in farming organisation. In pairs, decide what his main aims are. Do they include the improvements you suggested in question 2?

Gorbachev seeks key to farm revival

Anatoly Agenbegyan looks at efforts to give Soviet agriculture a new lease of life.

Rotting vegetables, unproductive labour, imported food; we all know that our farming is inefficient. But what is Mr Gorbachev doing about it? I spoke with planners and farmers about what is happening to our oldest industry.

Mr Gorbachev is reorganising agriculture from top to bottom. Under the old set-up one ministry would supply fertiliser to a farm and another would supply the machinery to spread it. But they usually didn't arrive at the same time. In order to simplify this central structure Mr Gorbachev has set up a new 'super ministry' (Gosagroprom) to co-ordinate planning. He has cut staff by half. This new ministry still creates plans and sets output targets but leaves decisions much more to local administrators and the farms.

Mr Gorbachev is trying to loosen the grip of central control in the farms. The farms are being made self-financing. They are being given incentives to produce more. For example, they are now allowed to sell 30 per cent of their planned output of fruit and vegetables outside the state system where they can charge higher prices. The farm accounting system is in the process of being modernised.

The government is trying to motivate farmers. Gorbachev is encouraging a team contract system. He would like farms to become genuine co-operatives. He wants financially independent teams and family groups to make a contract with the farm management. The team would rent plots of land and agree on levels of output to deliver to the collective. They would either keep the surplus to sell at the higher market price or sell it to the collective at a bonus price. Mr Gorbachev sees the worth of 'team contracts' and of making farmers 'masters of the land'. Three quarters of the agricultural labour force is now working under a team contract system. There are signs that production is improving. But teams and families still need improved tools, storage and equipment.

Mr Gorbachev is openly encouraging private plots. He would like collective farms to hand over more animals to their members for fattening; there is now no limit to the number of animals that can be kept on each plot. He is speeding up the allocation of plots (though these are often of poor quality) to city dwellers who want to grow food in their spare time.

Mr Gorbachev is still waiting for the giant leap forward. His target is to make the Soviet Union self-sufficient in food.

Work in a Soviet factory

In the Soviet Union, 38 million people work in factories producing goods for industry. One important industry is car assembly. Read on to find out how factory work is planned and managed in a command economy and how industry is changing.

Car assembly plants in the Soviet Union

Gulf of Bothnia
Baltic Sea
Moscow
Gorki
Izhvesk
Tol'yatti
Lutsk
Zaporozhye
Aral Sea
Black Sea
Caspian Sea

0   1000 km

Assembly shop at Volzhsky works, Tol'yatti

The Tol'yatti car plant

Car production started at Gorki in 1930. Later, factories were built at Moscow, Izhvesk, Lutsk and Zaporozhe. The largest car production plant is at Tol'yatti and covers 570 ha. Begun in 1967, it reached full production in 1974 and today produces over half the Soviet output of 1.3 million cars. Cars produced here are for export. Tol'yatti is named after an Italian communist leader and the factory was designed and equipped with the help of *Fiat* of Italy.

D

Alison Green, a journalist, recently visited the Tol'yatti car factory. Here, she gives her impressions of her visit.

The factory itself looks like any other – after all the way of putting a car together has not changed since Henry Ford. It is fanatically clean and impressive by its sheer size. The assembly building is 2km long and 500m wide with four tracks. A trolley bus service runs from one end to the other, making six stops to bring the workers to their position on the assembly line. All the basic production takes place at the site (forging, foundry, building the engines, pressing and assembly). But the plant needs 10,000 parts and components from 70 factories in the Soviet Union, Eastern Europe and Italy. There are difficulties getting supplies of the right quality at the right time. The factory has a large spare parts storage and distribution centre.

The factory employs 85,000 people, most of whom are production workers. They work in two shifts. Their life largely seems to be their work. Many of them live in drab twelve-storey tower blocks a short bus ride from the factory in the new town of Tol'yatti. The flats are provided by the company. Single workers sleep two to a tiny room and share a cooker and a fridge. The rent is very small, though – only seven roubles a month.

Tol'yatti is a model plant with an education centre for production technology and computer techniques. Workers can earn bonuses of up to 40% of their basic wage. Incentive and wage differentials are paid. Many workers have been decorated with orders and medals.

4 Study Source D. Describe the work being done in the photograph.

5 The list below shows the stages which exist in producing a car. Rearrange the list so that these stages appear in the correct order:
  • The foundry provides the engine plant.
  • The product goes to the test and check building.
  • The press shop supplies the body shop which supplies the paint shop.
  • The forge supplies the transmission plant.
  • The parts come together at the assembly plant.

6 The assembly plant needs car parts from 70 factories. What problems do you think this might cause?

7 Turn back to Source D on page 87. Would you rather be a worker in the Tol'yatti car factory in the Soviet Union, or in a microchip factory in Japan? Explain your answer.

A great deal of planning went into building the car factory at Tol'yatti. Capital, labour, land and suitable transport were required for the plant to be successful. The industrial planners were helped by experts from the Fiat car firm in Italy.

Choosing a location

1 a) A large car assembly plant needs 80,000 workers. The plant is best located near a large town. What choices did the planners have? Use an atlas to list the major towns in Source A in order of population.
   b) A large car factory needs land. Cheap, flat land near the river was available at Tol'yatti. On which river is Tol'yatti situated?
2 What transport costs are involved in moving COMPONENTS to the factory at Tol'yatti for manufacturing cars?
   a) On a tracing of Source A, draw five distance rings with Tol'yatti at the centre. Using your tracing, complete the table below Source A to show costs of moving components per tonne to Tol'yatti.
   b) Draw a graph to show the relationship between distance and transport costs, using the information in Source A. Comment on what your graph shows.
   c) Do you think the distances and costs involved in transporting components to Tol'yatti are too great?
3 What other factors do you think Soviet planners considered when deciding to locate the factory at Tol'yatti?

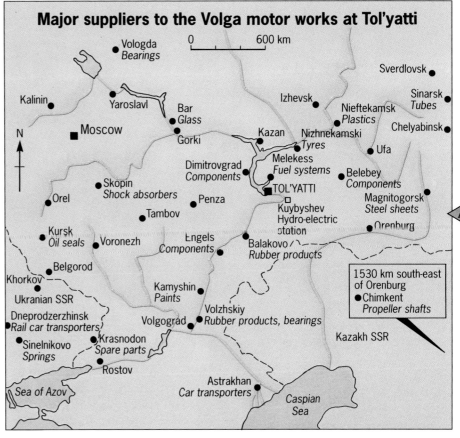

Major suppliers to the Volga motor works at Tol'yatti

Vologda *Bearings*
Kalinin
Yaroslavl
Bar *Glass*
Moscow
Gorki
Izhevsk
Nieftekamsk *Plastics*
Sverdlovsk
Sinarsk *Tubes*
Chelyabinsk
Kazan
Nizhnekamski *Tyres*
Ufa
Dimitrovgrad *Components*
Melekess *Fuel systems*
Belebey *Components*
Skopin *Shock absorbers*
Orel
TOL'YATTI
Magnitogorsk *Steel sheets*
Penza
Tambov
Kuybyshev Hydro-electric station
Orenburg
Kursk *Oil seals*
Voronezh
Engels *Components*
Balakovo *Rubber products*
Belgorod
Khorkov
Kamyshin *Paints*
1530 km south-east of Orenburg
Chimkent *Propeller shafts*
Ukranian SSR
Dneprodzerzhinsk *Rail car transporters*
Volgograd
Volzhskiy *Rubber products, bearings*
Sinelnikovo Springs
Krasnodon *Spare parts*
Kazakh SSR
Rostov
Sea of Azov
Astrakhan *Car transporters*
Caspian Sea

A

Scale of map in km				
0 300	800	1,500	3,000	km
5	10	15	30	

Roubles per tonne transport costs
(1 rouble = £1·10)

Tol'yatti and transport costs

Product supplied	Place made	Distance from Tol'yatti	Cost of moving 1 tonne to Tol'yatti

ПЕРЕСТРОЙКА
(Perestroika)
Problems and remedies

"We pretend to work and they pretend to pay us.
We have to work to centrally planned production targets. Factories are becoming rusty. We haven't got much in the way of new technology and computers. There is no competition – the threat of bankruptcy is nil.
We are good at investing but we don't put technology to the best use. We get bonuses for quantity not quality of production.
Factories are out of touch with their customers. Research is detached from the factory."

Leonid Ivanoff,
Soviet factory manager

Some possible solutions

- Invest in new technology and modernise existing factories.
- Reform the management systems.
- Limit the power of the ministries and abolish planned targets.
- Have less centralisation.
- Let the factories decide on investments.
- Develop new technology by funding more research.
- Increase links between factories and researchers.
- Let factories organise their own supplies.
- Allow competition between factories – risk bankruptcies.
- Encourage factories to produce what the consumers want.

Stage 1	Stage 2	Stage 3
Preparation 1985-7	**Transition 1988-90**	**Take-off 1991-?**
Anti-alcohol campaign Drive to replace incompetent and corrupt officials Merging of some ministries Foreign trade rights widened More legal scope for small private enterprises	Increase independence of industry Bring research closer to production Reduce bureaucracy Start price reforms Become familiarised with new system	Economic growth accelerates as motivation improves People still learning and adjusting

The planned pattern of perestroika

Chasing the capitalists

Soviet industry revs up

What's wrong with industry?

What does perestroika mean for industry?

How far along the road are we?

The Politburo and other powers

4 Read Source B to find out how industry is managed in the Soviet Union. Now write down which planning body is responsible for the following:
- Investment in agriculture or industry.
- Planning the future of an industry.
- Managing motor vehicle assembly.
- Investing in consumer industries.
- Deciding what goes into the Five Year Plan.
- Investigating technological developments in industry.
- Planning the location of a car plant.
- Amending original Politburo plans.
- Paying bonuses to workers.

5 In pairs, discuss the strengths and weaknesses of economic planning in a command economy.

6 You have been asked to write an article about *perestroika* for the Soviet newspaper *Izvestia*. It should concentrate on the problems of industry and the need for change. Use the information in Source C to write the article – it should be about 300 words long. Your editor has told you to use the sub-headings in Source D as a guide.

Shopping in the Soviet Union

A common feature of Soviet daily life is the need to queue for goods of all descriptions. A shopper in the Soviet Union probably spends at least six hours longer buying goods per week than a shopper in the UK. The Russian in the queue may well wonder why a country that can send astronauts on record-breaking space journeys seems incapable of providing an efficient retail service.

Retail is an important part of the service sector in the Soviet Union. (In all, 41 million people work in service industries.) This page and page 103 examine how retail is organised and how it is changing.

1   Study Source A. What differences exist in the way shops are run in the Soviet Union and the UK?

2   **a)** Study Source B. Using the statistics it gives, fill in the table below Source B.
b) How would you describe the organisation of shops in the Soviet Union?

Shops and the State

In communist states, particularly the Soviet Union, the shops are generally owned by the government. They are supervised by the Ministry of Trade. This means that no one makes a profit, so there is no reason to overcharge for goods. But there is no competition between shops either, nor between factories making the goods for sale. The government has a monopoly of all products and commodities. It does not build a whole row of shops where one will do. The customer has to buy from the state shops or do without. In the Soviet Union, if a shopper does not like the goods, he or she cannot cross the road or go round the corner to another shop. There is only one. The people working in the shop, so long as they do their job adequately, don't have to go out of their way to be polite or to help customers. They know the customers will have to keep coming anyway.

Queuing at the state-run meat market

Three Giant Powers, M Simons, Oxford University Press (adapted)

3   In pairs discuss how each of the following people might view shops and shopping in the Soviet Union:
a) Olga Alexis, a housewife in Moscow;
b) Anna Philipporna, department store manager at *Gum*, the state-owned store in Moscow;
c) Nikolai Andropov, assistant in a food shop;
d) Ivor Pralinsky, an official from the Ministry of Trade.

4   **a)** Look at Source C. What percentage of people in Moscow are employed in retail and service jobs?
b) How does this figure compare with that for the Soviet Union as a whole? Suggest reasons for any differences.
c) Compare the figures for retail and service employment in the Soviet Union with those in the United States.

B

Retailing in the Soviet Union		
A comparison with the UK	*Soviet Union*	*UK*
Total employed in retail services	7.5 million	2.3 million
Number of retail outlets	699,900	343,153
Total floor space	49.8 million m²	Not available
Total retail turnover	325,500 m roubles	£82.3m

Retail statistics	*Soviet Union*	*UK*
Average number of employees per shop		
Average turnover per shop		
Average turnover per worker		
Average turnover per square metre		
Average size of shop		

C

Employment by sector in the USA and Soviet Union		
	USA	*Soviet Union*
Services and retail	58%	29%
Industry	20%	27%
Agriculture	3%	25%
Others*	19%	19%

*including construction, transport and communications

Employment in Moscow: a percentage breakdown

Industry	25
Building	11
Transport and communication	10
Retail and service	9
Administration and public services	10
Health care	5
Education	7
Scientific and technical	20
Other	3

A free market?

Until very recently, the State almost completely controlled the buying and selling of goods. But people have been able to buy on the free market. Collective farmers have grown food on their private plots and then sold it at markets in towns for higher prices than in state shops.

5 Look at Source D and with a partner discuss:
  a) what is being sold.
  b) where it is being sold.
  c) who is buying.
  d) who is selling.
6 Using an atlas to help you, draw a map to show where the sellers at this market have come from. Comment on what your map shows.

At Moscow central market (above), farmers sell produce from collective farms and private plots. They come from as far away as Uzbekistan, Azerbaydzhan and Armenia. There are 30 private markets in Moscow selling large quantities of potatoes, vegetables, fruit, meat and poultry. Eight thousand such markets exist in the Soviet Union.

The Soviet Union and the private sector

Mr Gorbachev has been pushing for co-operatives – which really means for small private businesses. In 1986 it became legal to run a private taxi and to rent rooms. The Soviet Union now has nearly 14,000 co-operatives employing 150,000 people who do anything from hairdressing to key cutting. The average income of a co-operative member is around 50 roubles more than the average Soviet worker's wage.

But would-be entrepreneurs have faced many obstacles. Until 1988, the laws were restrictive. Many Russians are deeply hostile to the idea that members of co-operatives can make a lot of money. 'Nobody wants to help the co-operatives', complains a member of a popular co-operative boutique, 'although everybody says they have to be helped.'

From the beginning of July 1988, co-operatives were given – in the eye of the law, at least – equal status with state enterprises. There are no longer restrictions on their size, there are now few limits to the industries and services they can be involved in, and (apart from whatever tax rates are finally settled on) none on the amount members can earn. Members can arrange to share income: not just according to the amount of work contributed, but also according to the amount of capital invested. To stop this looking all too capitalist, there is a rule that only those who work in the co-operatives can draw an income from them. Co-operatives will not have to fulfil a plan and will be able to set their own prices. Some may even be granted foreign-trade rights.

It is hoped that co-operatives in the countryside, operating as parts of the big collective farms, will help to revitalise agriculture. As differences in income increase, the profit motive, competition and high-quality service will become more powerful influences throughout the economy. But Gorbachev's opponents are right: the co-operatives are capitalist wolves in socialist clothing.

Elmar and Virve Lepp are the owners of this café

Towards capitalist values?

Since 1988, the government has passed laws which encourage initiative in the service sector of the economy. The benefits of co-operatives and small private businesses are being stressed. Such developments show a fundamental change in state policy.

7 Imagine you are a radio reporter working for the BBC and have been sent to Moscow to find out more about these changes. Using Sources E, F and G, write a talk of around 350 words. Your piece should examine:
  • how Gorbachev has gone about encouraging private enterprise in the service industries.
  • how successful he has so far been.
  • an example of how the changes have affected an individual.
  • whether the co-operatives really are 'capitalist wolves in socialist clothing'.

A profit-making restaurant

Andrei Fyodorov used to be a state restaurant manager. Recently, he was involved in setting up one of the hundred co-operative restaurants in Moscow, the Kropotkinskoye café, located in an elegant, aristocratic town house. . .

"State restaurants are like railway stations. But this is cosy and subtly lit with friendly staff. There are seven of us running the café and we employ a further 21 people. We divide the profits among the partners. The director earns £600 a month and the chef £500. We aim to pay back our bank loan in five years' time.

We had some problems to begin with in getting a licence and premises from the local council, but now we've decorated and furnished the place. We recruited our own co-operative members and decided our own wages.

Prices are still high. We have to buy our ingredients from the expensive free markets. But at the moment, we are trying to arrange a formal contract to buy direct from one particular collective farm."

Adapted from Martin Walker, *The Guardian*

PLANNING AGAINST THE ODDS

The development of Norilsk

A major problem for the Soviet Government has been persuading people to settle in areas which are unattractive to live in, but have great industrial potential. This page and page 105 look at the example of Norilsk, an area rich in mining, which lies north of the Arctic Circle. Read on to find out more about the problems the government has been faced with in developing Norilsk over the past 60 years.

In 1930, rich deposits of copper and nickel ores were discovered at Norilsk. Coal was believed to exist nearby. The Soviet Five Year Plan of 1932–36 set out plans to mine the area and build a city near the mines.

Special labour regions in the Soviet Union

Arctic Ocean

Baltic Sea

● Moscow

● Norilsk

Arctic Circle

Caspian Sea

Aral Sea

Sea of Okhotsk

Areas where workers receive additional payment over and above basic wage

A

1 Look at Source A and Source B. In small groups, and with the help of an atlas, list the main difficulties which would face people who lived and worked in Norilsk.

Imagine you are a planner and your job is to provide a workforce for the new development at Norilsk. Over the years, the type of problem you have to deal with will change. In groups, discuss your responses to each of the situations in questions 2, 3 and 4.

2 It is 1935 and the dictator Stalin is in power. The plan is to mine nickel ore and also to begin work building a town and railway. All this will require 140,000 workers.
a) Where do you think the workforce might come from?
b) What labour problems do you think you would be likely to face?
c) How would you set about recruiting workers?

3 It is now 1960 and you need to attract efficient workers to Norilsk. You aim to increase the workforce by 19,000 every year.
a) What incentives would you offer to try and attract good quality workers?
b) Design a poster which appeals to socialist principles. Emphasise that it is the duty of loyal subjects to help the Soviet Union prosper and exploit its industrial opportunities.

4 The year is 1965. You have attracted workers to Norilsk, but you want to make sure they remain there permanently. To help do this, you need to improve the standard of living. The main problems are:
● the poor rate of house building.
● a shortage of living space.
● alcohol-related problems.
● undernourishment amongst children.
● poor medical facilities.
● overcrowded primary schools.
● overwork among women, who are in full-time jobs and responsible for families.

Which of these problems do you think most urgently requires a solution and is most likely to prevent workers leaving Norilsk?

B

Train passing through the city of Norilsk

Keeping the workers happy

5 Look at Source C. The survey shows problems identified by workers in Norilsk in 1975. What remedies could you suggest for each problem? Which problem do you think would be the most difficult to deal with?

Norilsk today

In the 1980s the population of Norilsk grew steadily and is likely to reach 250,000 by the early 1990s. But because of the introduction of labour-saving technology, the government is no longer trying to increase the workforce. It is quality rather than quantity which now matters most.

Problems identified by workers

- Many workers were unhappy about working conditions. There were complaints about dust, loud noise, toxic chemicals and the general monotony of the work.
- Graduates mentioned the lack of opportunity for higher education, the dearth of shopping facilities and poor shopping services.
- Higher level employees were dissatisfied with the quality and availability of nurseries, housing, shops, and recreational and cultural facilities.

Hydro power station, Norilsk

The view down Lenin Avenue

6 Source D shows the town of Norilsk today. How would you set about attracting the most highly skilled workers to Norilsk? Suggest ways in which it would at the same time be possible to control the growth of the city so that there is less pressure on amenities.

7 You have been asked to summarise the problems you faced and the solutions you proposed in planning labour for Norilsk. The idea is to help other planners in the Soviet Union.

a) Make a large copy of Source E. On it, add the following labels in the appropriate problem box.

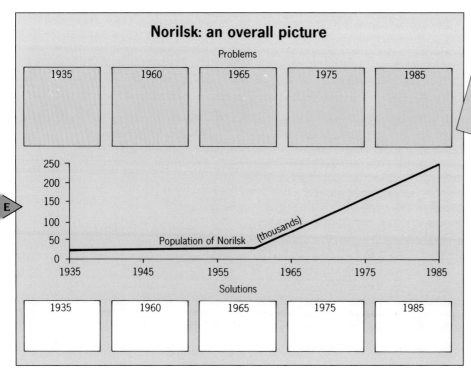

Keeping labour

Recruiting labour

Attracting efficient labour

Keeping labour satisfied

Responding to changed labour conditions

b) Add your main solutions in the relevant solution box.

c) State briefly why the problems you dealt with changed between 1935 and the present day.

Norilsk: an overall picture

Problems

1935	1960	1965	1975	1985

Population of Norilsk (thousands)

250
200
150
100
50
0

1935   1945   1955   1965   1975   1985

Solutions

1935	1960	1965	1975	1985

DOES COMMUNISM CREATE A FAIRER SOCIETY?

The Soviet Union: wealth indicators by republic								
	% of people in towns		Income – % above/below average Soviet wage	Expenditure – retail spending per person, 1984 (roubles)	Welfare, measured by the number of doctors per 100,000 inhabitants			
Name of republic	1913	1982			1940	1960	1970	1984
Estonia	19	71	+12.6	1,800	100	239	331	455
Latvia	38	70	+2.1	1,800	132	264	359	480
Lithuania	13	64	−0.7	1,400	67	174	275	424
Belo Russia	14	59	−7.7	1,200	57	164	258	367
Ukraine	19	63	−8.4	1,200	84	199	277	405
Moldavia	13	42	−17.5	1,200	42	143	205	363
Georgia	26	53	−12.6	1,200	133	330	364	525
Armenia	10	67	−5.6	1,000	175	240	287	371
Azerbaijan	24	54	−17.5	800	100	237	250	369
Kazakstan	10	56	−1.4	1,200	43	140	218	363
Turkmenistan	11	48	−1.1	800	76	187	213	311
Uzbekistan	24	42	−15.4	800	47	139	201	327
Tadjikistan	9	34	−17.5	600	41	127	159	260
Kirgizia	12	39	−14.7	800	38	154	208	324
RSFSR	17	71	+5.6	1,240	82	208	290	441

The Soviet Union, J Cole (Butterworth); Economist Supplement, 1988;

Before and after 1917

Before the revolution the Soviet Union was in many ways a poor and backward country. After 1917 it industrialised fully. People moved to the towns to work in factories. Changes in farming and industry were planned.

1 One way of measuring modernisation is to examine the number of people living in towns. Using Source A, draw a graph to show the percentage of people living in towns in each republic in 1982. How similar are the figures for each republic? Does your graph suggest that the degree of modernisation in the Soviet republics was roughly equal in the early 1980s?

Social and geographical differences

2 Now use Source A to draw graphs which show the pattern of wages, expenditure and welfare in the republics. To what extent do significant inequalities exist?

3 Rank each republic according to wage, expenditure and welfare levels. Add the ranks from each republic and divide by three to get an overall picture. Display your results on a map of the Soviet Union. Use three different colours to shade the five most prosperous republics, the middle five and the poorest five. Comment on the pattern your map shows.

In 1917 the Soviet Union inherited many social and geographical inequalities from the old Tsarist (imperial) government. Access to welfare was unequal. For example, the number of doctors per person in republics like Latvia and Georgia was 45 times greater than in the Central Asian republics.

4 Using the welfare data in Source A, draw a graph like the one on the right to show changes in numbers of doctors per thousand people from 1940 to 1984 in each republic. Two have been done for you (Source B). Does your graph suggest that inequalities in access to welfare are decreasing?

5 It is difficult to get data for many aspects of life in the Soviet Union. What other difficulties do you think exist in trying to assess whether geographical and social inequalities are decreasing?

6 Do you think that by the year 2000 a command economy like the Soviet Union could produce a completely equal society?

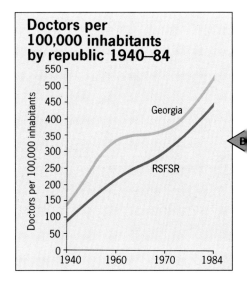

Doctors per 100,000 inhabitants by republic 1940–84

A MIXED ECONOMY: SIERRA LEONE

Upland rice farming in Sierra Leone

Swamp rice farming

How do people earn a living?

People in Sierra Leone are poor. Rural people are the poorest of the poor. Three quarters of the country's working population are employed in agriculture, which does not bring much income.

1 Look at the photograph of upland rice farming on page 107.
   a) What work is being done? What is being produced?
   b) Who is doing the work?
   c) What evidence is there that these are poor people working in difficult conditions in a hostile environment?
   d) Now look at the photograph of swamp rice farming on page 107. In what ways is the work similar to or different from upland rice farming work?

Eighty-one per cent of all farmers in all parts of the country produce the staple crop rice. The two main ways of growing rice are *traditional upland rice* and *swamp rice farming*.

Upland rice farming	Swamp rice farming
• Upland areas consist of bush and forest land. Individual farmers work farms (averaging 1.5 ha) made up of scattered fields. No water control is used.	• Much labour is needed to clear and level the land as well as building banks and water control systems. Once completed it need not be done again.
• A 0.2 ha field is made from bush and woodland cleared and burned, mainly by the men, in the dry season. Much of the work is done in groups and only hand tools are used.	• High yielding types of rice seeds are sown in nursery beds and then transplanted to the paddy fields.
• Native varieties of rice seed are scattered on the newly-cleared land. Rice is grown with other crops. Women do most of the weeding. Children scare the birds away. Harvesting is done by both sexes.	• Mechanical methods are used to prepare the fields. Advisors help the farmers to get the best out of their land.
• After a year the land is used for other crops.	• 77 per cent of the cost of the development of swamp rice is paid for from International Development Associations.
• At least seven years are needed to return the soil nutrients before the land can be recleared and used to grow crops again.	• Fertility is maintained by careful fertiliser input and yields are improved by use of pesticides.
	• Rice fields vary in size from 0.5 ha to 100 ha. These fields may be cultivated by many individual growers.

▷ B

2 Using Source A draw a sketch map to show land use around the village.
3 There are differences in the way rice is grown in upland and swamp areas. Use Source B to compare cultivation methods in each case.

Draw a table using the following headings to display your findings: location; farm size and field size; labour (methods and people); technology and capital.

Farming in central Sierra Leone

Traditional upland rice farming (using bush fallowing system)

Swamp rice farming (using flood water and controlled water)

Granite rocks
400   600m

Savanna, woodland

Woodland vegetation

200mm rain mainly May November

Humidity
May 80%
January 50%

Temperature
January 15°C
July 27°C

◁ A

Advanced secondary forest

1-2 year regenerating forest   Upland rice   Regenerated forest

Forest   Cassava

Upland rice   Village   Garden

Vegetables   Swampy ground

Land cleared for cultivation   Vegetables

Vegetables   Cassava   Swamp rice

Advanced regenerating over 2 years

Swamp rice

Marshland

Rice production: labour requirements (working days per hectare)		
Type of work	Upland	Inland swamp
Brushing (December–January)	22	—
Felling (January–February)	17	—
Cleaning and burning (April–May)	15	—
Nursery	—	5
Ploughing (April–May)	25	50
Harrowing	25	37
Transplanting	—	44
Fencing	10	25
Weeding	47	30
Bund repairs	—	2
Pest scaring (May–December)	44	50
Harvesting and seed processing (October–December)	52	62
Total labour requirements	257	304

Inputs and outputs		
Input/output measures	Upland	Swamp
Current yields (lbs per hectare)	2,224	4,448
Expected yields with improved technology (lbs per acre)	3,460	5,930
Income per hectare with improved yields (2.35 leones per bushel)	135.50	232.30
Cash inputs (leones per hectare)		
Seed rice (2.5 leones/bushel)	6.18	4.94
Pesticides		3.71
Fertilisers	8.90	12.60
Tools and machines	1.24	5.00
Return after cash input deducted	119.20	206.10
Development costs		14.90
Returns after development costs deducted	119.20	191.30
Labour input (working days per hectare)	257	304
Returns per workday (leones)	1.13	1.60

How hard do people work?

4 Both upland rice and swamp rice farming need much work (Source C).
a) Draw two circular farming calendars to show the work done in both systems.
b) How much labour is required for each type of rice farming?
c) Which requires more?
d) Which jobs are done by men, which by women and which by children? (Look back to Source B.)

How do people produce food?

Both upland rice and swamp rice farming need inputs, e.g. labour and cash, to produce outputs.

5 Using Source D and the information on the right, draw a systems diagram to show the inputs and outputs of each type of rice farming.
6 Which is the better system? Think about cash input and costs, returns, labour, returns for each day worked, and investment for following years.

• Normally there are sharp divisions of labour between the sexes: brushing, selling and clearing are male tasks whilst weeding is a female occupation. Harvesting is done by both sexes.
• Children are important in the family farming system – they scare birds and fire pellets.
• There is a long tradition of work groups. The village decides which land to burn and which to cultivate. People work together to do a job.
• In upland rice farming, 82-man days come from the family and 22 from hired labour.

How can people produce more?

Swamp rice farming seems to be more productive than upland farming. The government is encouraging farmers to grow swamp rice. Some of their reasons are given by a government official (Source E).

7 Using Source E, design a government poster encouraging farmers to grow swamp rice.

Swamp rice growing can conserve the environment. Upland rice wastes land and leaving hillsides bare can mean more erosion. Swamp rice doesn't use as much land or cause erosion.

The World Bank loans us money for agricultural development schemes. This helps us to train farmers and buy the necessary fertilisers, pesticides and high yielding seeds.
The money also pays for training advisers and improving roads and bridges. Health care and education also are improved as part of these schemes. Everyone benefits from this and it is much easier to develop swamp rice areas than upland rice.
We have a lot of people who eat rice as their main food. We have to import expensive rice at the moment so money goes out of our poor country. Swamp rice is very productive. It would solve these problems although it is difficult to change old ideas, systems and practices.
It is politically important we get as much rice as possible. The people want rice at reasonable prices. There have already been riots over food in Freetown, the capital. 99

One farmer's view against growing swamp rice

- In our village no one cultivates a swamp.
- When we cut down the trees in the traditional way, we can sell the firewood.
- I haven't got much time to think about the poor town people who need rice.
- If I want to produce crops for sale, I won't grow rice. I'd grow cassava or vegetables for the local market.
- Swamp rice tastes so inferior.
- We produce other crops with our rice.
- It is not sensible to grow just rice as the swamp rice people do.
- I think it's harder work and it's unpleasant. It is unhealthy and when one person is sick it stops others working.

One farmer's view for swamp rice cultivation

- I prefer the swamp rice. I don't have to guess when the rains will come and guess when to burn and plough. I can plant over a larger period of time.
- There is less work weeding.
- There is less need for bird scaring. The children do this. But we've got fewer children in the family and they are at school.
  It isn't too difficult to level the flats and control the water flow.
- I don't need to work in a large group as with upland rice farming.
- With water controlled, it means you cut down on the uncertainty of the weather.
- The rice yield is up nearly 50% because I can get two or three crops in a year.

A

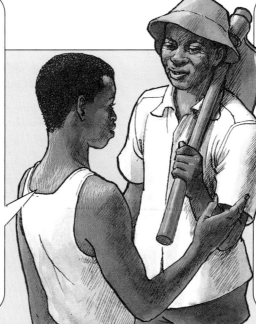

		What are the farmers' attitudes to ...							
	Risk	Amount of work	Type of work	Who does the work?	Increased production	Sale of product	Group decisions	Change in general
Farmer who is for swamp rice cultivation								
Farmer who is against swamp rice cultivation								

Farming changes

The government wants to encourage more rice production by swamp rice methods of cultivation. Not all farmers are in favour of this. What are the difficulties?

1 Study Source A. Show the attitudes of the two farmers by completing a large copy of the table above.
2 Some women may have different attitudes to that of the male farmers in Source A.
   a) Look at Source B. Would the female farmer support the government plan to introduce swamp rice?
   b) What reasons would she give?
   c) Are these the same reasons as the male farmer's?

3 Some farmers accept change; others do not. In groups, discuss the following:
   a) Why might you find it difficult to change your attitudes? Are there sometimes good reasons for a person not doing so?
   b) In the case of the Sierra Leone farmers, how would you encourage them to change their attitudes and work patterns? (Think of: force, education, publicity, persuasion, negotiation, incentives.)

B

I need to produce a lot of rice for sale. With the money I can help my children – I have to pay their school fees.

I like the swamp rice method. I find it difficult to fit in with the labour groups growing the upland rice. It's difficult for the women to negotiate with the men.

Farmers' choices

Farmers have a choice. They can choose to change or not to change. But the government wants changes in certain directions. Sierra Leone has a mixed economy. Economic decisions are made both by the State and by individuals. The information on this page will help you to find out how the State influences changes in rice farming in order to increase the food supply for many people.

4 a) Look at Source C. In pairs, explain to each other what is happening.
b) In what ways does the State affect farming?
c) How might the following benefit or not benefit from the influence of the government: peasant farmers; the consumer; the State?

Change is difficult when people are poor

Three quarters of Sierra Leone's 3.5 million people live in the countryside. Rural incomes are low. People find it difficult to meet basic needs. They are very poor and have few employment opportunities. Life expectancy is only 34 years.

How can we measure the poverty of people in a country? The poor are:
● those who earn less than the official minimum wage (absolute poverty).
● those whose income puts them in the bottom 10 per cent or 15 per cent of the population (relative poverty).
● those who do not have an income which is enough to satisfy their basic needs.

What are the basic needs of an average family of five living in the rural areas of Sierra Leone? They need food (the amount varies by age and sex) and non-food basics, such as fuel and clothing.

5 Look at Source D.
a) What are the total yearly basic needs of a rural household of five?
b) How much is spent on food per year?
c) How much is spent on non-food basic needs per year?
6 a) Present this information as a bar chart in money or percentages. Subdivide the food section to show how

much is spent on each individual.
b) Now sub-divide the non-food basic needs section to show how much is spent on each item per year.
c) Comment on how this expenditure compares with your own family expenditure.

7 In rural areas, 70% of people do not have enough income for their basic needs. Suggest how these people manage.

The influence of the State on the agricultural free market

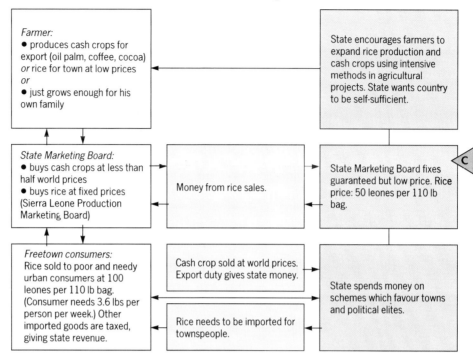

Basic needs of a rural household of five			
Food needs (per month)			
Member of household		Recommended calorie intake per day	Average monthly cost of minimum food basket (leones)
Male		2,700	9.74
Female		2,200	7.93
First child 10–14 years		2,200	7.93
Second child 5–9 years		1,600	6.92
Third child 0–4 years		1,100	5.12
Non-food basic needs (per month) in Leones			
Fuel	Kerosene for lighting and cooking		2.00
Clothing	Amount actually spent on clothing and footwear		5.00
Health	One visit per household per month to a government health centre or hospital plus prescribed medicines		1.40
Education	Cost of keeping two children at school (one primary, one secondary) – school fees, books, uniform		5.50
Transport	Average cost of one return journey per month per household to nearest market centre		0.80
Total food and non food basic needs (per month)			52.34
Yearly household expenses on basics			628.08
Average yearly expenses per head			125.62

National Diamond Mining Company – Sierra Leone Limited: (DIMINCO) Open cast mining: drag-line machines sift gravel and diamond-bearing gravel is washed, sorted and concentrated. This is passed over greased shaking tables to which the diamonds stick. DIMINCO operates at 13 different sites and employs 45 people at each mine, with 33 at each plant. The plants produce three quarters of a million carats per year. Diamonds go through the government diamond office at Kenema where they are washed, graded, checked and bought for export.

Diamond mining	Alluvial Diamond Mining Scheme	DIMINCO
Land (amount used)		
Labour (organisation/ numbers employed)		
Capital invested		
Technology used		
Amount produced		
Marketing arrangements		

Alluvial Diamond Mining Scheme: Four thousand licensed diggers sieve for diamonds along river swamps or build small dams in the dry season. The recovery rate is low. Each digger employs a gang of eleven men. They work for a proportion of the diamonds won. The only legal means of disposal of stones is through the government diamond office. Private African miners make three quarters of a million carats per year. The government diamond exploration company also prospects within the scheme area.

Extraction big and small

Some people in rural areas can earn a living by digging for diamonds. These and other minerals provide important exports for the country. A country like Sierra Leone with a mixed economy encourages private initiative in digging for diamonds. But the State also plays a part in production and marketing.

1 Study Source A and Source B. How is production organised to involve both private and public activity?
2 How has the State influenced the marketing system?

Digging for diamonds
3 Using Sources A and B, compare the organisation of work in the diamond mining industry in the Scheme areas and DIMINCO. Do this by completing a copy of the table above.

The organisation of the diamond mining industry has been in both public and private hands.

4 Use Source C to draw up a table which shows ownership of diamond production from 1935 to today. Divide up your table into 'public' and 'private' ownership columns. In the 'public' column use the headings: 'Colonial government (Britain)' and 'Sierra Leone government'. In the 'private' column, use the headings 'Small-scale legal' and 'Large-scale legal'. Then answer the question 'who owned it?', by ticking the relevant entry.

History of diamond mining in Sierra Leone

Diamonds were discovered in 1930. In 1935 the colonial government gave a private British company, the SLST, a 99-year concession to mine diamonds. This gave the company exclusive rights to prospect for, produce and market. It paid an annual rent and 25 per cent of profits went to the government.

The company monopoly was ended in 1956 and the Alluvial Diamond Scheme was set up to give leases to allow small-scale mining by local people (see source A). Fifty per cent of the SLST production had to be marketed via the government diamond office. It paid royalties and taxes to the government.

In 1970 the private SLST was NATIONALISED (51 per cent of the shares were owned by the government) and renamed DIMINCO. Today minerals make up 70 per cent of the export trade and diamonds account for 60 per cent of this trade.

Systems and the state

How has the State influenced the marketing and selling of diamonds abroad?

5 Using Source D, draw a simple sketch map of Sierra Leone to show where diamonds are found.

6 a) Draw a large outline copy of the block diagram (Source E). On it mark the origin of the diamonds and the present day location of diamonds.
b) On a tracing overlay, draw in colour the internal system of inputs and outputs.
c) On a second tracing overlay, in a different colour, draw the world economic system.

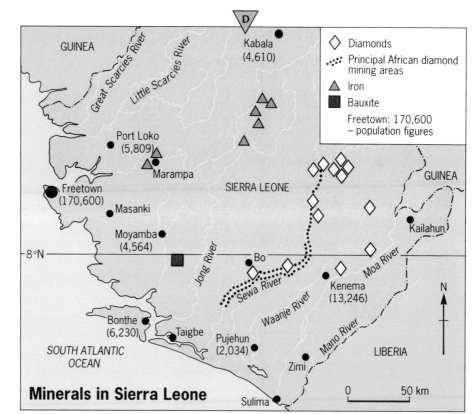

Minerals in Sierra Leone

Legend:
◇ Diamonds
⋯ Principal African diamond mining areas
▲ Iron
■ Bauxite
Freetown: 170,600 – population figures

Diamond marketing system

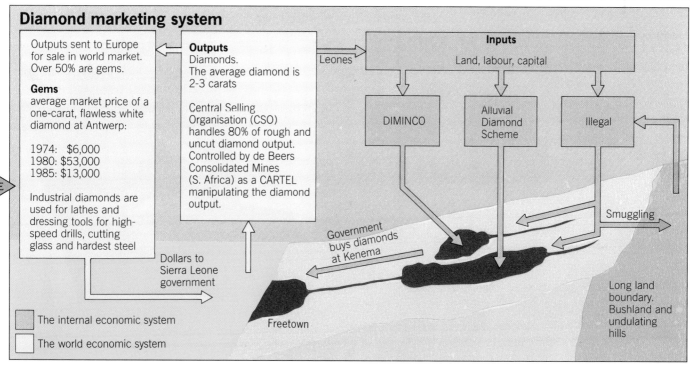

Outputs sent to Europe for sale in world market. Over 50% are gems.

Gems
average market price of a one-carat, flawless white diamond at Antwerp:

1974: $6,000
1980: $53,000
1985: $13,000

Industrial diamonds are used for lathes and dressing tools for high-speed drills, cutting glass and hardest steel

Outputs
Diamonds.
The average diamond is 2-3 carats

Central Selling Organisation (CSO) handles 80% of rough and uncut diamond output. Controlled by de Beers Consolidated Mines (S. Africa) as a CARTEL manipulating the diamond output.

Inputs
Land, labour, capital

Leones

DIMINCO

Alluvial Diamond Scheme

Illegal

Dollars to Sierra Leone government

Government buys diamonds at Kenema

Freetown

Smuggling

Long land boundary. Bushland and undulating hills

☐ The internal economic system
☐ The world economic system

Changes

7 In groups, discuss what would happen to diamond production and work in Sierra Leone if:
a) There were changes in the physical system. For example, suppose a new volcanic diamond pipe was found.
b) There were changes in the world economic system:

- South Africa flooded the market with diamonds:
- substitutes were developed for diamond drills;
- fashionable people in the West no longer valued gem diamonds;
- several selling organisations broke up.
c) There were changes in the internal economic system:

- larger licenses for private extraction were given;
- more modern technology was used;
- a military government came to power.

8 Smuggling is a form of private enterprise. Should the government stop smuggling? Discuss how it might do this.

WHAT WORK IN MANUFACTURING INDUSTRY?

Some people earn their living in manufacturing, industry and handicrafts. These people make up less than five per cent of the workforce, but the government is encouraging small-scale and large-scale industry. This page and page 115 investigate how the government is doing this and look at work in manufacturing industry.

Private and small scale

1 Source A shows the main types of small-scale manufacturing industry in Sierra Leone. Describe the work that is being done in the photos.

Investigation

The government of Sierra Leone has to make a decision. Should it encourage small-scale manufacturing industry? Or should it encourage large-scale manufacturing industry? It needs information to make a sensible decision. Researchers gathered the information in Source B.

2 Your job is to write a report for the government to give details of the main characteristics of small-scale manufacturing industry. Your report should include:
   a) a list of existing small-scale industries.
   b) the location of these industries (include a map).
   c) your view on whether they have a future.
   d) suggestions to the government as to whether they should encourage small-scale manufacturing industry. Give your reasons.

Large-scale manufacturing

3 Read Source C. Why does the government want to encourage larger industries?
4 Study Source D. Make a list of the larger industries found under the following headings: food and drink, chemical and pharmaceutical, building and construction, metal and light engineering and others.
5 What methods can the government use to encourage industrial development?
6 Three quarters of manufacturing activity is in Freetown. What are the advantages and disadvantages of this?
7 Should the government encourage foreign investors to set up manufacturing industry in Freetown?

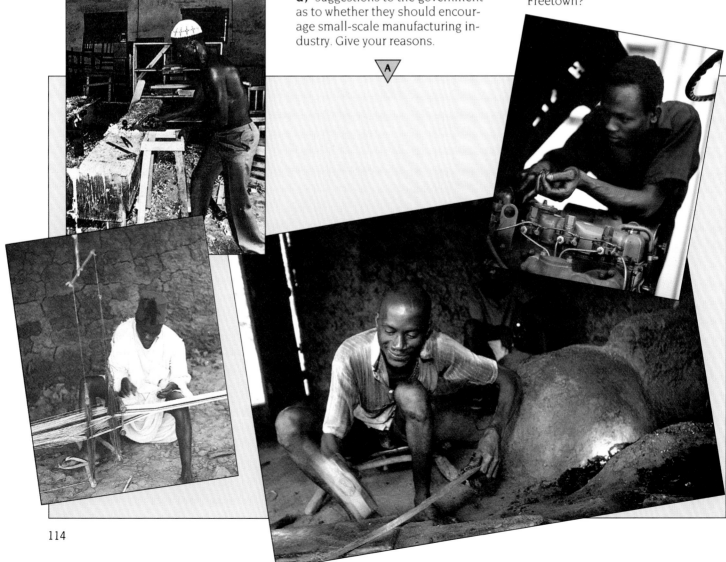

A

Small-scale manufacturing research data

What is the type of small-scale manufacturing in towns?
(% of total small-scale manufacturing)

	Clothing	Woodwork	Metalwork	Food	Repairs	Other
Largest town: Freetown	65	11	4	2	14	4
Large towns: 20–50 000	42	20	4	12	16	6
Small towns: 2–20 000	41	22	4	23	9	1

Growth in small-scale manufacturing industry
over a 6-year period (%)

	Establishments	Employment
Food	+17	+23
Clothing	−1	+2
Woodwork	−3	+6
Metalwork	+4	+4.5
Repairs	+12	+12

Size of firm (%)

Nos employed	Freetown	Large towns	Small towns
1	27	21	25
2–5	54	61	67
6–9	16	14	6
10 or more	4	4	2

How old are the firms? (%)

Less than 3 years old	35
More than 15 years old	4
More than 30 years old	1

Do they last?

	Opening rate (% per year)	Closure rate (% per year)
Freetown	11.0	9.5
Large towns	11.0	11.1
Small towns	9.5	11.1
Villages	6.5	11.1

Do people show initiative?
(over a 5-year period)

47.6% had restyled goods and services (e.g. created new fashion in clothing; new kind of packaging for bread).
38.5% had created new products (e.g. a carpenter would start making cupboards in addition to table and chairs).
34.5% had transformed their workshop.
22.5% had bought new machines.

'One baker in Freetown had shut down his electric oven and built a brick oven instead. Another had converted his electric oven to wood firing by installing a firebox at the rear end and distributing heat in the baking chamber by means of water tubes.'

B

Do people reinvest?

Profits are ploughed back for the purchase of tools, equipment and raw materials. Tailors reinvested 12 per cent of their total profits and carpenters 11 per cent. (These figures are markedly below those reported for other countries. 'Some of the profits not reinvested were channelled into private use, the education of family members or other ventures.')

We are keen to set up larger scale manufacturing. Our reasons for this are:

– to expand the economy
– to achieve a favourable BALANCE OF TRADE
– to encourage self-sufficiency
– to encourage job creation in rural areas
– to reduce migration to Freetown, which is overpopulated
– to promote local growth

No industry employs more than 1,000 people. The government pamphlet shows you the types of industries our country has.

Industrial development

The Mabole Fruit Canning industry

How government encourages industry:

- Grants development certificates to industries important to the economy.
- Creates industrial estates.
- Develops roads and other INFRASTRUCTURE.
- Welcomes foreign investors.
- Gives tax concessions, especially to industry creating jobs using local raw materials in rural areas.
- Widens the small local market by economic union with Liberia and other West African countries.

Industries in Sierra Leone

Industries established now number about 40 and these include plastic footwear, knitted garments, tinned fruits, juices and jams, cane sugar, suitcases, metal assembly, wheat flour, perfumes, soap, diamond polishing, fisheries, beer, distilled spirits, confectionery, paints, petroleum, cosmetics, pulp and paper and high quality office and household furniture.

There are two large palm mills operated by the Sierra Leone Production Marketing board. There is also a palm kernel oil mill; rice mills; groundnut oil mills and a mineral water bottling plant.

D

The Guardian, 1987

A quarter of Sierra Leone's 3.5 million population live in towns. A large percentage of them live in Freetown, the capital city. Urban incomes are low. The people are poor. They find it difficult to meet basic needs. But they do have more employment opportunities than rural people.

- What are these employment opportunities?
- How poor is poor in a town?

Earning a living in Freetown

1 Source A shows people at work in Freetown. In pairs describe the type of job and the work being done.

2 **a)** Look at Source B. Which of the jobs in Source A do you consider to be part of the informal economy?
b) Look at Source C. How many people work in the informal economy of Freetown?
c) What percentage of the workers of Freetown are part of the informal economy?
d) What link is there between job type and earnings?

3 Using the sources and your own ideas, what do you think the advantages might be of working in the informal economy? What are the disadvantages?

A

Street hawker at work

Woman spinning cot

Selling at Freetown market

B

Informal economy
That part of an economy which performs productive, useful and necessary labour without formal systems of control and payment and which operates beyond official recognition. The term is normally reserved for activities carried out alongside the formal (controlled, paid and recorded) sector.

Dictionary of Human Geography, Blackwell

Jobs and earnings in the Freetown area vary a great deal as the table shows.

Jobs and earnings in Freetown

Occupational group	Number (thousands)	%	Average income per person (leones per year)
Hawkers	45	18	222
Unskilled labourers	40	16	425
Street sellers	40	16	525
Artisans	35	14	571
Semi-skilled workers	27	11	630
Skilled workers	19	8	895
Clerical workers	15	6	2,333
Retailers	14	6	4,143
Professional/managerial	6	2	6,500
Entrepreneurs	5	2	9,800

C

Basic needs of an urban household of five

Food needs

Member of household	Recommended calorie intake per day	Average monthly cost of minimum food basket in leones
Male	2,700	12.60
Female	2,200	10.17
First child 10–14 years	2,200	10.17
Second child 5–9 years	1,600	7.93
Third child 0–4 years	1,100	5.91

Non-food basic needs (per month)

Fuel and rent Low cost two-room dwelling plus fuel for lighting/cooking	9.00
Clothing Actual expenditure on clothing and footwear per household	5.00
Health One visit per household per month to government health centre or hospital plus prescribed medicines	1.40
Education Cost of keeping two children at school (one primary, one secondary), school fees, books, uniforms	5.50
Transport Within the Greater Freetown area by public transport	4.00
Total food and non-food basic needs (per month)	71.68
Yearly household expenses on basics	860.16
Average yearly expenses per head	172.03

◁ D

Jobs and earnings in Freetown

Occupational Group	Number (thousands)	%	Average income per person (leones per year)	Income for each family member, assuming each worker supports five people
Hawkers	45	18	222	40.40

◁ E

Evidence of urban bias?

Average urban household income is three times greater than rural income.

Low spending on agricultural development: only 17% of all Development Plan expenditure

Access to safe drinking water:
1% of rural population
75% of urban population

Poverty: two-thirds of households in rural areas live below the poverty line. Nearly a quarter of young children are chronically undernourished.

Hospital services:
Average urban hospital serves 31,119
Average rural hospital serves 78,506

Rural farmers make up 70% of the population, yet they receive only 16% of public investment.

◁ F

Basic needs in towns

People in Freetown earn money in both the formal and informal economy. Is what they earn enough for their basic needs?

An average family of 5 living in Freetown needs food (the amount varies by age and sex) and non-food basics, such as fuel and clothing. Source D shows that, for each individual, minimum basic needs would cost 172.03 leones per year.

4 a) What are the total yearly basic needs of an urban household of five?
b) How much is spent on food per year?
c) How much is spent on non-food basics per year?
d) Present this information as a bar chart in money or percentages.
e) Sub-divide the food section to show how much is spent on each individual each year.
f) Sub-divide the non-food basic needs section to show how much is spent on each item each year.

5 a) Copy Source C, adding another column on the right-hand side, as is shown in Source E.
b) On your completed table, mark with a red line the basic needs figure of 172 leones.
c) What number of people have incomes below the basic needs poverty line? What number above the line?
d) What percentage of people are above and below the line?
e) What occupations do the people have below and above the line?

6 How do basic needs in rural and urban areas compare?
a) Use Source D on page 111 and Source F on this page. In what ways are food needs and non-food basic needs the same for the rural and urban people? How do they differ?
b) People have different incomes in rural and urban areas. What percentage of rural people are below the basic needs poverty line? What percentage of the urban people are below the basic needs poverty line?

7 Both rural and urban people are poor. Rural people have moved to the towns in search of a higher standard of living.
a) Using Source F, give four pieces of evidence which suggest living standards are higher in urban areas.
b) Some observers talk of 'urban bias' toward investment. Suggest why the government might favour urban people. The following points might help:
- Better-paid people in towns
- Concentration of people
- Politically powerful urban elite
- Concentration of educated people
- Concentration of problems
- Easily mobilised population

How evenly is wealth distributed?

This page and page 119 look at variations in the quality of life in different areas of Sierra Leone.

1 What does Source A tell you about life expectation for children in Freetown and in rural areas?

Urban–rural health disparities in Sierra Leone

	Freetown (%)	Rural (%)
Infant mortality	20.0	33.3
Significantly underweight children	18.3	32.4
Malaria parasites in blood	4.0	36.2
Chronically undernourished children	10.3	26.6

A

Indicators of regional disparities in Sierra Leone

Region	Area (sq. km)	Population	Primary-school students per 10,000 population	km of roads per 1,000 sq. km	Number of doctors	Number of electricity outlets
Sierra Leone	27,928	3,000,000	620.3	158.5	180	23,498
Western Area						
incl. Freetown	261	982,000	1,254.8	862.3	89	15,140
Northern Province	13,923	1,046,000				
1 Bombali			554.0	134.4	10	846
2 Kambia			389.2	239.0	3	262
3 Koinadugu			251.7	83.5	3	261
4 Port Loko			468.2	224.9	12	461
5 Tonkolili			589.4	135.0	9	389
Southern Province	7,868	196,000				
6 Bo			820.5	258.2	9	1,756
7 Bonthe			714.6	20.4	4	283
8 Moyamba			601.6	135.8	3	232
9 Pujehun			424.1	167.2	3	205
Eastern Province	5,876	776,000				
10 Kailahun			690.5	224.9	8	167
11 Kenema			541.2	209.3		1,495
12 Kono			456.8	113.6	9	2,001

B

2 a) Study Source B. Using the information it gives and Source C, draw four choropleth maps to show the distribution of primary school students, roads, doctors and electricity outlets throughout Sierra Leone.

b) Do your maps suggest that there are significant regional inequalities in the quality of life? If so, give examples.

3 Using your atlas, try to explain the pattern your maps show. (You may find the information on pages 111 and 117 helpful.)

Measuring quality of life

4 In pairs, decide which indicator in Source B is most important in assessing quality of life. Give reasons for your conclusions.

5 How might the Government of Sierra Leone try to even out regional inequalities? What problems do you think it would face?

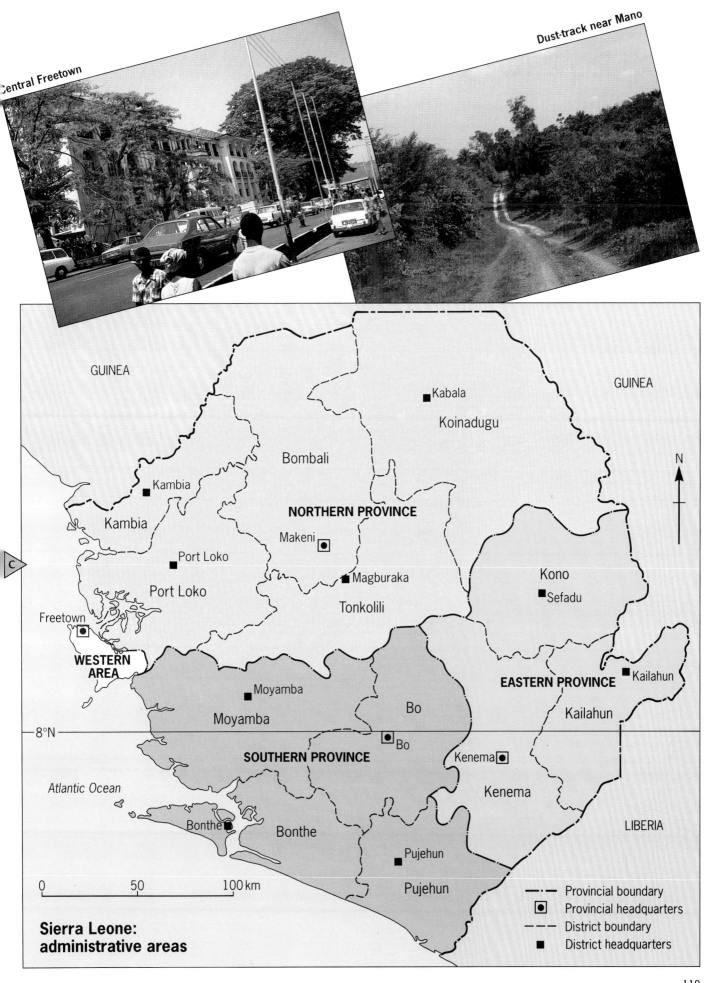

Central Freetown

Dust-track near Mano

GUINEA

GUINEA

Kabala

Koinadugu

Bombali

Kambia

N

Kambia

NORTHERN PROVINCE

Makeni

Kono

Port Loko

Sefadu

Port Loko

Magburaka

Freetown

Tonkolili

WESTERN
AREA

EASTERN PROVINCE

Kailahun

Moyamba

Bo

Kailahun

Moyamba

8°N

Bo

SOUTHERN PROVINCE

Kenema

Atlantic Ocean

Kenema

Bonthe

LIBERIA

Bonthe

Pujehun

0   50   100 km

Pujehun

—·—·— Provincial boundary
⊙ Provincial headquarters
– – – District boundary
■ District headquarters

**Sierra Leone:
administrative areas**

10 HOW TO INTERPRET A PHOTOGRAPH

You have studied work in a poor country. Sierra Leone is an economically developing country. It works a mixed economy. In this chapter, you have seen photographs of life and work in the country and the town. To conclude this Unit, the authors have chosen one final photograph. We could have chosen a picture of industry encouraged by the State, or a picture of a public government scheme. Instead, we have chosen a picture of private enterprise in a market, showing people going about their daily work. This photograph can be used as *evidence*. It gives information.

How can we analyse this photograph? Use all the skills you have learned so far to draw an annotated sketch of it. Use the questions at the bottom of the photograph to build up a picture of *jobs*, *work*, *employment* and *the quality of life* in this part of West Africa. Consider the following questions and discuss your answers with a partner:

1 Who took the photograph?
2 Why do you think it was taken?
3 What is the main message of the photograph?
4 What issues does the photograph raise in your mind?
5 Write a brief caption for the photograph. Compare your caption with that of other people in the class. Which is the most *accurate*, *informative* and *interesting*?

You could take a similar photograph of your local market and annotate it in the same way. Note any similarities and differences with the scene in Sierra Leone.

King Jimmy market, Freetown

WHAT?
Is this work?
Employment?
Self-employment?
Job?
Goods traded?
Methods used?
Organisation?
Sounds?
Smells?

WHERE?
Continent?
Country?
Place?

WHEN?
Time of day?
Season?
Weather/climate?

WHO?
Which people?
Age?
Sex?
Ethnic group?
Class?
Clothes?
Shoes?
Wealth?

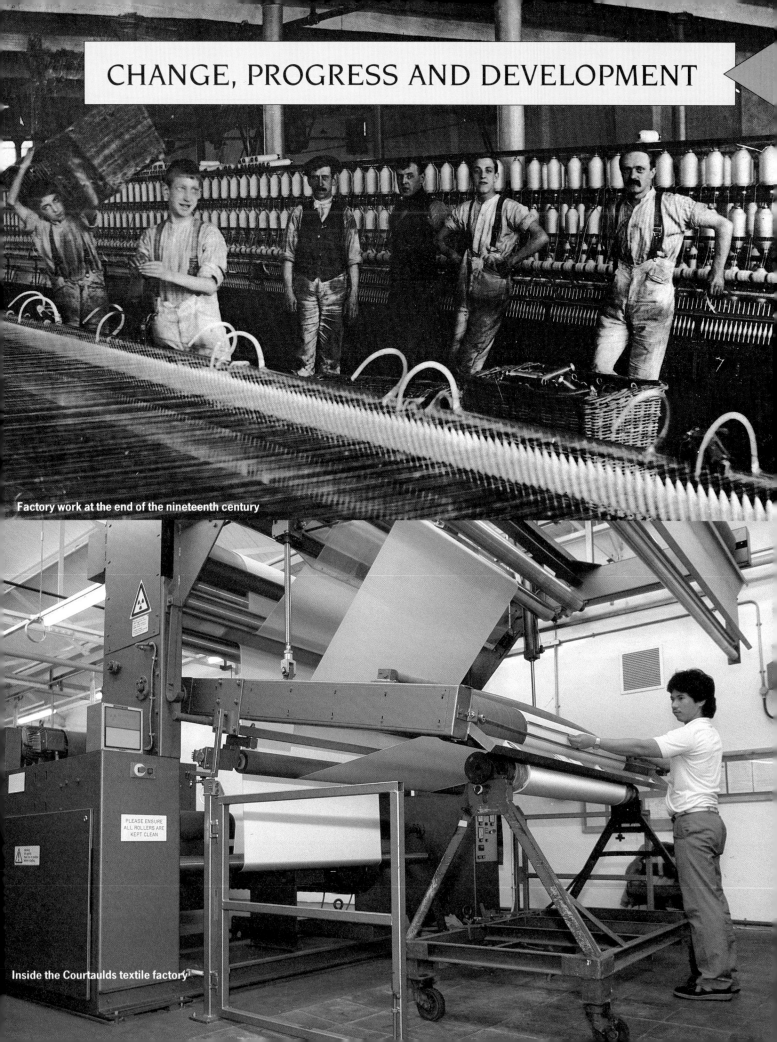

CHANGE, PROGRESS AND DEVELOPMENT

Factory work at the end of the nineteenth century

Inside the Courtaulds textile factory

PLEASE ENSURE
ALL ROLLERS ARE
KEPT CLEAN

The map (Source A) shows an area in the Midlands in the early 1800s. Oak woods would have covered the gently rolling land if the land had been left in its natural state. But over hundreds of years the landscape has been changed, as a result of decisions made by many different people. What changes have people made to this land? Who made the changes? Who gained?

Changes to the land

1 **a)** Draw a sketch map to show the main features of *change* in the area by the early nineteenth century. Think about *roads* (including a Roman road), *canals, abbeys, churches, settlements,* (farms, villages and towns) and *industries* (quarries, brickyards and collieries). Use different colours to show these features.

   b) Try to suggest a sequence in which these changes would have occurred. What would be the oldest features? Which features would have been quite new in the early 1800s?

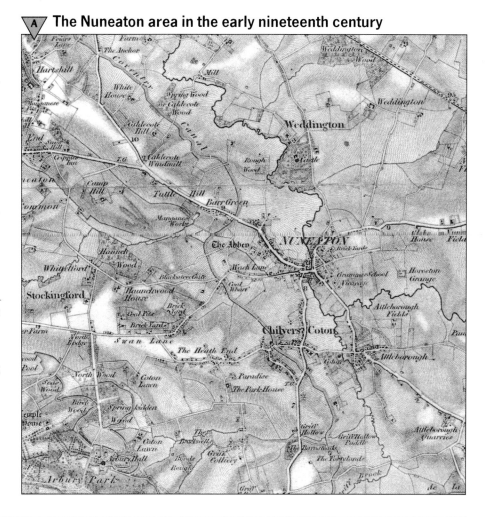

A **The Nuneaton area in the early nineteenth century**

Who made the changes?

By the 1800s Nuneaton was changing from a rural agricultural area to one where raw materials were dug out of the ground. Nearby factories were built. But changes such as these cost money and few families in a district were wealthy enough to invest in new ideas. Some people, however, were able to do so. In the Nuneaton area the principal investor at the end of the eighteenth century was Sir Roger Newdigate, a large landowner.

2 Where did the money for investment come from?
   Using Source B, list the sources of income for Sir Roger Newdigate. Which of these were local and which came from further afield?

3 How did Sir Roger invest his money? Which investments in Source B were ones he had inherited and which were ones he had initiated himself?

4 Sir Roger's investments would have brought no profit if there had been no market for his products. What changes to the local community did his investments bring? What were the wider effects?

Who gained, who lost?

5 **a)** In groups, using Source B and Source C, discuss how the people on the right might have been affected by Sir Roger's investments.
   b) Who seems to have benefited most and who least?

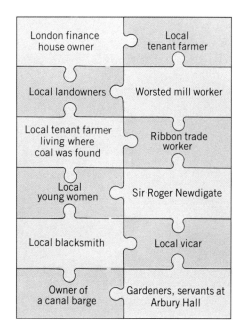

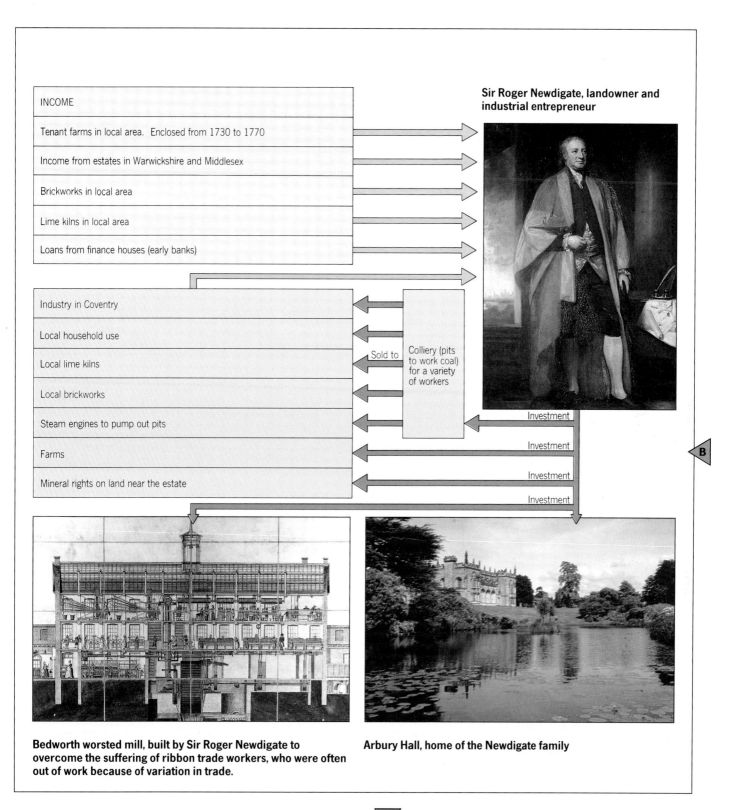

INCOME

Tenant farms in local area. Enclosed from 1730 to 1770	
Income from estates in Warwickshire and Middlesex	
Brickworks in local area	
Lime kilns in local area	
Loans from finance houses (early banks)	

Sir Roger Newdigate, landowner and industrial entrepreneur

Industry in Coventry

Local household use

Local lime kilns

Local brickworks

Steam engines to pump out pits

Farms

Mineral rights on land near the estate

Sold to → Colliery (pits to work coal) for a variety of workers

Investment

Investment

Investment

Investment

B

Bedworth worsted mill, built by Sir Roger Newdigate to overcome the suffering of ribbon trade workers, who were often out of work because of variation in trade.

Arbury Hall, home of the Newdigate family

C

Working conditions in factories 1810	
Hours of work per day – adults	no limit by law
Hours of work per day – children	12 – but difficult to enforce
Age at which children could begin work	5
Average child wages per week	4 shillings
Average adult annual income	£13

6 Sir Roger's investments led to major changes in the landscape and for the people. Would you call these changes improvements?

The rest of this Unit tries to help you understand what change, progress and development might mean.

The Nuneaton area looks very different 180 years later and people no longer work in the same activities. The map (Source A) covers the same area as the earlier map on page 120. What changes have there been in this time? Whose decisions brought about these changes?

Changes

1 Using tracing paper and Source A do the following.
a) Outline and shade the built-up area.
b) Draw in different colours the main roads, railways and canals. Place your tracing over the map on page 133. List the main changes that have taken place since the early nineteenth century.
c) Compare the two maps. List those features which were on the earlier map and can still be seen now.

2 The pie-chart (Source B) shows how the local people earn a living. For each type of activity give a map reference showing where this activity might be found today.

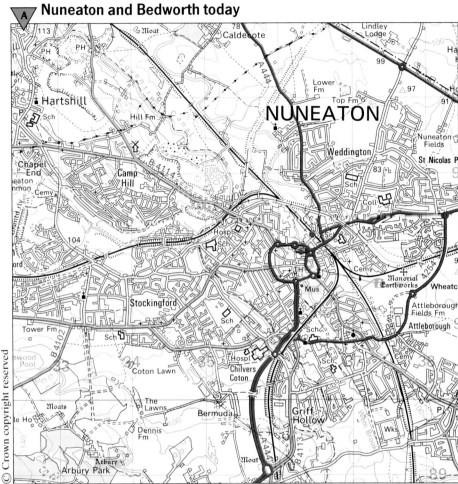

A Nuneaton and Bedworth today

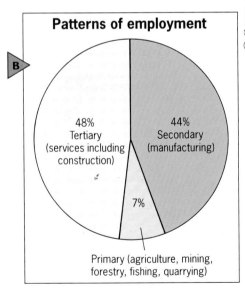

Patterns of employment

B

- 48% Tertiary (services including construction)
- 44% Secondary (manufacturing)
- 7% Primary (agriculture, mining, forestry, fishing, quarrying)

Decisions

Look at the photographs (Source C). They show some changes in the Nuneaton area. They are the result of decisions made by different people or organisations locally and elsewhere.

3 Complete the table below by filling in information about each of the photographs. One example has been done for you.

4 In groups, look at each of the photographs (Source C). Do you think local people are more or less important in making decisions that lead to change now than they were in the past?

Why not investigate?
So far Nuneaton had been used to show how decisions bring about change. This process of change benefits different groups of people. In a similar way you can investigate your local area.

Title of photograph and grid square	Nature of change	Type of change (economic, social)	Who made decision – private or public sector?	Where was decision made – locally, nationally, internationally?	When was the decision made?
Opencast mine (3589)	A new coal mine	Economic	Public sector – British Coal	Nationally	1986
Camp Hill					

Sudeley opencast mine, near Bermuda village, opened by British Coal, a nationalised industry.
Date: 1986

Federal Express, a large Public Limited Company, occupies a site on the Bermuda Industrial Estate. It is a local authority (Borough Council) scheme to supply industrial space to various size companies. It was formerly a clay works.
Date: 1980

Gypsy Lane roadstone quarry is owned by Tarmac, a multinational company.
Date: 1930s

Courtaulds acetate factory, part of a multinational organisation with headquarters in London and branches throughout the UK and the world.
Date: 1920s

Brick and tile works – a private company, still in local ownership.
Date: 1930s

St Nicolas Park, a local private housing scheme.
Date: 1970s

Camp Hill council housing – a local authority rented housing scheme.
Date: 1950s

St Nicolas' school, a local authority first school.
Date: 1962

The changes in Nuneaton were part of a wider process of change taking place throughout the country. Economic change was dominant, both in agriculture and industry, but at the same time, social changes were occurring. What were the main economic and social changes taking place in Britain?

The change from agriculture to industry

In the 1800s farming provided a living for 25 per cent of the working population. A lot more were dependent on supplying the farms and processing the goods from the farms. Today, barely 2 per cent of the working population earn a living from farming. The UK is less self-sufficient in food, but farming still needs a large supply and processing industry. (Remember these links in Unit 6.)

Many people left the land at the beginning of the nineteenth century because there was less work. The enclosure of farmland meant they had too little land to work economically. Many people went to the towns to look for work in the new factories. Today, factory work too has changed a great deal.

A A harvest team in Suffolk at the turn of the century

B Harvesting today

1 In pairs choose *one* of the photographs about farming (Source A and Source B).
   a) Discuss what you think life would have been like for the people in the photograph you have chosen. Think about the work involved, the effect of the seasons on its nature, the length of the working day, living conditions, and pay.
   b) Join with another pair who discussed the other farming photograph. Exchange your views on what your photograph showed.
   c) What changes in farming have taken place this century? Are these improvements? What progress has been made?

2 Look at the two photographs of industry on page 119 and, in pairs, carry out a similar exercise to question 1.

3 Your comments have been based on photographic evidence.
   a) What are the advantages and limitations of photographs as evidence?
   b) What other types of evidence would you need to make more detailed comments about change, improvement and progress?

   c) What are the main points you would make about the change from agriculture to industry since 1800?

What social changes occurred?

These economic changes were important to the prosperity of the country. But these changes had social consequences too. Some were more beneficial than others. People left the land to work in factories. This work was found in towns. New housing was built to accommodate the influx of people. Towns grew rapidly and conditions were not always pleasant.

Town growth is not so rapid today, but a large proportion of people still live in urban areas.

4 Look at Source C and at the photographs of school life (Sources D and E). Work in small groups.
   a) Discuss the problems schools faced 180 years ago.
   b) Discuss what a school day would have been like in Source D.
   c) Compare this with a day in your school life.
   d) What are the main differences?
   e) Are these differences examples of change, improvement and progress?

Education 180 years ago

'Except in Scotland, no public money was spent on elementary teaching. Most was done by charity schools or village dames or by the Sunday School movement ... or private effort. ... Teaching in the public schools was almost always restricted to the classics, and life was often brutal and undisciplined. ... Though there were some good grammar schools, a mass often suffered from the absence of any central body to see they were honestly administered.'

Better health care

At the beginning of the nineteenth century life expectancy was low, infant mortality was high and many endemic diseases existed. The level of health care was poor. If hospital treatment was needed, voluntary or public hospitals were used. Voluntary hospitals were paid for by people who gave money of their own free will. Patients paid what they could afford. Public hospitals were funded by local and government money. After 1948 all hospitals were reorganised under the National Health Service.

5 The photographs (Sources F and G) show health care at different times. In small groups discuss:
   a) what some of the reasons were for poor health statistics at the beginning of the nineteenth century?
   b) the changes that have taken place in health care over the past 100 years.
   c) the changes that have occurred in the organisation of health care. (refer back to Unit 2).

What do the changes add up to?

6 You have looked at social changes (developments in health care and education) and economic changes (developments in agriculture and industry) in Britain since the early nineteenth century. You have discussed whether these changes add up to progress. Now write a paragraph on whether you think they add up to development.

> **A definition of development**
> Development is the process of improving people's lives.

A grammar school in 1899

Medical care at the end of the nineteenth century – the quality of treatment varied from place to place.

A comprehensive school today – all children from ages 4–16 are entitled to a free education

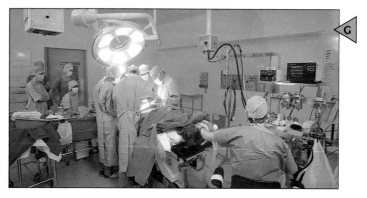

Today the National Health Service offers treatment to all, but resources are often scarce and many people are treated in private hospitals.

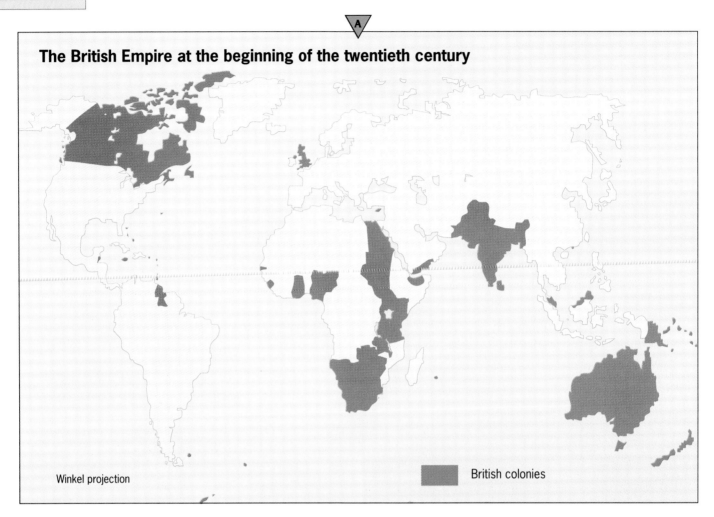

A

The British Empire at the beginning of the twentieth century

Winkel projection

British colonies

The Empire

During the nineteenth and twentieth century Britain developed. British workers and industrialists invested skill and money to make this happen. Britain also built up an empire of COLONIES across the world (Source A). Without the empire, Britain might not have achieved these economic and social advances. Some historians and commentators believe Britain's wealth and progress were based on the empire. Britain relied on the colonies as:

- a source of raw materials to make manufactured goods in Britain.
- a ready market for British made goods.
- somewhere to invest.

B

	Selected colonial raw materials and industries		
Raw material	Country name in 1900	Company	Industry in Britain
Sugar	Jamaica	Tate & Lyle	Sugar-refining in East London
Oil palm	Nigeria	United African Company	Soap-making at Port Sunlight
Cocoa beans	Gold Coast	Cadbury	Chocolate-making – Bournville, Birmingham
Cotton	Egypt	Arkwright	Cotton textiles in Preston
Tea	India	Brooke Bond	Brooke Bond in Croydon
Jute	India	Cox	Sack-making in Dundee
Rubber	Malaya	Dunlop	Tyre-making in Birmingham
Diamonds	South Africa	de Beers	Diamond-polishing in central London

1 Look at Source B.
  a) On a world map find the countries mentioned. Draw the sea routes by which the raw materials would have come to Britain.

  b) Use reference books to add further examples of raw material supply to Britain.

  c) Who might have owned the ships which brought these goods to Britain?

An ideal market

2 a) Using Source C complete the table on the right.
b) What sorts of goods might be exported to the colonies?
c) What were some of the 'other places' referred to in the table?

Opportunities for investment

3 Source D shows investments made by Britain in 1914. This was money (capital) used to set up and develop industries and services.
a) What was Britain's total investment overseas?
b) Where was the money invested? Rank the areas in order of importance.
c) How evenly spread around the world was the investment?
d) Did most investment go into the colonies?

4 Look back at Unit 10 on Sierra Leone. Discuss with a partner whether your investigation of work and employment in Sierra Leone supports the view put forward in Source E.

Britain – imports and exports	% of imports	% of exports
From the British Empire To the British Empire		
From other places To other places		
Total		

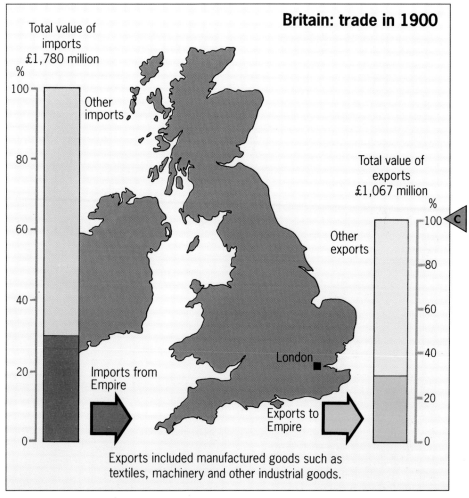

Britain: trade in 1900

Total value of imports £1,780 million

Other imports

Imports from Empire

Total value of exports £1,067 million

Other exports

London

Exports to Empire

Exports included manufactured goods such as textiles, machinery and other industrial goods.

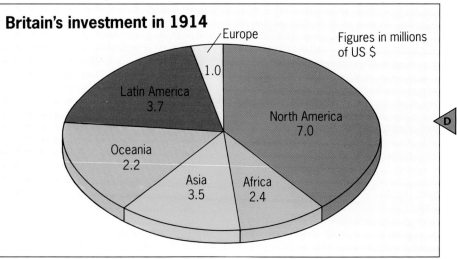

Britain's investment in 1914

Figures in millions of US $

Europe 1.0
Latin America 3.7
Oceania 2.2
Asia 3.5
Africa 2.4
North America 7.0

Yes it's true, the people of Africa have worked to provide cheap raw materials for Britain. These have been the basis of many of your manufacturing industries. You made things like textiles and clothes and sold them to us. This helped you but stopped our young industries from developing. You have invested in Africa and this has helped some of our people get jobs, but you have taken back the profit for your shareholders. Many Africans who study history as I have soon realise you have exploited us so that your people could develop.

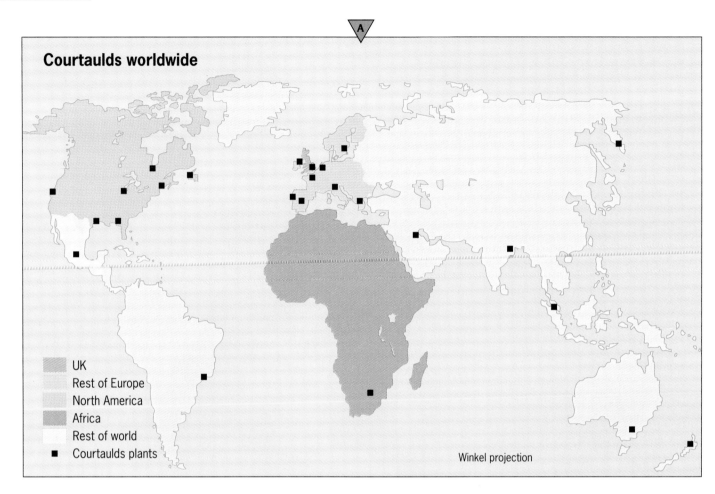

Courtaulds worldwide

UK
Rest of Europe
North America
Africa
Rest of world
■ Courtaulds plants

Winkel projection

Britain invested heavily abroad and this led to a large import and export trade. Much of this investment was made by individual companies and they made connections with various parts of the world. They still need these connections. In what way do British companies today need the world?

The Courtaulds example

Courtaulds, a UK MULTINATIONAL, started in 1816 weaving silk from the Far East. Today it produces a variety of goods, from textiles to paint. It operates in 25 countries, employing a total of 65,000 people.

Location

1 Look at Source A. Draw a map to show where Courtaulds plants are found. Use an atlas to locate places as accurately as possible.

Courtaulds – performance figures 1987

Manufacturing location	Turnover 1987 (£ million)	Profit 1987 (£ million)	Investment 1987 (£ million)
United Kingdom	1,394	115	446
Rest of Europe	440	46	103
North America	264	5	84
Africa	127	30	80
Rest of world	152	15	48
Total	2,377	211	761

Investment

2 Where do Courtaulds have investments? Look at Source B.
a) Which two regions had the largest investments in 1987?
b) Roughly what proportion of Courtaulds' total investment is this?
c) Estimate the proportion of investment which was overseas.
d) Which areas make up 'the rest of the world'?

Profit

3 Courtaulds, like any other company, judges its success by how much profit it makes. Where are the profits made? From the table (Source B), work out:
a) which two areas make the biggest profit.
b) the proportion of profits made overseas.

Expansion

Some idea of the success of a company can be gained by comparing profit and turnover. For example, the more profit (return) made for every £ of turnover (total sales of the company) the better. It is also better if more profit (return) is made for every £ of investment.

Courtaulds wants to increase its profits by expanding.

4 The Board of Directors of Courtaulds in London are to discuss the expansion of the firm. You have been asked to recommend where future investment should be made. You must try to increase the profit of the firm. More profit means better returns for the shareholders. Complete copies of Source C and Source D to help you make your choice.

5 Present your recommendations about future investment to the Chairman of the Board. Include a map and full reasons for your choice.

Prospects for future investment (1)

	World	UK	Rest of Europe	North America	Africa	Rest of world
Investment (£ million)	761	446	103	84	80	48
Profit (£ million)	211	115	46	5	30	15
Return on investment	£0.277					

The return on investment is found by dividing the profit made by the investment. For the world example, this is the same as saying that the return (profit) is £0.277 (about 28 pence) for every £1 invested.

C

Prospects for future investment (2)

	World	UK	Rest of Europe	North America	Africa	Rest of world
Turnover (£ million)	2,377					
Profit (£ million)	211					
Return on turnover	0.0887					

D

Return on turnover is found by dividing the profit made by the turnover. For the world example, this is the same as saying that the return (profit) is £0.0887 (about nine pence) for every £1 turnover.

The Colodense print plant at Whitchurch, Bristol, part of Courtaulds Packaging

E

◀ Visibles (goods) which have been made in the UK are exported to other countries.

▶ Visibles are imported into the UK.

◀ Invisibles (services) sold to other countries are exports for the UK.

▶ Invisibles bought from other countries are imports for the UK.

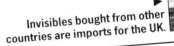

A

The UK's prosperity and continued development depends on trading.

1 The photographs (Source A) show various goods and services which the UK imports and exports. From Source A, name the visible import, visible export, invisible import and invisible export. Give one other example of each of these types of imports and exports.

Balancing the figures
The BALANCE OF TRADE is the difference between the import and export of goods (visibles). The CURRENT BALANCE is the difference between total imports and exports – goods as well as invisibles (services). When imports are greater than exports, the UK has a *deficit*. When exports are greater than imports, the UK has a *surplus*.

B

UK current account (£ million)				
Year	Current balance	Exports	Imports	Invisibles balance
1985	+2,888	78,111	80,289	+5,066
1986	−944	72,843	81,306	+7,517

2 From the table (Source B) answer the following questions:
   a) Was there a deficit or surplus on the balance of trade in 1985 and 1986? Explain your answer.
   b) Why was there a deficit on the current balance in 1986 but not in 1985?

Partners in trade
The UK is the fifth largest trading nation after the USA, West Germany, Japan and France.

3 Look at Source C.
   a) On two world maps, show the UK's ten main export markets and import suppliers.
   b) What similarities and/or differences are there between the two maps?
   c) How important is trade with the EEC?
   d) What might be the effect on the UK's trading pattern of removing all trade restrictions within the EEC in 1992?

C

The UK's 12 major trading partners		
Country	% of exports	% of imports
United States	14.7	11.7
Ireland	4.6	3.3
Belgium and Luxembourg	4.3	4.7
Netherlands	9.4	7.7
Norway	—	5.2
Sweden	3.8	2.9
France	9.9	7.8
Spain	2.0	2.0
Italy	4.4	5.1
Switzerland	—	2.8
West Germany	11.4	3.1
Japan	—	4.8
Others	35.5	38.9

The trading pattern of the UK		
Area	Imports	Exports
EEC	46	46
Other West European countries	17	13
North America	15	17
Other developed countries	7	5
Oil-exporting countries	4	8
Rest of world	11	11
Total	100%	100%

The global economy

The UK's trade and prosperity is firmly placed in the developed world. This is part of a world pattern of trading – the global economy.

4 What is the world pattern of trade? Look at Source D. Think back to other Units in this book and answer the following questions.

a) What is meant by: developed market economies; centrally planned economies; developing countries; OPEC (The Organisation of Petroleum Exporting Countries)?

b) On a world map, use four colours to shade in these different economic groupings.

c) Name five countries in each of the groups.

5 a) Use Source D to complete a copy of table I.

b) Rank the trading groups in order of total trading.

c) Now, take each group separately and rank the groups they trade with in order of importance.

d) Comment on any differences/similarities.

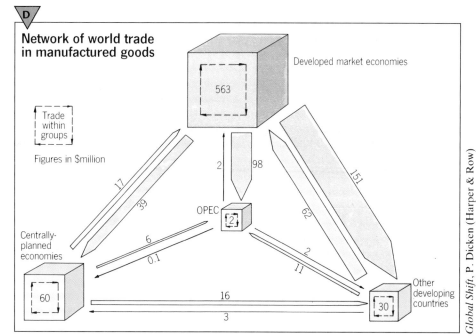

D Network of world trade in manufactured goods

Trade within groups

Figures in $million

Developed market economies — 563

OPEC — [2]

Centrally-planned economies — 60

Other developing countries — 30

17 · 39 · 2 · 98 · 151 · 62 · 6 · 0.1 · 2 · 11 · 16 · 3

Global Shift, P. Dicken (Harper & Row)

6 Some groups benefit and some lose (have larger imports than exports) from this trading pattern.

a) Complete a copy of table 2 to show surpluses and deficits in trade.

b) Which trading group benefits most from trade in manufactured goods?

c) Which group loses out?

d) Where deficits occur, how do you think these are made up? (Think about what OPEC means.)

Here is the News. The main story is about the UK's balance of payments and world trade.

E

Table 1 – trade in manufactured goods

From To	Developed	Centrally planned	Developing countries	OPEC	Total
Developed	563.0				
Centrally planned		60.0			
Developing countries			30.0		
OPEC				2.0	

Table 2 – who benefits or loses?

From To	Developed	Centrally planned	Developing countries	OPEC	Total
Developed	not applicable	+			
Centrally planned		not applicable			
Developing countries		−	not applicable		
OPEC		−			

7 You work for a TV news company. It is your job to produce a three minute slot on the evening news programme where the main item is UK trade (Source E). The information on this page and page 132 is what you must produce the item from. The newsreader will need three minutes of commentary (about 400 words) and there will be an opportunity to include graphics (maps, tables, graphs and photographs) which the newsreader can refer to. Whatever graphics you use should appeal to your viewers.

a) Write out your commentary.

b) Select the graphics you will need.

c) Decide where the graphics will come during the commentary.

d) In groups choose a commentary to read out. Discuss the points it puts across. Is there anything that could be added?

11 ASPECTS OF DEVELOPMENT

This Unit has looked at the meaning of *change, improvement, progress* and *development* in the UK. There are a number of aspects to development shown in the diagram (Source A). These change over time.

1 In small groups read through Source A. (There are three statements for each aspect.)
a) Decide which three statements go with each aspect of development.
b) Put the statements in chronological order for each aspect of development.
c) On a large copy of Source B write out each statement in the appropriate place on the diagram.
(d) Do you think this diagram adequately sums up development in the UK? What other information might you need to know to build up a complete picture of development?

Progress for all?

We have seen that the UK has changed, improved and developed.
● It has changed its agriculture.
● It has developed its industries and services.
● It has increased trade with the rest of the world.
● It has improved the quality of life of its people.
● It has developed democratically.

We have asked whether economic, social and political developments have benefited everyone. The following Units show that other countries are developing. The Gambia, South Korea and Nicaragua are in different parts of the world. They are developing in different ways. As you study these countries, ask yourself whether the UK developed in a similar way. Think about whether the economic, social and political developments are benefiting the whole population.

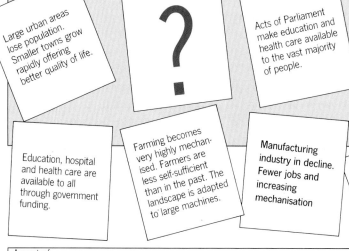

Britain was world's leading manufacturing nation as the factory system developed.

Massive movement of people to towns and cities took place for work in new factories.

?

Increasing introduction of machinery on farms leads to decreasing workforce in farming.

?

Trade with European partners and with other developed countries becomes very important.

One quarter of the workforce is employed in farming – great dependance on manual labour.

Continued urban growth – rapid expansion of towns, **especially the suburbs**

Colonial trade is very important. Britain is a major trading nation, with little international competition.

Manufacturing industry becomes outdated. Britain is overtaken by other countries in the production of basic goods.

Britain loses export trade to international competition as other countries become industrialised.

?

Large urban areas lose population. Smaller towns grow rapidly offering better quality of life.

?

Acts of Parliament make education and health care available to the vast majority of people.

Only wealthy people have access to health care and education.

Education, hospital and health care are available to all through government funding.

Farming becomes very highly mechanised. Farmers are less self-sufficient than in the past. The landscape is adapted to large machines.

Manufacturing industry in decline. Fewer jobs and increasing mechanisation

?

A

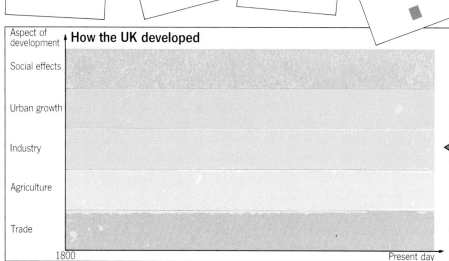

Aspect of development	How the UK developed
Social effects	
Urban growth	
Industry	
Agriculture	
Trade	

1800   Present day

B

Women drawing water from the village well in Jurunku

Location of The Gambia

The Gambia

Senegal

Guinea Bissau

Mali

Guinea

Burkina Faso

10°N

Atlantic Ocean

Sierra Leone

Liberia

Ivory Coast

Ghana

N

0   500 km

TRADE AND 'POOR' COUNTRIES

Abrahim surveys his groundnut crop...

A

C

Groundnuts in The Gambia

Year	Groundnut production (tonnes)	Groundnuts for export (tonnes)
1968		150,000
1970	129,000	
1973–77		132,000 (average per year)
1978	105,000	78,000
1980	103,000	
1981	130,000	46,000
1982	151,000	
1983	106,000	
1984	114,000	55,000
1985	120,000	

Major markets for Gambian groundnuts

UK	28%	Belgium and Luxembourg	13%
Netherlands	21%	France	8%
Portugal	14%	Others	16%

Most economically developing countries are poor if we define 'poor' by how much the people earn, how many things they own and how much they eat. But they are part of the global economy just as much as the UK is. The governments of economically developing countries need to know: What can we trade? How can we borrow? How can we raise our living standards?

This Unit helps you to answer these questions by studying one small country in West Africa – The Gambia. It also shows how *trade, aid* and *self-help schemes* are being used to improve the quality of people's lives.

Which crop to grow?

Gambian farmers like Abrahim (Source A) cultivate a number of different crops. They grow millet (a cereal grass), maize and rice to feed their families. They

also grow crops which are sold to the rest of the world (on the world market).

1 Look at Source A. What is Abrahim growing? Why is it important to him? Describe the landscape.

2 Abrahim lives in the village of Dunkunku, on the north bank of the River Gambia. His family, like other farming families grow food and CASH CROPS. Source B shows where in the area these are grown. Use Source B to complete a copy of the table on the left. (You can estimate the size of the area by tracing a ½km grid over the map.) You could also draw a transect from A to B as a cross-section to show where the crops are grown.

Type of crop	Estimated area	Approximate distance from village	Type of land used
Rice			
Groundnuts and food crops			

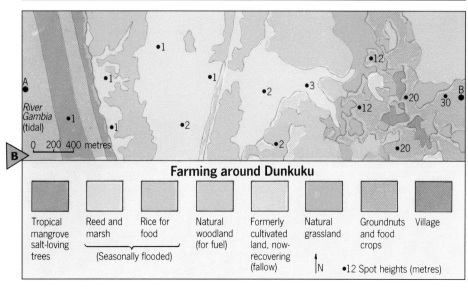

Farming around Dunkuku

Tropical mangrove salt-loving trees	Reed and marsh	Rice for food	Natural woodland (for fuel)	Formerly cultivated land, now-recovering (fallow)	Natural grassland	Groundnuts and food crops	Village

(Seasonally flooded)

●12 Spot heights (metres)

A
River Gambia (tidal)
0 200 400 metres
B
B

Groundnuts for export

Groundnuts are important to the Gambian farmer. He sells them to the Gambia Produce Marketing Board. They are then mainly sold in Western Europe to be made into cooking oil, salad dressing, margarine, soap and cattle cake. The farmers in Gambia hope they will fetch a good price.

3 **a)** Using Source C, draw two line graphs to show groundnut production and export.
b) What conclusions can you draw from your graphs?
c) Draw a bar chart to show the major markets for groundnuts in Europe.

4 **a)** Using Source C and Source D copy the table on the right. Work out the selling price of groundnuts and the amount of money received from exports in 1984. (Take the selling price to be the highest price for the year.)
b) Assume that in 1987 Gambian farmers exported the same amount of groundnuts as in 1984. How much revenue would these exports bring in?

Year	Amounted exported (1)	Price of groundnuts (2)	Amount received (1 × 2)
1984			
1987			

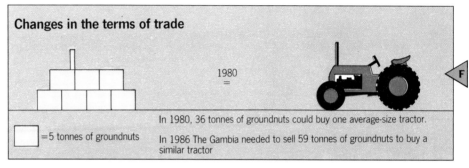

Groundnut prices 1978–87

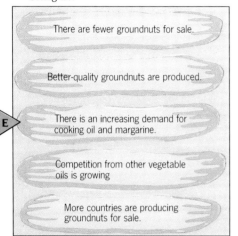

There are fewer groundnuts for sale.

Better-quality groundnuts are produced.

There is an increasing demand for cooking oil and margarine.

Competition from other vegetable oils is growing

More countries are producing groundnuts for sale.

Changes in the terms of trade

1980
=

□ = 5 tonnes of groundnuts

In 1980, 36 tonnes of groundnuts could buy one average-size tractor.

In 1986 The Gambia needed to sell 59 tonnes of groundnuts to buy a similar tractor.

5 **a)** The statements in Source E show that the price of groundnuts varies each year. Pick out the statements which you think would lead to a price rise and those which you think would result in a fall in price.
b) Can Gambian farmers affect these influences on world prices? Give reasons for your answer.

Affording imports

Gambia uses the money it gets from exporting groundnuts to buy goods on the world market. It must pay the world price but prices of goods are higher than in the past.

6 **a)** Look at Source F. It shows how the TERMS OF TRADE have changed.
b) Draw a similar diagram to show the 1986 figures.

c) Why does it now take more groundnuts to buy the same amount of goods? (Think about the world price of groundnuts compared to the world price of tractors.)

The terms of trade affect the whole Gambian economy, because they apply to all goods bought by The Gambia, not just to tractors.

7 Look at Source G and do the following:
a) Rank the exports in order of importance.
b) Rank the imports in order of importance.
c) Why is there such a wide range of imports and such a narrow range of exports?
d) What is the difference between import spending and export earnings?
8 In groups, use the information on this page and page 136 to outline what you see as The Gambia's trading problem.

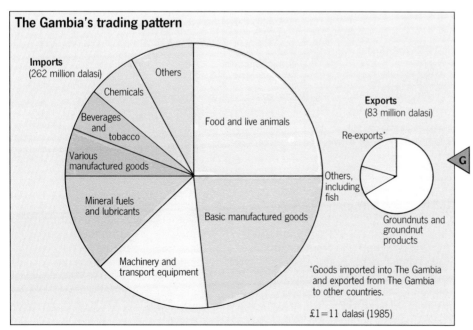

The Gambia's trading pattern

Imports (262 million dalasi)

Others
Chemicals
Beverages and tobacco
Various manufactured goods
Mineral fuels and lubricants
Machinery and transport equipment
Food and live animals
Basic manufactured goods

Exports (83 million dalasi)

Re-exports*

Others, including fish

Groundnuts and groundnut products

*Goods imported into The Gambia and exported from The Gambia to other countries.

£1 = 11 dalasi (1985)

All countries need to borrow in order to develop. But the problem is particularly serious in 'poor' countries like The Gambia. They need to pay for development plans but money from trade is not enough. Poor countries need to borrow from different world institutions and commercial banks. To find out what is involved, read what a Gambian economist, says in Source A.

In England, people go to the High Street bank to borrow money for a particular purpose. They have to pay back the sum they borrow plus the interest.

We need capital to put into projects, but the money we get from selling our groundnuts is going down. We don't export much else. Few other ways of gaining money exist so the government has borrowed. It borrowed from world institutions like the WORLD BANK and the INTERNATIONAL MONETARY FUND (IMF).

Now we're £175 million in debt. We hope to pay this back over a number of years, but we have problems. This is a large amount for a small country. We have to pay back £9 million every year. Some countries have tried to help us by cancelling our debt and giving us aid.

A

B

invest

Investors

Deposits

Interest

Bank

Loan made
Money (e.g. £100) borrowed – the principal

Borrowers
apply for loans
Bank assesses risk

The original sum borrowed, and the interest, are paid back £100+£10

Borrower pays 10% interest over a year

Borrowing from a bank
People borrow from a bank or other financial institutions. The amount you pay back depends on the interest rate you are being charged. The time period of the loan will also vary.

The state of The Gambia

People	Economy	Trade and debt
Population = 686,000 Growing at 2.6% per year Percentage in towns: 21% Urban growth rate: 5% per year Adult literacy rate: 20% Life expectancy: 36 years	Mixed economy GROSS DOMESTIC PRODUCT falling National income per person: £181 p.a. Growth rate of income 1965–83: 1.4% Labour force in agriculture: 78%	Exports: groundnuts 67% fish 8% Total exports: £28 million Total imports: £81 million Debt: £175 million Debt service charges: £9 million per year

Society
Religion
Muslim 85%
Christian 8%
Other 7%
Ex-British colony
Independent since 1966
	Living standards
	Consumer prices 1983–85: 40% rise
	Food supply:
	   1960: 2300 calories per day
	   1961–71: 2348 calories per day
	   1980–82: 2223 calories per day
		Politics
		Multi-party democratic republic
		People's progressive party has ruled since 1962
		Attempted coup by Muslim dissidents in 1971; ministers charged with corruption as a result
		Since 1982 there have been close ties with Senegal

C

The process of borrowing

1 Source B shows how an individual might borrow money from a bank. Draw a similar diagram to show how a country might borrow from a world institution. (The glossary gives more information about these world institutions.)

We have seen how money *can* be borrowed. But in order to decide whether to lend a country money and how much to lend, the world's banks and financial institutions work out whether that country is a 'high-risk' one. Such a country may have problems in the future paying the money back.

2 Imagine you are the head of an international financial institution to which the government of The Gambia has applied for a loan. Using Source C, write to the government explaining why you are reluctant to grant the loan.

A problem of debt

THE GAMBIAN TIMES

Imports grow and groundnut prices drop

HOW CAN £143 million DEBT BE REPAID?

INCOME: £115 million EXPENDITURE: £127 million

The Gambia borrows again

ECONOMY WORSENS – *Living standards drop again*

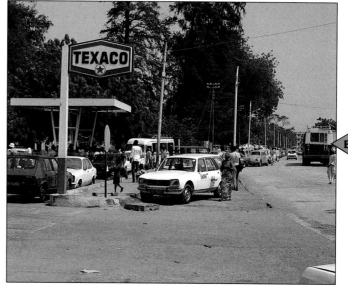

Banjul, capital of The Gambia: the inhabitants have been hit hard by economic crises

3 What does Source D tell you about the problems facing The Gambia?

4 Look at Source F. What choices does it suggest are open to The Gambia? Working in small groups, discuss the advantages and disadvantages of each choice. Say which one you think would be the best and why.

Another loan?

5 Read Source G. Do you think The Gambia should take out another IMF loan? In your answer, consider that, whilst it may make good economic sense, the loan may be politically unacceptable. Think about its effects on the Gambian people (Source E).

6 The Gambian President decides that an IMF loan is essential. Write a speech for him in which he tells the people why he has made this decision, despite the problems a loan may bring.

Memo to: **Minister of Finance and Trade**

From: **President**

Your briefing yesterday told me all about the problem. The papers tell me all about the problem. But what should we do?
I can see four choices:
- borrow more money to pay the interest we owe.
- try to get the date changed so we have longer to pay back our loans.
- try to get the debts written off.
- stop all payments.
I'm not an economic expert like you. What other choices do we have? Which one is best in the circumstances?

Memo to: **President**

From: **Minister of Finance and Trade**

I would recommend you go for an IMF loan. I think they will give us another one. But they make conditions.
They will say we have got to adopt a recovery programme. This means:
- cutting back on government spending (like health and education).
- controlling wages.
- getting rid of food and public transport subsidies.
- increasing taxes.
- raising interest rates.
- devaluing the currency. This will put prices up and reduce some imports (especially the non-essential ones). It should make the values of our exports go up.
If we do these things I'm sure we can get a loan. But it's important to remember that although the IMF charge less interest, they are strict on repayments. A loan certainly makes economic sense. But what about the wider implications?

139

As well as trading and borrowing, The Gambia has been given foreign aid to help the economy. Richer countries have provided money and experts to help development, particularly in agriculture (Source A).

1 **a)** One country that has helped The Gambia is Taiwan. Use Source B to explain what sort of help was given.
   b) Suggest reasons why Taiwan wanted to give aid to The Gambia.

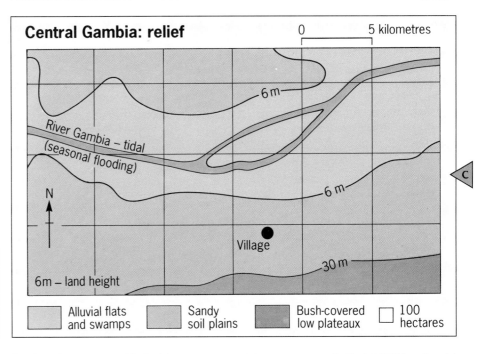

An irrigated rice scheme in The Gambia A

Asia helps Africa

In 1966 The Gambia and Taiwan signed an aid agreement. The aim was to increase The Gambia's food production and cut back on expensive imports. Taiwan was to provide money and technical expertise to help develop rice farming. A 'rice mission' was set up near Georgetown. This was to help farmers develop their own village-based irrigation systems and to allow double-cropping (growing two crops a year).

Gambian farmers were shown how to build bunds (raised banks) and canals. They would then cultivate their small farms. Each group of farmers were given a free pump. They had access to Rotovators (machines for breaking up soil). They were given free fuel, seed, fertiliser, and pesticides for the first season. There was a 'rice rush'. By 1974, 1,200 ha of land had been opened up to irrigated rice.

B

Central Gambia: relief

0   5 kilometres

River Gambia – tidal (seasonal flooding)

6 m
6 m
N
30 m
Village
6m – land height

| Alluvial flats and swamps | Sandy soil plains | Bush-covered low plateaux | 100 hectares |

C

Foreign aid – a proposal

To increase food production, Lisa Schmidt, a foreign agricultural expert, visited central Gambia. Her visit was financed by a rich country. She noticed villagers growing food crops such as millet and sorghum (a coarse grain). She saw women growing rice for food in the nearby swamp lands and men growing groundnuts on the sandy soil up to 3km from the village. She noticed that up to 6km from the village the woodland had been cleared for fuel and occasional cultivation.

2 Imagine you must help Lisa prepare a report on how farming can be made more productive.
   a) Make a copy of Source C and draw concentric circles of a 3km and 6km radius around the village.
   b) In these circles label the traditional land uses, naming food crops, cash crops and cleared land.
   c) Draw a sketch section to show how farming is affected by the form of the land and its soils.

Lisa recommends that 1,200 ha should be used for irrigated farming. This land will be prepared by villagers. It will be irrigated by small pumps, taking water from the river. The farmers will be able to grow two crops a year.

3 **a)** On your map choose a suitable location and draw 100-ha grid squares to show this scheme.
   b) Why have you chosen this location?
   c) Why might a grid layout be suitable?

Success?

You have seen how a foreign aid irrigation scheme could be put into practice in a country like The Gambia. In the last 50 years there have been four irrigation projects (Source D).

4 Using Source D draw a table to show the achievements of these projects. Use the following headings: project; location; Who helped?; When?; evidence of success/failure.

5 There have been problems with the projects. The major ones seem to be *irrigation, fields, machinery, labour* and *pests*. Which in your view seems to have been the most difficult problem? Give reasons for your answer.

What makes a good foreign aid scheme?

6 a) Divide into four groups representing male African farmers, female African farmers, foreign agricultural experts helping with a scheme, and government officials. You have been asked to say what the characteristics of a good aid scheme are in your group's view. Produce a statement starting 'A foreign aid scheme should . . .'.

b) Compare your group's views with those of the other three groups. What are the main differences?

Irrigation projects and their problems

1931 Persian wheel irrigation scheme, Georgetown Scheme abandoned 1945

1948 Colomar Development Corporation scheme for irrigated rice around the Patcharr-Wallikunda swamp and the Kudang swamp area. Abandoned 1958

1966 Taiwanese rice scheme at Yoro-Beri Kunda. Little sign of activity today.

1972–77 World Bank scheme of rice, Georgetown.

By 1982 only 20 of the original 50 schemes remained.

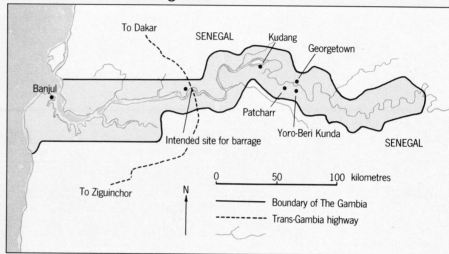

The Gambia and surrounding areas

Every irrigation project organised in The Gambia during the last 50 years has run into serious difficulties. It has proved impossible to establish irrigated rice as a popular crop amongst farmers. The time, effort and investment of many years now lies wasted in empty fields, choked canals and broken-down machinery. The government goal of national food self-sufficiency is as remote as ever. The main reasons why the irrigation schemes failed seem to be:

- poor irrigation systems – there is a lack of flood protection and drainage facilities. Canals are often badly built.

- badly organised field layouts – many plots of land are very small and low-lying, or too far from the irrigation pumps.

- unsuitable machinery – pumps and tractors are often unreliable and inefficient. Ploughing equipment is generally too heavy for local soils and conditions. There is a lack of spare parts and it can be extremely difficult to replace old or broken machinery.

- labour difficulties – women are unwilling to give up cultivating swamp rice (over which they have control) for the sake of irrigated rice, which the men control. A plot of rice can take up as much as 3 ha of land which would otherwise be used for cultivating other crops. Many male farmers do not believe the sacrifice to be worthwhile, even though rice prices are good compared to other crops. The demands of irrigated rice are therefore considered by many people to be too great.

- pests – no safeguards were ever made for the protection of crops from pests. The cost in time and money of bird-scaring and pest-shooting has cut deeply into farm budgets.

A proposal

A recent five-year plan for The Gambia concluded that:

- The country needs to be self-sufficient in food.
- A barrage should be built at Yelitenda. The water would be used for double-crop rice irrigation over an area of 24,000 ha. It would cost £44 million.

- An experimental scheme should be put into effect, involving 15,000 farmers and costing £11 million. The aim is to irrigate 1520 ha – 560 for pump injection and 960 for controlled swamp rice farming. Machinery will be available for farmers.

E

7 Do you think the scheme outlined in Source E has a better chance of succeeding than previous ones? If so, explain why.

We have seen that foreign aid from banks has financed large schemes and that these schemes have had their difficulties. But aid also comes from charities. These organisations try to assist small scale improvements and encourage self-help. These pages look at ways in which the Gambian people might be able to help themselves.

Action Aid steps in

Momodou Wurri Jallow works for Action Aid. This is a UK organisation which aims to help the many people who live in village communities in countries like The Gambia. He is an agricultural assistant working with farmers, helping them to improve their farming and their standard of living.

Wurri is about to visit the village of Jurunku, 25km east of Banjul, the capital of The Gambia. After crossing from Banjul to Barra by an early ferry he faces a drive along dirt roads to the village.

1 Look at Source A and answer the following questions:
   a) How many people live in the village?
   b) What is found at the centre?
   c) What crops do the villagers grow?
2 Wurri wrote a report on his visit to Jurunku. From his notes and pictures (Sources B to D) on this page and page 143, answer the following questions:
   a) What are the houses and buildings like?
   b) Which buildings do you think are the most important? Say why.
   c) What do you think are the main strengths of traditional village life?
   d) What seem to be the main difficulties facing the villagers?
3 Wurri has been asked to suggest what could be done to make life better for the people in the village. What do you think he might recommend? Remember that Action Aid has limited funds.

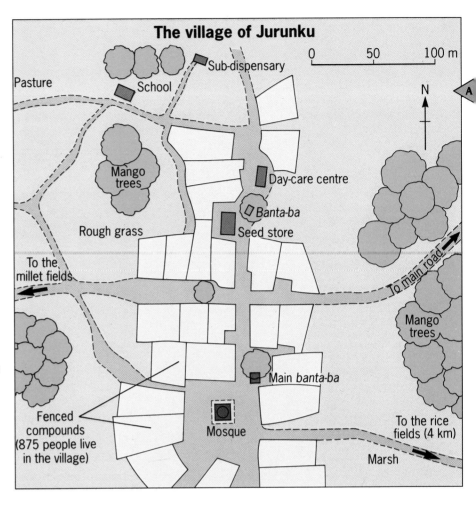

The village of Jurunku

Pasture · Sub-dispensary · School · Mango trees · Rough grass · To the millet fields · Day-care centre · Banta-ba · Seed store · To main road · Mango trees · Main banta-ba · Fenced compounds (875 people live in the village) · Mosque · To the rice fields (4 km) · Marsh

0   50   100 m

N

A

A tradition of co-operation

Jurunku's mosque, complete with fence to keep out straying animals

The people speak the Mandingo language. They live in 50 compounds (settlements) each enclosed by woven bark fences. The people in the compound are all one family. They are Muslim so it is traditional for the male head of the compound to take up to four wives in his lifetime. Each wife has a separate house within the compound. This group of people forms the main farming and social unit of the village.

People are used to working together. The women join together as a co-operative to grow vegetables. The main meeting place is the *banta-ba*, a raised platform under a shady tree. The village has a head man. Some of the houses are round huts about 4m in diameter. They are built by the people out of dried mud blocks. They have dirt floors and roofs of grass. Some of the better-off families have thin corrugated iron

costs £40 to cover a house plus £5 for nails. There is one cement block compound owned by the *Imam*, the Muslim religious leader of the village. The villagers paid for and built the mosque. It is large and solidly constructed out of mud blocks.

B

Farming for a living

The other two main public buildings are the seed store and the sub-dispensary. The seed store keeps the groundnut seeds for the next season, and is designed and financed by the government. The sub-dispensary has a young man trained to give injections.

The village owns the land. The main food crop is rice, with some millet, sorghum and maize. Groundnuts are grown for cash. The men till the groundnut land by hand, although there are a few ox-drawn ploughs and seeders drawn by donkeys. They belong to a co-operative which sells the groundnuts. It also loans them money during the difficult season of the rains when food is scarce.

The women grow rice and vegetables. They walk 4 km each day to the rice paddies, often wading through swamps. They work the heavy, wet clay by hand. They carry the harvest back to the village on their heads. They prepare the grain for cooking. Children help in the fields and look after the goats, sheep and long-horned cattle.

The vegetable garden is irrigated land. It grows garden-egg, tomato, bitter tomato, okra (a pod plant), cabbage, peppers, lettuce and onions. There are two small shops.

There are four wells – the water is poor and a constant health risk to children. The women queue to draw water. Sanitation is not good – only a few compounds have any pit latrines.

The sub-dispensary, which is situated near to the existing school

The village seed store

Women walk to the rice fields, often with children on their backs

Education

The school is a small, two-classroom block (4m × 2m) built by the villagers. Over 100 children want to go to school but only 24 of these will get a primary education. The building is made of cement-plastered mud block walls with a corrugated roof. Furniture is basic. The teacher is from the local community and has had four years of secondary schooling in Banjul.

Parents pay 50 pence per month for each child at school. The children learn to read and write and do arithmetic. They read the Koran and have Islamic studies in both the local language and Arabic.

Jurunku's school committee line up outside the school building

DEVELOPMENT – WHO BENEFITS?

Development agencies like Action Aid encourage self-help ('te-sito') by the community. In Jurunku the community decided they wanted a bigger school. Action Aid helped them build one by providing school staff and materials (Source A). Action Aid has also funded other self-help development projects in Jurunku. Three of these were the building of a causeway construction (raised path) to the rice fields, well-digging and improving vegetable gardening. Read on to find out about the benefits these projects have brought.

Building a new school

Changes in Jurunku

1 **a)** Turn back to Source A on page 142. Draw a sketch map of Jurunku.
b) On your map outline the area covered by houses.
c) Mark the main meeting place at the centre of the village.
d) Now add a causeway through the marsh which leads to the rice fields. This is situated in the south east of the village.
e) Add two wells, 25m apart, 200m to the east of the school.
f) Draw in a vegetable garden around the wells, approximately 100m × 100m.

The causeway

2 Draw a sketch of Source B. Add notes about the causeway to your sketch. Think about the following: what is it built of?; where has it been built?; what can you say about its design?; what is its purpose? Do you think the photograph was taken in the wet season or the dry season?

3 **a)** How far is a return journey to the rice fields?
b) From June to December one person goes to the rice fields and back five days a week. How far does that person walk every week?

A new well

4 Look at the photograph on page 135.
a) Who is using the well? What are they doing?
b) What does the well seem to be made of?
c) How is the water being brought to the surface?
d) Suggest some of the problems which might be associated with this well.

5 Now look at Source C.
a) How does the new well differ in construction from the older one?
b) Suggest the benefits the new well might bring and who gains.

A causeway helps women to reach the rice fields in remote swamp areas

Action Aid have provided the villagers with a new well

The vegetable garden

Annual village inputs

Women farmers' group manage all local resources

▶ Labour

▶ Seeds

▶ Other expenses

▶ Marketing costs

▶ Credit repayment (over three year period)

Total = D55,424

Action Aid inputs

▶ Fencing (barbed wire) to keep out animals

▶ Permanent cement-lined wells to provide water in dry season

▶ Technical support – advice and follow-up services

Total cost D15,400

Action Aid – provides national assistance and the Technical support not available locally.

Annual garden outputs

▶ **Vegetables**
sold for cash
Dry season –
onions, tomatoes, chillies, cabbage, aubergines and green leaves
Wet season –
chillies, bitter tomatoes, okra and green leaves

▶ **Vegetables**
exchanged for rice and millet

▶ **Vegetables**
consumed

Total D68,300

For every woman vegetable farmer 14 other people benefit through the food consumed or exchanged.

---

6 a) Look at Source D. Draw a large diagram like the one above and show the inputs to the vegetable garden by both Action Aid and the women farmers group. Describe the vegetable garden and give details of what it produces.

b) What benefits do you think Action Aid's inputs have brought to the vegetable garden?

7 'New developments may bring benefits: they may also bring costs to particular groups.'

a) In groups, and using Source E, discuss this statement with reference to women.

b) In view of how busy the women already are, how could new crops or new land be cultivated?

A woman's work is never done

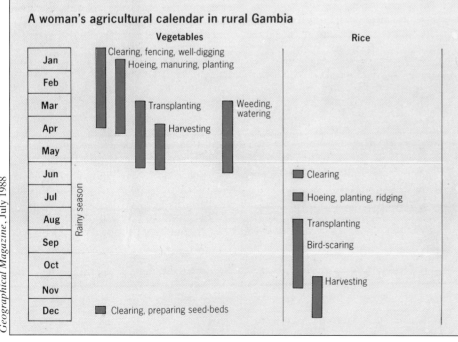

A woman's agricultural calendar in rural Gambia

	Vegetables	Rice
Jan	Clearing, fencing, well-digging / Hoeing, manuring, planting	
Feb		
Mar	Transplanting / Weeding, watering	
Apr	Harvesting	
May		
Jun		Clearing
Jul		Hoeing, planting, ridging
Aug		Transplanting
Sep		Bird-scaring
Oct		
Nov		Harvesting
Dec	Clearing, preparing seed-beds	

Rainy season

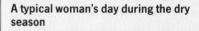

A typical woman's day during the dry season

5am Wake, wash, dress and eat

6am Leave for fields

7am Start work in fields
During the day, breaks are taken for breastfeeding, lunch and rest periods

3pm Collect fuelwood and other bush products

4pm Leave for home

5pm †Collect water
†Pound millet

6pm Prepare evening meal

7pm Eat evening meal

7.30 †Wash up, launder, clean kitchen, bath children

9pm Bath and retire for the night

†*There is a rotation of these jobs among the women.*

Milling Machines Revolutionise Workload

Results of a recent project suggest that if African women were released from the many hours of drudgery that most of them face, they would use the extra time to grow more food.

The project, funded by the United Nations Development Fund for Women (Unifem), has supplied milling machines to 15 Gambian village communities. These machines grind millet, the coarse grain, into flour which serves as their main food. For millions of Africans, millet, a drought-resistant crop, is all that stands between life and death. Turning millet into flour is a job that African women traditionally do by hand. This usually means about four hours of laborious, hand-blistering pounding each day. Before pounding the millet, the women thresh the grain and remove the husks. In all, about seven hours' work is needed.

In the village of Njau, close to the border with Senegal, Ms Farna Ceesay, 40, used to rise before dawn to thresh and dehusk millet. 'I used to go to the fields with the pounding hanging over me, waiting for me when I got back home', she said.

Today, she and the other women of Njau village pound no longer. Instead of processing millet by hand they take it to a shed that houses a small, diesel-powered mill. The machine grinds the millet in five minutes. The women view this saving of time with delight and astonishment. One

Using a new milling machine in The Gambia

said, 'It's a miracle. It has freed me from drudgery.'

It is what the women do with the time they save that has important implications for African agriculture. Ms Farna Ceesay said the energy she would have put into pounding she now puts into the fields, weeding more and growing more. She has planted maize and beans, some of which she sells. This has given her a cash income for the first time in her life. In another village the president of a women's group said: 'Before the mill came, we were sometimes short of food. Now we have food and some left to sell.'

This extra locally-grown produce should help The Gambia to cut imports of food, especially rice. 'If women get the technology, The Gambia could become self-sufficient in food,' said a field-worker.

The West German-made mills cost about £800 each and a community that receives one saves an equivalent amount over five years. This is then paid back to Unifem, allowing the agency to buy mills for other villages. The machines are at the moment rare in Africa. But possibilities exist for saving yet more time. In Njau village a woman said: 'I'm thankful for the mill, but it's still a full day for us. What we need now is a thresher that can save us a further two hours a day.'

---

1 Look at Source A. Milling machines like the one in the photo have been introduced into The Gambia for grinding millet. Read the newspaper article to find out about the effect these machines have had on the quality of people's lives. When you have read Source B, work through the questions:

> Where is technology being introduced?
>
> Why is it needed?
>
> What sort of technology is it?
> What are its characteristics?
>
> Who has introduced it? How? When? To whom?
>
> What results has the technology had? Weigh up the costs and benefits. Are there any problems?
>
> What effect will it have on the future?

2 Now use the same questions to investigate the impact of another piece of technology (your group can obtain information for this by writing to a Local Intermediate Technology Group).

SOUTH KOREA: A SUCCESS STORY

Seoul, capital of South Korea

Family planting rice on their small farm in the Chollanamdo area of South Korea. The average farm size is 1 ha. Farms have been small since 1948 when large estates were broken up. The largest farm allowed is 3 ha.

Agricultural changes in South Korea		
Year	Agricultural population (%)	Calories per person per day
1970	51	2,500
1984	34	3,000

Co-operative success?

In many farming areas, family units have organised in groups. Co-operatives have been set up. Farmers agree among themselves to grow a cash crop at the same time with the same methods. Jointly, they buy machinery and subsidised fertilisers and sell graded produce to specially selected markets.

One of these co-operatives is Ha-ee, 280 km from Seoul, the capital of South Korea, and 12 km from Chongu town, the local market. Hwang Se-Yeon is leader of the Ha-ee village group. This is one of 4,500 *co-operative unit farming groups* (called Jak Mak Bhan) in South Korea.

Efficient farming is the basis of South Korea's economic development. Is this because of enterprising individual family farms or because of co-operative group farming? Or is it a result of government protection?

1 **a)** Which crop is being grown in the photograph (Source A)?
b) What work is being done?
c) What evidence is there to suggest that this is intensive farming?

2 Enterprising farmers have made South Korea self-sufficient in rice. How does Source B show that Korean farming has become more efficient?

3 Family farms can also have their problems. Suggest what some of these might be.

4 With the help of Source C and the text above, answer the following:
a) Describe six main features of a co-operative farm.
b) What advantages does a co-operative have over an individual family farm?

An interview with Hwang Se-Yeon

Q: *Who belongs to the village group?*
HS-Y: We have 47 households, mostly bearing the same surname.
Q: *How did the co-operative start?*
HS-Y: We reclaimed land in the 1950s. We set up a chopstick factory to earn money when farming was slack. I introduced the idea of growing vegetables under plastic sheets in the cold season. We got together to buy supplies, assess and sell produce; later we brought our own trucks. As we grew larger we could bargain better with buyers.
Q: *What do you grow?*
HS-Y: We grow rice. We grow CASH CROPS like squash,* lettuce, Chinese cabbage, cucumbers and yellow melons. We have a slogan: 'Let land not become idle for more than ten days.'
Q: *How do you make up your minds about what to grow?*
HS-Y: We meet once a year to decide. We take

into account what other areas are growing, what seeds are being sold, the weather forecasts, the prices different crops are fetching, what people want, and government policies.
Q: *How and where do you market your produce?*
HS-Y: We grow eleven crops for the market, but squash is the most profitable. We only sell as a group, and all produce must be assessed and packed to the group standards. We fine people when standards aren't met. We have contracts with five wholesalers in Seoul, and with one or two transporters. We make 4,000 journeys a year. We also have a village person at the markets to tell us about price changes.
Q: *Have you been successful?*
HS-Y: Oh, yes. The average income of our members has increased four times in eight years and we earn above average levels. All this is mainly due to group marketing.

*squash = a marrow-like vegetable

2,000 Days

Comparison of group and individual prices and marketing costs for squash	Group marketing per box (£)	Individual marketing per box (£)	Difference (£)
Price obtained at Seoul market	4.10	3.70	
Total marketing costs	1.00	1.40	
Made up of sorting and grading	0.28	0.33	
packaging and materials	0.33	0.34	
transport	0.16	0.41	
loading and unloading	0.03	0.03	
administrative fees	0.20	0.29	
NET RETURN	3.10	2.30	

D

E

Interference or protection?

The government limits competition by putting taxes (called tariff barriers) on cheap imported foods. This means prices are kept high inside South Korea. The consumers pay more for their foods, but the farmers get more income. The government also buys and sells large amounts at high prices.

More than one in three of our people live in the countryside – we must help them and keep them happy.

We need farming so that we can feel secure against threats from communist North Korea.

We need to stop migration to the cities.

Government protection supports inefficient farmers.

Other countries will put up tariff barriers against our goods.

We need balanced development – agriculture and industry.

High food prices push up the cost of living, and people want higher wages. Then you get inflation.

Farm organisation

5 **a)** One product marketed by the group is a vegetable called squash. Complete the table (Source D) to show the differences in marketing costs between individual and group farms.
   b) Which type of farming has the highest net return?
   c) Which type of farming has the lower marketing costs?
   d) Why are its costs lower?

6 *Ha-ee* is a successful co-operative family group. Some factors which might have helped its success are:
   ● a strong leader
   ● group decision making
   ● a need to co-operate
   ● a willingness to carry out group decisions
   ● improved farming methods
   ● planned farm management
   ● power through group size
   ● honesty in dealings
   ● family loyalty
   ● a tradition of co-operation

   In pairs, discuss how each of these elements make a group farm successful. Rank them in order of importance. Compare your results with other pairs. Can you think of any other factors which help make groups successful?

Government support?

7 Why should a government protect its farmers? Why might it decide not to do so? To help you answer these questions, sort out the statements in Source E into those that are for and those that are against protection.

8 *Who gains from protection? Who loses?*
   Decide whether each of the following people would be for or against government support and give reasons for your decisions: South Korean rice farmer, South Korean villager, South Korean town dweller, South Korean industrialist, South Korean politician, South Korean planner, US citrus (tropical fruit) farmer, US beef farmer, Thai rice exporter.

13.2 THE GROWTH OF INDUSTRY

Many economically developing countries want to start industries. These provide the basis for economic improvement. Twenty years ago, South Korea began to produce textiles and shoes for export. You may well own a pair of South Korean trainers. This page and page 151 investigate why industries like textiles and shoes developed in the 1960s, how these industries are changing and the ways in which they form part of the 'global economy'.

1 Find out if you, or anyone in your group, owns or has owned a pair of South Korean trainers.
   a) Count the number of people who own trainers.
   b) Find out where they were made. (You may need to look inside for a label!)

c) Group them into countries of origin.
d) In pairs discuss what you think of the Korean trainers. Consider their characteristics (e.g. price, quality, durability, appearance, comfort).
e) Score each characteristic on a five-point scale.
f) What general conclusions can you draw?

The past
2 South Korea has been making footwear since the 1960s. What original advantages did the country have which helped it develop its shoe-making and exporting industry? Look at the cartoons (Source A). List five advantages Korea had for making and exporting shoes.

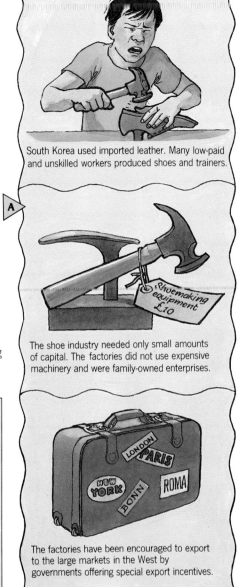

A

South Korea used imported leather. Many low-paid and unskilled workers produced shoes and trainers.

The shoe industry needed only small amounts of capital. The factories did not use expensive machinery and were family-owned enterprises.

The factories have been encouraged to export to the large markets in the West by governments offering special export incentives.

B

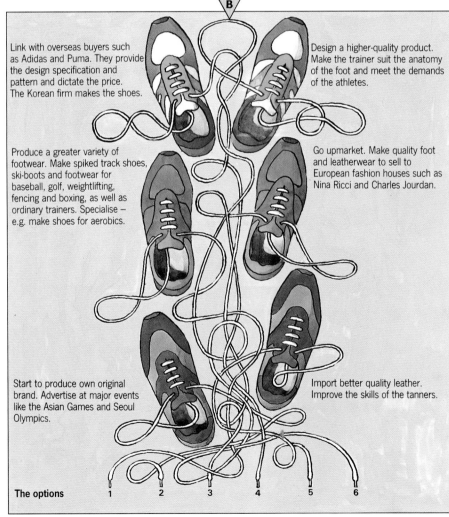

Link with overseas buyers such as Adidas and Puma. They provide the design specification and pattern and dictate the price. The Korean firm makes the shoes.

Design a higher-quality product. Make the trainer suit the anatomy of the foot and meet the demands of the athletes.

Produce a greater variety of footwear. Make spiked track shoes, ski-boots and footwear for baseball, golf, weightlifting, fencing and boxing, as well as ordinary trainers. Specialise – e.g. make shoes for aerobics.

Go upmarket. Make quality foot and leatherwear to sell to European fashion houses such as Nina Ricci and Charles Jourdan.

Start to produce own original brand. Advertise at major events like the Asian Games and Seoul Olympics.

Import better quality leather. Improve the skills of the tanners.

The options  1 2 3 4 5 6

The way forward
3 The time is 1980. You are a manager of a South Korean shoe exporting firm. Your product has a poor reputation in the major markets. How can you make it a different story? You have to decide the way forward for your firm.
   a) Look at Source B. In pairs, discuss the choices you have. For each choice, discuss what the advantages and disadvantages would be for the firm. Make a list.
   b) Which one option would you choose for the next ten years? Say why.
   c) Rank the other options in order of priority.

Towards 2000

What prospects are there for the Korean shoe industry as the year 2000 approaches? You are part of a group of young workers in a Korean shoe factory in Seoul. You make shoes for export and want to know something about the prospects for the industry by the year 2000. Your job might be affected by any developments. You ask a sympathetic economist, Chung Lou-Yun for her predictions. She suggests that the shoe workers should have a 'teach-in' in the canteen (Source C), to find out what the future might hold. She presents you with some facts and a graph (Source D) and then asks you to do the following:

4 Draw three graphs to show what might happen to Korean shoe exports:
  a) if present trends continued
  b) if exports levelled off
  c) if exports declined.

Economist Chung Lou-Yun plans a 'teach-in' for Seoul shoe workers.

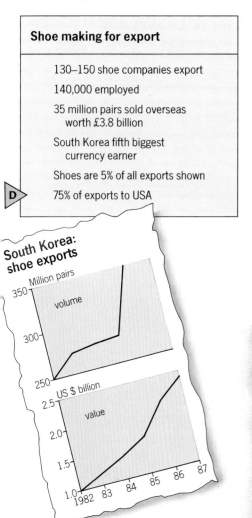

Shoe making for export

130–150 shoe companies export

140,000 employed

35 million pairs sold overseas worth £3.8 billion

South Korea fifth biggest currency earner

Shoes are 5% of all exports shown

75% of exports to USA

South Korea: shoe exports

Million pairs — volume — 350, 300, 250

US $ billion — value — 2.5, 2.0, 1.5, 1.0 — 1982 83 84 85 86 87

5 Discuss in small groups what might happen to the Korean shoe industry if:
  a) There was *increased competition*. (Think about where this would be likely to come from and why.)
  b) There was an increase in *foreign demand*. (Where from? Why?)
  c) There was a *decrease* in foreign demand (perhaps because the USA had restricted imports).
  d) There was an increase in *raw material costs*.
  e) There was an increase in *domestic demand*. (Think about why this might happen.)
  f) There was an increase in *wages* paid to the workers.

  g) There was a change in *technology* which altered the way shoes were produced.
6 Chung Lou-Yun shows you a newspaper article from Leicester, in the UK, where the shoe industry is important (Source E). Discuss the attitude of European countries and firms to shoe imports and production. How might this affect the Korean shoe industry?
7 'Get involved! Try to influence decisions', advises Chung Lou-Yun. In the light of this, think about how your firm might prepare for the year 2000. Write a letter to the management of the firm setting out your ideas.

Worries over rise in shoe imports

A massive surge in imports of footwear from the Far East is setting alarm bells ringing among British footwear manufacturers, including those in Leicestershire.

During the first eight months of this year imports into the UK from Taiwan were up by 37 per cent, from South Korea up 50 per cent and from China up 187 per cent.

Imports from all three seem set to reach record totals for 1987, says the British Footwear Manufacturers'

by John Stone

Federation.

The UK already has quotas on most kinds of footwear imports from China while an industry-to-industry agreement with South Korea sets ceilings on certain categories.

A similar agreement with Taiwan industry lapsed three years ago when the employers' federation there was unable to ensure that it was observed.

Leicester Mercury, 30 November 1987

Today, many South Koreans work in other industries apart from shoe-making and textiles. Newer industries grew up between 1961 and 1979 when South Korea went through an 'economic miracle'. It became an 'NIC' – a newly industrialising country. People worked long hours for low wages. They were a disciplined workforce. The factories used advanced, large-scale technology. The firms were reliable and produced goods quickly for the world market. How has the Korean 'economic miracle' come about? Is it the result of private enterprise or of government help?

Hyundai

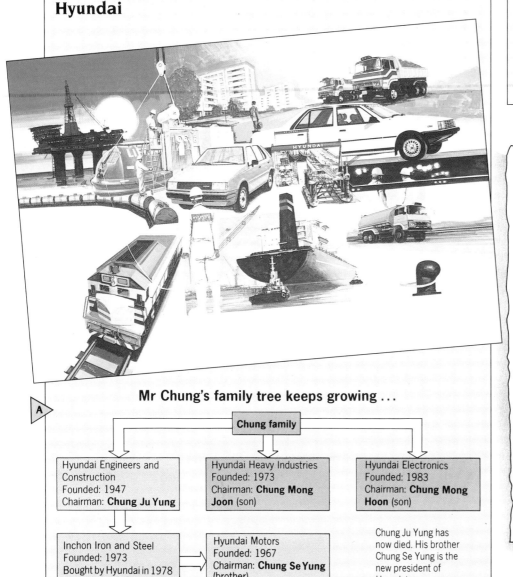

B

Chung Ju Yung explains how Hyundai grew up.

'I borrowed some money from a friend and I got started in the building industry. When the Korean war started in 1950 my workmen built runways for the US Air Force. After the war I made my money helping to rebuild the country. The firm grew and we added new businesses. In 1967 we moved into making cars. We are one of the oldest and biggest conglomerates. The company is still run by the same family. We are leading Korea into the next stage of industrialisation.'

C

Foreign surprise at Korean car output

Ulsan will never be the same again.

Hyundai has invested in a large car-assembly plant not far from the sea in this south-eastern settlement. The story began in 1967 when enterprising Hyundai started the assembly of medium-sized saloon cars. These were made under licence from Ford (Europe). There were plenty of workers willing to put in long and hard hours in the rapidly expanding plant. Then, knowledgable engineers, imaginative designers and exciting decisions by the management led to the company introducing the Pony. This was the first home-bred, home-built car in Korea. But Korea only had a population of 40 million so the home market for cars was small. As the factory had to be large to produce cars efficiently, most of the cars rolling off the assembly lines were for export.

By 1987 Hyundai was producing nearly half a million cars a year. They sold well in the USA, where at $5500 they were $1000 cheaper than the nearest Japanese rival. Hyundai is now producing cars in Canada. Hyundai serves as a good example of the fruits that enterprise, initiative and hard work can bring.

1   Look at Sources A and B.
   a) The older industries of Korea are shoe-making and textiles. Hyundai makes different things. List the products made by Hyundai. Mr Chung was an 'opportunist' (he took advantage of the opportunities offered).
   b) How did he start Hyundai?
   c) How did the firm grow inside South Korea?
   d) What opportunities is it taking now?
   e) Hyundai is a large conglomerate. What do we mean by the term 'conglomerate'? Think about the range of goods Hyundai produces.

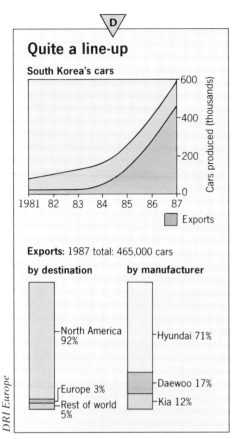

DRI Europe

Quite a line-up

South Korea's cars

[Line/area chart: Cars produced (thousands), y-axis 0 to 600, x-axis years 1981 82 83 84 85 86 87]

■ Exports

Exports: 1987 total: 465,000 cars

by destination | **by manufacturer**

North America 92%
Europe 3%
Rest of world 5%

Hyundai 71%
Daewoo 17%
Kia 12%

The car industry

Hyundai produces cars for the global economy. How has it done this? Is it through private enterprise (business initiative) or has the government helped and protected it?

2 a) The newspaper article (Source C) tells us Hyundai is an enterprising private firm. What examples of enterprise are given?
b) Why did Hyundai choose Ulsan for the location of a car factory?
c) Why did firms like Hyundai decide to export?

3 Look at Source D and answer the following questions.
a) How many cars a year does Hundai produce? (Refer to 1987 figures.)
b) How many cars does Hyundai export?
c) What per cent of cars are exported?
d) Where are the cars exported to?
e) How has the export of cars changed since 1981?
f) Has Hyundai been successful?

Government action and American reaction

4 How does the South Korean government help its car industry? From the interview (Source E), find six sentences to show six different ways in which the government helps. Complete the table in Source F by matching the technical terms and the definition with your sentences.

5 a) In pairs, discuss how a South Korean might reply to the arguments of the American in Source G. Illustrate your ideas.
b) In groups, discuss the merits of your illustrations. Choose the best points made. Now draw an agreed group illustration.

An American view ...

❝A few years ago it was the Japanese. Now it's the South Koreans. They're selling their cars unfairly in our country because their government has helped them so much. It gives firms money to produce cars. It kept them in business when the *Pony* sold in the USA at $5500, a full $1000 cheaper than a Japanese car. Firms cannot produce cars at that price without help. In 1962 the government banned the import of cars. It wanted to encourage the growth of the country's young industry.

Imported parts for cars were made expensive as a matter of policy, as the government wanted to help its own car-parts makers. When Korean firms produced cars for export, they paid only minimal tax. The banks were given no choice but to lend money to car exporting firms. The government said only Koreans could own a car assembly company and forced car companies to join together to become large.❞

◀ E

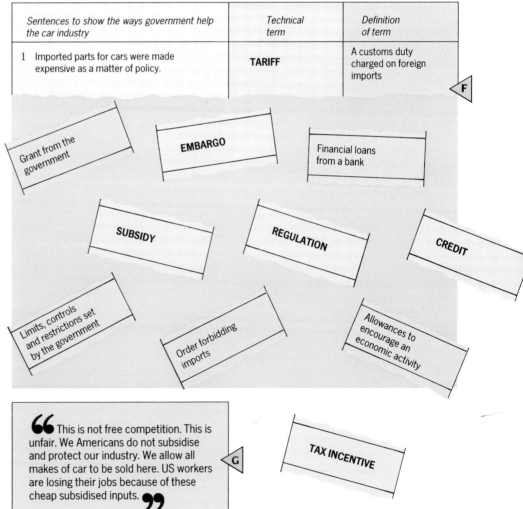

Sentences to show the ways government help the car industry	Technical term	Definition of term
1 Imported parts for cars were made expensive as a matter of policy.	TARIFF	A customs duty charged on foreign imports

◀ F

Grant from the government

EMBARGO

Financial loans from a bank

SUBSIDY

REGULATION

CREDIT

Limits, controls and restrictions set by the government

Order forbidding imports

Allowances to encourage an economic activity

TAX INCENTIVE

❝This is not free competition. This is unfair. We Americans do not subsidise and protect our industry. We allow all makes of car to be sold here. US workers are losing their jobs because of these cheap subsidised inputs.❞

◀ G

Assembly workers in an electronics factory and a supervisor

Electronics has been one of the great export growth industries during the last 20 years. It is based particularly on the microchip (semiconductor). Firms like Hyundai, Daewoo, Samsung and Lucky Goldstar produce a quarter of all manufactured output in South Korea. Electronics makes up 16% of the country's exports. There are 16,000 people employed in microchip plants. Who benefits from this work? Is it the worker, the local company or the international corporation?

1 What does Source A tell you about work in a microchip plant in South Korea? In pairs answer the following questions:
   a) Who is employed (think about numbers, age, sex and skill levels)?
   b) How is the work organised and carried out?
   c) What is the relationship between workers and management?
   d) What do you think it would feel like to work there?

Conditions of work

Source A does not tell you all you want to know about work in an assembly factory in South Korea.
Read Source B which adds further detail. Many firms still refuse to recognise the new trade unions, which are not company run. In some cases, workers have been striking for higher wages and the right to form a union. Many of the strikes are still illegal. Riot police have been called in and tear gas used.

2 These two pieces of evidence (Source A and Source B) can be seen in different ways.
   a) An industrialist sees that South Korea has many labour advantages for assembling microchips. List them.
   b) A worker sees that Korean industrialists neither value the workforce nor treat them fairly. What evidence is there of this?

Workers sceptical of economic miracle

South Koreans work the longest hours in the world. Some work a 72-hour week. During an eleven hour working day, 50 minutes are allowed for lunch and ten minutes for a mid-afternoon tea break.
   'I'm so tired in the mornings that I feel like a machine,' said one worker.
   The country's economic miracle has been built on low wages which account for 8 per cent of the average company's cash. Many workers earn less than the minimum wage of £80 per month.
   Women are in a particularly bad position. They make up 40% of the workforce and are in low-paid and unskilled jobs. Most are young and unmarried, often from rural areas and poorly educated. The average female wage of £76 a month is 48% of a man's average pay. Little career structure exists for women. In a society with a CONFUCIAN religion, many are expected to retire at 25 when they marry.

Who owns the microchip industry in East Asia?

Local and foreign ownership patterns

Country	GNP per head (US$)	Wages per hour (US$)	Population in urban areas (%)	Number of locally-owned microchip plants	Total employed in locally-owned microchip plants	Number of US-owned assembly plants	Employment in US-owned assembly plants
Hong Kong	5,100	1.33	92	6	4,000	8	4,552
Indonesia	530	0.35	22	Not available	Not available	2	3,200
South Korea	1,700	1.19	57	17	15,500	5	8,800
Malaysia	1,840	0.84	Not available	2	1,450	14	38,136
Philippines	790	0.63	37	14	18,000	11	13,112
Singapore	5,240	1.58	Not available	1	240	11	10,397
Taiwan	Not available	1.36	Not available	19	8,000	9	15,296
Thailand	770	0.43	17	2	900	4	6,470

◁ C

3 Some assembly industry is owned by local business people. Look at Source C.
a) List the number, workforce and average size of locally-owned assembly industry.
b) On a map of East Asia, show the number of locally-owned microchip plants. To your map, add the number of people employed in these plants.
c) Which economically developing countries in East Asia do not have a locally-owned microchip industry?

4 Some assembly industry is owned by foreign companies, particularly from the USA.
a) List the number, workforce and average size of foreign-owned plants in South Korea.
b) On another map of East Asia show the number of foreign-owned microchip plants and add the number of people employed.

5 Among the reasons put forward by US business analysts for setting up plants in East Asia were availability of cheap labour and the fact that there was a market for the product. In groups of three, use Source C to test these ideas by drawing one scatter graph each to show:
a) the relationship between the number of US-owned plants and national wealth (GNP). (This might measure the market.)
b) the relationship between the number of US-owned plants and average hourly wages. (This might measure the cost of labour).
c) The link between the number of US-owned plants and the percentage of the urban population. (This might measure availability of labour.)
d) Discuss what your graphs show. What do they hide?
e) Summarise your conclusions.

Locating in East Asia

6 Source D shows the Board of a USA corporation which makes microchips. Their plans for East Asia include:
- six assembly plants.
- one specialised test facility plant. (This plant will test selected products from all the assembly plants.)
- seven regional sales offices, equally spread in the area.
- two marketing headquarters. These will make decisions about selling the products in the area.

The Board has narrowed down the choice to eight countries (Source C). Using Source C, Source D and an atlas, write a report to explain where you would locate your plants and offices. Include maps to illustrate it.

Politics matters. Our firm will be welcomed by many countries.

I think we all agree. We will build in East Asia. But we must remember that not all the countries are politically stable. We must spread our plants across different countries.

We can make the circuits and send them abroad. An overseas assembly plant can make them into an assembled circuit which we can then import. We are only charged customs duty on the value added overseas.

We're looking to expand. There seems to be a large market for our product in East Asia. Our competitors have set up assembly plants in some countries there.

There are large reserves of labour in these countries. The women are good workers – they are willing to work long hours.

▽ D

13.5 A MODEL FOR ASIA?

Images of change

" Within a generation, South Korea has changed from being one of the poorest countries to a country with some measure of social wealth . . . more people than ever before are at work and at higher real incomes: a nation of peasants has become one of urban workers. **"**

Seoul, almost completely rebuilt after the Korean War

Left, a new development in a Korean town; right, children going to school

1 Read the quotation in Source A. In pairs discuss the way the information on this page supports it. Think about the photographs, too. Write a paragraph outlining the changes which have taken place in South Korea in the last 25 years.

2 In pairs, use Source B to design a poster for the South Korean Overseas Information Service showing the economic and social progress made by your country between 1963 and the mid 1980s. The government has also asked you to include their predictions for the year 2000. You may like to

concentrate on the most important figures and show these as graphs or headlines. Create a strong visual image.

3 You support an opposition party in South Korea. What do Source A and Source B not tell you about modern life there?

Political change

▼ **pre 1945** ▼	
Part of Japanese empire	
▼ **1945** ▼	
End of Second World War Korea split into North and South	
▼ **1950–53** ▼	
Korean War	
▼ **1953–60** ▼	
Political unrest and military control	
▼ **1961–79** ▼	
Economic miracle: political repression under a dictator who was murdered in 1979	
▼ **1987** ▼	
Free (?) elections	
▼	
? 2000 ?	

Figures of change and government predictions

			1963	1984	2000
Economic change	Wealth (GNP per head)	US$	82	2,000	5,100
	Employment				
	Agriculture	% of jobs	63	27	20
	Manufacturing	% of jobs	9	24	20
	Services	% of jobs	28	49	60
	Unemployed	% of population	8	4	3
	Self-employed	% of population	n.a.	50	40
	Working women	% of population	n.a.	39	50
Social change	Population	million	25	40.6	49.4
	Average life-span	years	n.a.	66	72
	House ownership	% of population	n.a.	67	82
	Cars	per 100 people	n.a.	1	26
	Telephones	per 100 people	n.a.	12	39
	Refrigerators	% of population	n.a.	38	90
	Hours worked	av. per week	n.a.	54	41

A fair distribution of wealth?

4 The graph (Source C) is called a *Lorenz curve*. It shows how income in the developed countries is distributed. It tells us that the top 20% of the population have 41% of the wealth, the top 80% of the population have 94% of the wealth and the bottom 20% owns 6%.
a) On a copy of Source C, draw a line to show how the income of South Korea is distributed.
b) How fair is the South Korean distribution of wealth?
c) On the same graph, add information for one other Asian country, one African country and one South American country. (Refer to Source D.)
d) Compare South Korea with these countries.

5 It is often claimed that in LDCs (less developed countries) and NICs (newly industrialising countries), 'the rich get richer and the poor get poorer'. That is, only a small élite group benefits from development. Using Source C and Source D and what you have learned in this Unit, decide whether this is true for South Korea, and if not, why not.

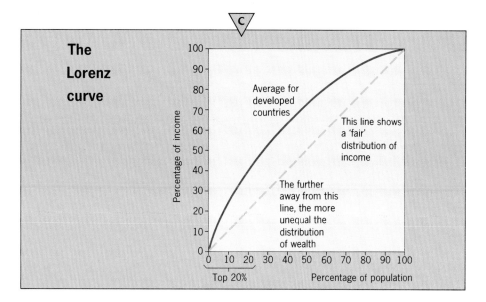

The Lorenz curve

Average for developed countries

This line shows a 'fair' distribution of income

The further away from this line, the more unequal the distribution of wealth

Percentage of income

Percentage of population

Top 20%

Wealth distribution throughout the world

Population	Average for developed countries (%)	South Korea (%)	Brazil (%)	Peru (%)	Malaysia (%)	Hong Kong (%)	India (%)	Kenya (%)	Tanzania (%)	UK (%)
Top 20%	41	45	67	61	62	47	50	60	61	46
Middle 60%	53	49	31	37	34	48	43	37	37	48
Bottom 20%	6	6	2	2	4	5	7	3	2	6

6 Slums have been removed to make the buildings in Source A possible. Look at Source E. In groups, answer the following questions:
a) What happened in Chong Shin Dong?
b) Who decided what should happen?
c) How was the decision carried out?
d) What were the effects?
e) Who benefited?

Resignation in the face of destitution – but militancy is growing among slum dwellers

Seoul's slum clearance games

Scene: the Seoul slum city of Chong Shin Dong one September Sunday.

One mother, Cho Kum Sang, said: 'I was sleeping and my small children were beside me. My husband was not there because of threats he had received. Suddenly a teargas cylinder was fired into the room.

'When I got the children out, it was total panic. It was pouring with rain and all we could see was police.

'In the morning, everything was ruined. Our home was destroyed by men using sledgehammers. One of our friends injured his spine when he was beaten up. Yet all we wanted to do was stay where we were. We weren't bothering anyone.'

Officially, of course, the incident did not happen. No mention of it has appeared in the state-controlled media.

This operation was typical of the brutality with which Seoul is stepping up its huge redevelopment scheme to push its 3.5 million slum dwellers out of sight.

The result of the redevelopment programme is that the sturdy, but often overcrowded slums, nearly all of which have water and electricity, are being razed en masse to make way for large, multi-storey blocks for the capital's rapidly growing middle classes. The extraordinary growth of the city over the last ten years – Seoul now has more than ten million people – has also sent property prices soaring.

The President, government officials, police and construction firms all want to 'move the people on'.

In Chang Shin Dong, the 600 families had resolutely refused to budge, despite threats, bribes and other forms of intimidation, such as cutting off water and electricity supplies. Many know they were not illegally occupying the land their houses were built on and say they could see no justifiable reason why they should move.

Alternative accommodation offered by the government was either too expensive or too far out of the city and from their place of work.

It has now become clear that many people have had more than enough of a government which has based its power on a system of injustice, brutality, repression and spying. They are no longer convinced that it matters that saying anything against the government brands them as a North Korean spy. But they do believe that the United Nations' declaration entitling everyone to a roof over their heads should apply to them, too.

Adapted from *The Guardian*, 31 October, 1987

7 Is South Korea an Asian success story? Look back over the whole of this Unit. Present your view.

13 TENSION IN KOREA AND EAST ASIA

Development for many countries in the world has not been either easy or peaceful. Between 1950 and 1953 Korea was devastated by war. Today, the country is still divided between communist-backed North Korea (the Democratic Republic of Korea) and the USA-backed South Korean Republic. The two sides are separated by the *demilitarised zone* (zone with no military presence – see Source A). Korea is a cause of the tension between the superpowers.

1   Korea is like many other developing countries: it uses some of its wealth for military expenditure.
a) Using Source B, draw bar graphs to show the percentage of GDP (gross domestic product) allocated by Asian developing countries to military spending.
b) In groups, discuss the advantages and disadvantages to a country in spending for military purposes.

B

Country	Military spending as a percentage of GDP 1986/87
USA	6.4
USSR	?
UK	5
China	1
Japan	1
South Korea	5
North Korea	9
Taiwan	6
Philippines	1.5
Hong Kong	0.5
Thailand	5
Malaysia	6
Singapore	6.5
Indonesia	3
Burma	3
Vietnam	?
Kampuchea	?
Laos	?

2   Korea is divided into two small countries. There is tension between North and South Korea. Both countries are heavily armed and each is supported by a different superpower.
a) Using Source C, provide the missing figures for the table opposite.
b) Is there a balance of armed forces between North and South Korea? Does one exist between the Communist and Western blocs?

3   The small countries of East Asia have had their own social and cultural history, but they have been ruled by COLONIAL powers. They are part of wider present day *political and economic groupings*.
● Using your library and newspapers, find out which external powers have affected Korea in the past and which economic and political groupings the Koreans belong to today.

A

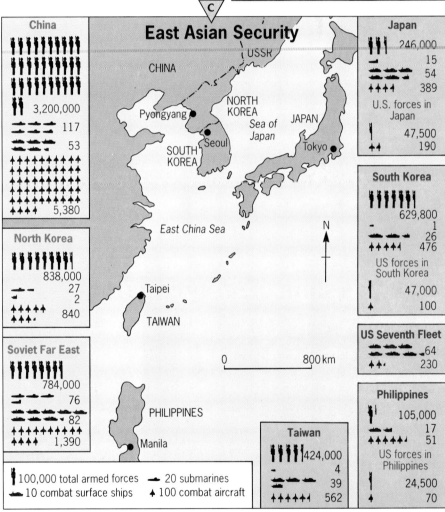

C

East Asian Security

100,000 total armed forces ⟶ 20 submarines
10 combat surface ships ▲ 100 combat aircraft

China
3,200,000
117
53
5,380

North Korea
838,000
27
2
840

Soviet Far East
784,000
76
82
1,390

Japan
246,000
15
54
389
U.S. forces in Japan
47,500
190

South Korea
629,800
1
26
476
US forces in South Korea
47,000
100

US Seventh Fleet
64
230

Philippines
105,000
17
51
US forces in Philippines
24,500
70

Taiwan
424,000
4
39
562

Type of force	North Korea	South Korea	Total Communist bloc	Total Western bloc
Armed forces				
Submarines				
Combat surface ship				
Combat aircraft				

A farm in pre-revolutionary Nicaragua

It takes a lot of courage and some strong reasons for ordinary people to rebel against their rulers and overthrow them. In 1979 the people of Nicaragua did just this. Since then, they have struggled to develop as a SOCIALIST society. This Unit helps you to understand the difficulties of a socialist path to development.

Pressure for land

Many people lived in the countryside. What were conditions like there before 1979?

1   Imagine the revolution has not yet taken place. Look at the photograph on page 159. Tomas Gonzales is thirty-seven and inherited the estate seven years ago. To him, it is productive and well-organised. Draw a sketch of the photo and on it label the following:
    ● fertile land
    ● cultivated fields
    ● efficient farm management.

2   Peasants also live in this countryside. Using Source A, list six objections Juan Sevilla sees in the system of land organisation.

Peasants grew food (beans, corn, and vegetables) and reared animals (chickens and pigs) on small plots of land. Large landowners introduced cash crop and livestock farming. As a result peasants were pushed off their land. They moved further and further into central Nicaragua. First the large landowners developed coffee estates, then beef ranches, then cotton estates and cattle ranches. The peasants tried to produce their own food on small plots but they also had to do seasonal labouring work on the large estates to earn a living.

Who owned the land?

3   Look at Source B.
    a) Draw a sketch map to show the land ownership and land use pattern in the Central Highlands of Nicaragua.
    b) Who owns most of the land?
    c) Who does not own much land?

Juan Sevilla, a 45 year old peasant, describes life before 1979 in the interview.

❝ There are seven of us in the family. We are like most people here. We live in the country. We are poor – we do not own land and find it difficult to feed ourselves. Other peasants who rent or own a small plot also suffer from food shortages. We live in a one-room shack. There is no electric light, no toilet and no clean drinking water. The floor is the dirt on the ground. None of us can read or write. I would like my sons to learn, but there is no school here. Anyway, they must work. My wife has lost five children since we married. Diarrhoea weakened them and then measles killed them.

We borrow from the money lender so that we can buy crops, cooking oil, sugar, salt and kerosene (paraffin). He makes us pay back half as much again. We all work at harvest time on the coffee, cotton and sugar estates. I started picking coffee when I was six. If you fill a ten-kilo basket you can earn 16 cents. I work from sunrise to sunset. I earn a dollar. We live in the modern barracks here and then move on. Working on the coffee estates is hard but picking cotton is even worse. The cotton estates are lower down near the coast. The sun is baking. There is nothing to protect you from the cotton branches, the dry spray they put on the bushes or the swirl of gnats and jiggers (fleas).

Am I unhappy? I talk to the priest a lot. He tells me that there is enough land for everybody but that it is owned by a few big landowners. They don't even all *live* in the countryside. The land is fertile but they waste it by grazing cattle and then they export the cattle. They do not grow food for Nicaraguans. ... ❞

Land use in the Central Highlands 1978
(East of the inter-American highway near Jinotega and Matagalpa)

rugged terrain

hardwood forest

peasant small holdings cut out of forest

village inhabited by landless peasants

poor soil

rented lands (25 ha) for coffee worked by local people

medium size coffee estate (100 ha)

for food crops (maize grasses, some cattle)

owned by absentee landowner

One of 6 owned by an absentee landowner

small coffee estate (55 ha) owned by local small landowner worked by existing local labour

500   400   300   200   100   0 metres

500   400   300   200   100

Unfair and unjust?

4 Look at Source C.

a) Name five groups who lived in the countryside.

b) What percentage of land was owned by large landholders (those owning over 350 ha)? How did this compare with the rest of the population?

c) What were the two most important cash crops grown on the largest farms? How did this differ from cash crops grown on farms of less than 35 ha?

d) What percentage of the rural income did moderate and large landowners receive?

e) What percentage did landless people who worked on other people's land get?

f) What was the calorie intake of the richest and poorest 50%?

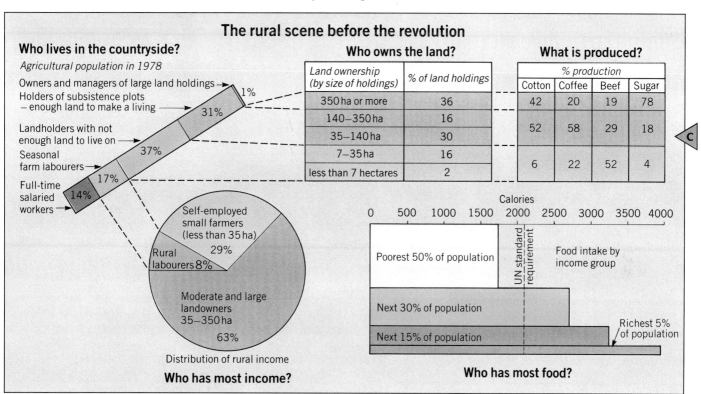

The rural scene before the revolution

Who lives in the countryside?

Agricultural population in 1978

- Owners and managers of large land holdings → 1%
- Holders of subsistence plots – enough land to make a living → 31%
- Landholders with not enough land to live on → 37%
- Seasonal farm labourers → 17%
- Full-time salaried workers → 14%

Who owns the land?

Land ownership (by size of holdings)	% of land holdings	% production			
		Cotton	Coffee	Beef	Sugar
350 ha or more	36	42	20	19	78
140–350 ha	16	52	58	29	18
35–140 ha	30				
7–35 ha	16	6	22	52	4
less than 7 hectares	2				

What is produced?

Pie chart:
- Self-employed small farmers (less than 35 ha) 29%
- Rural labourers 8%
- Moderate and large landowners 35–350 ha 63%

Distribution of rural income

Who has most income?

Food intake by income group (Calories: 0, 500, 1000, 1500, 2000, 2500, 3000, 3500, 4000)
- Poorest 50% of population
- Next 30% of population
- Next 15% of population
- Richest 5% of population
- UN standard requirement

Who has most food?

C

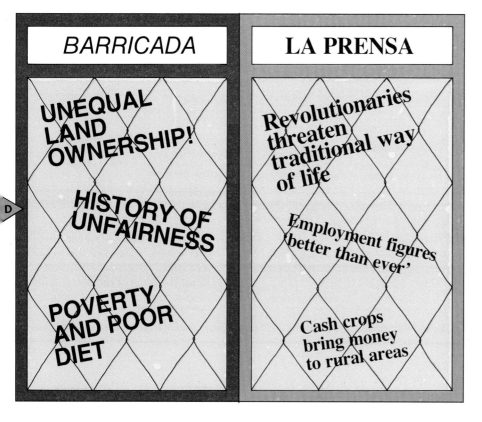

BARRICADA

UNEQUAL LAND OWNERSHIP!

HISTORY OF UNFAIRNESS

POVERTY AND POOR DIET

LA PRENSA

Revolutionaries threaten traditional way of life

'Employment figures better than ever'

Cash crops bring money to rural areas

D

Groupwork

5 You are four journalists working for newspapers in pre-revolutionary Nicaragua. Two of you work on *Barricada*, a revolutionary newspaper. You think that the peasants have good reasons for wanting change in the countryside. Two of you work on *La Prensa*, a newspaper which supports the government and large landowners. You believe revolution would bring disaster. Using Source D to help you, write your article. Include headlines, a clear text and illustrations if you wish.

6 Many people thought these rural conditions were unfair.

a) It is 1978. You live in a village in the central highlands near Matagalpa (see Source B). Discuss with other villagers what you could all do to make this a fairer farming area.

b) Choose the best suggestions. Draw a block diagram to show how the valley would change.

Ownership and organisation

In 1979 there was a socialist revolution in Nicaragua and the Sandinistas came to power. (However, there are still people, called the Contras, fighting against the new government.) Has the revolution changed the ownership of land and the organisation of agriculture?

Harvesting coffee at *La Unidad* state farm in the central highlands

An interview with Felichieve Garcia

Q: You work on *La Unidad* STATE FARM. How did the farm come into existence:

FG: The land was owned by someone who lived in Managua. It was left idle and unproductive.

After the revolution the State took over his land. Land that was idle could be taken over. We grow coffee for export and we need large farms to do this.

Q: If the State owns the land how does this benefit the workers?

FG: Workers still pick the coffee and do the hard work. But we get higher, fairer wages and three free meals a day.

Q: How is the farm run?

FG: The farms are managed centrally by government in Managua. But we have monthly meetings here where we discuss the work plan. The workers make decisions. They can get rid of inefficient farm administrators.

Q: Some people say state farms are BUREAUCRATIC, that they are run from the top down and that they are inefficient. What do you think?

FG: Well, I am a socialist. State farms in a revolutionary country like Nicaragua mean ordinary people can have a say in how things are run.

But it is true that some state farms produce less than CO-OPERATIVES in certain places. So the government is trying to have a mixture of state farms, co-operatives and private farms – both large and small.

Q: So this area has different types of farm. They are not all state farms?

FG: That's right. There are co-operatives. One type of these is the credit and service co-operative. On these farms the people work sections of land as individuals. They have grouped together to buy pesticides and machines more cheaply.

The other type of co-operative is the production co-operative. The people share the land and they share the work. I would not like that because some people work harder than others.

Q: Did you also say that private farms exist?

FG: Yes. The government allows private farmers to exist if they use all their land; if they live near their holdings; if they produce crops. The government buys their crops at a fair price including a profit for the farmer.

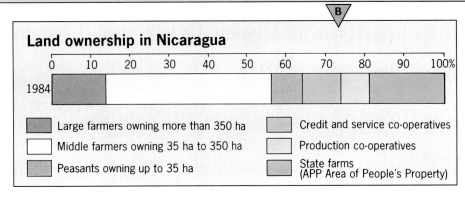

Land ownership in Nicaragua

0 10 20 30 40 50 60 70 80 90 100%

1984

- Large farmers owning more than 350 ha
- Middle farmers owning 35 ha to 350 ha
- Peasants owning up to 35 ha
- Credit and service co-operatives
- Production co-operatives
- State farms (APP Area of People's Property)

Type of holding	Percentage of crop production from different types of land holding	
	1984	2000
State farms	16	30
Production co-operatives	3	20
Credit and service co-operatives	18	20
Large private farms	14	5
Small private farms	49	25

1 The interview, Source A, gives the characteristics of state farms, credit and service co-operatives, production co-operatives and private farms. With a partner discuss what might be the advantages and disadvantages of each of these four ways of organising farming.

	Advantages	Disadvantages
State farms		

2 **a)** Copy the bar chart of land ownership (Source B).
b) Look back at Source C on page 161. Draw a similar bar chart of land ownership in 1978.
c) Describe the main changes in land ownership between 1978 and 1984. Give reasons for these changes. (You need to consider Source A.)

3 Source C shows the production of crops in 1984, and what the government would like to see by the year 2000. What does it tell you about the aims of the Nicaraguan government for crop production and land holdings?

Export earnings from agriculture

Before the 1979 revolution Nicaragua depended on the export of unprocessed primary commodities. Has the revolution affected agricultural export earnings? Or have world prices made a difference?

4   Look at Source D.
    a) Which three agricultural commodities were produced for export in 1978?
    b) Describe where they were produced.

After the revolution Nicaragua continued to earn money by exporting these products.

5   **a)** Use the tables of statistics (Sources E and F) to complete column 1 and column 2 of the table below them.
    b) Work out how much money these crops brought to Nicaragua in 1978 and 1984. Fill in column 3.
    c) The amount of money brought in by the two crops has changed. This could be because the revolution affected production. Does this seem to be true? Why might this have happened?
    d) Or it could be because the world prices changed. Is this true? Why might this have happened?
    e) Which of these two explanations best fits the data?

6   Did the revolution affect where Nicaraguan exports went?
    a) Use Source G to rank the countries buying Nicaraguan goods in order of importance in 1970 and in 1985.
    b) What are the main changes in trading partners?

7   What evidence is there in Source G to show that:
    a) The USA did not support the revolutionary government and its changes. It had a policy of economic boycott or blockade.
    b) Other developed countries did not agree with the USA.
    c) Socialist countries actively supported Nicaragua.

8   Read Source H. Draw a diagram to show the change in the purchasing power of Nicaragua's exports.

D

cattle		height m
coffee		1000
cotton		200
highway		0
railway		

HONDURAS · Pto Cabezas · N · NICARAGUA · Jinotega · Tuma · Chinandega · León · L. Managua · Boaco · MANAGUA · Juigalpa · Rama · PACIFIC OCEAN · Diriamba · Granada · Bluefields · San Juan del Sur · Ometepe I. · L. Nicaragua · CARIBBEAN SEA · COSTA RICA · 0 km 100

Nicaragua's major agricultural exports *(thousands of tonnes)*				
	1969	1978	1981	1984
Coffee	30	51	57	47
Cotton	69	132	81	90

E

Prices of major export crops *(dollars per tonne)*				
	1969	1978	1981	1984
Coffee	n.a.	3360	2720	2700
Cotton	n.a.	1000	1420	1480

F

		Column (1) *Amount of crop exported (tonnes)*	Column (2) *World market price (dollars per tonne)*	Column (1) × (2) *Income (dollars)*
Coffee	1978			
	1984			
Cotton	1978			
	1984			

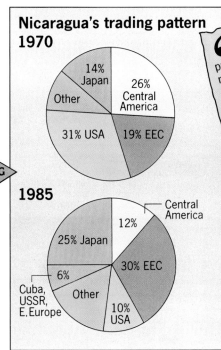

Nicaragua's trading pattern

1970

14% Japan · Other · 26% Central America · 31% USA · 19% EEC

1985

Central America 12% · 25% Japan · 30% EEC · 6% Cuba, USSR, E. Europe · Other · 10% USA

G

H

"However much we work to double or triple production it will never give us enough to cover the needs of a normal economy. The revolution has been working with the support of the whole of the people right from the start to recover the volume of production (to pre-revolutionary levels) but the price of our products (relative to other goods) has continued to fall.

● Ten years ago with 1012 kilos of coffee you could buy a jeep. Today you would need 3816 kilos.
● Ten years ago you could buy a tractor with 4816 kilos of cotton, today you would need 13 846 kilos."

Jaime Wheelock, Nicaraguan Minister for Agriculture, February 1985.

9   With a partner discuss what you have learnt from this page and explain why the purchasing power of Nicaragua's exports has changed.

de cero a **15 mil libras de carne de cerdo DIARIAMENTE** **98% PROPIEDAD DEL PUEBLO**

'From zero to 15 thousand pounds of pork a day – 98% property of the people.'

Billboard in Managua, April 1982

Harvesting maize

Food supply

Total production of food				
	1977	1980	1984	1986
Maize (million kg)	394	375	514	264
Beans (million kg)	90	86	119	71
Rice (million kg)	105	94	226	124
Beef (million kg)	49	54	40	45
Pork (million kg)	3	4	6	14
Poultry (million kg)	6	6	11	10
Milk (thousand litres)	21	10	10	n.a.
Eggs (thousand dozen)	4	12	19	n.a.

World Development, 1987

Food availability per person			
	1977	1980	1984
Maize (kg)	82	79	75
Beans (kg)	18	21	22
Rice (kg)	18	26	37
Beef (kg)	14	10	9
Pork (kg)	2	3	2
Poultry (kg)	2	4	3
Sugar (kg)	50	41	n.a.
Eggs (dozen)	5	6	6
Milk (litres)	17	24	23
Cooking oil (litres)	45	42	47

J. Collins, *Nicaragua*, Grove Press

Poor people like Juan (Page 160) did not eat well. One of the aims of the revolution was to improve the food intake of everyone in Nicaragua. Billboards like the one in Source A are found in many places. Production and consumption of pork, chicken, eggs, rice and other foods had increased significantly by 1982. But there have been production failures since then and nutritional gains are increasingly being threatened by the economic crisis resulting from the war against the American-backed Contra guerrillas.

1 a) In small groups choose four foods from the figures in Source B and draw graphs to show production and availability per person from 1977 to 1984. Which foods do you think are most important?
b) Which foods are people getting less of than they were in 1977? Why do you think this is?
c) Summarise your general conclusions.
2 The Nicaraguan Government want people to be better fed. Three general ways they could do this are shown in Source C.
a) Where does Source A fit into this system?
b) Source D shows details of what the government did. Use the statements in Source D to match with the three general ways of increasing food. In groups discuss which measures in your view are more important than others. Which would you do first? Which do you think would be most difficult to implement?

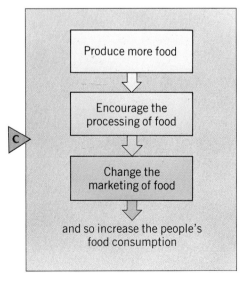

Produce more food
⇩
Encourage the processing of food
⇩
Change the marketing of food
⇩
and so increase the people's food consumption

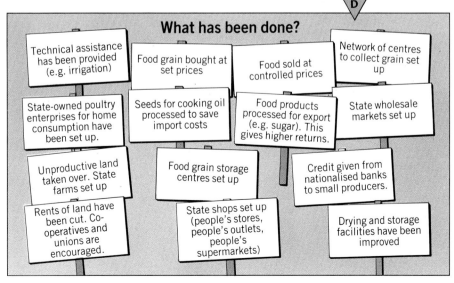

What has been done?

Technical assistance has been provided (e.g. irrigation)

Food grain bought at set prices

Food sold at controlled prices

Network of centres to collect grain set up

State-owned poultry enterprises for home consumption have been set up.

Seeds for cooking oil processed to save import costs

Food products processed for export (e.g. sugar). This gives higher returns.

State wholesale markets set up

Unproductive land taken over. State farms set up

Food grain storage centres set up

Credit given from nationalised banks to small producers.

Rents of land have been cut. Co-operatives and unions are encouraged.

State shops set up (people's stores, people's outlets, people's supermarkets)

Drying and storage facilities have been improved

Manufacturing industry

State textile factory in Managua, producing for the whole country

Like most economically developing countries, Nicaragua has spent some money in improving manufacturing industry. Its aim is to produce food and clothes by processing its own resources for local needs.

Before 1979 Maria Fernando worked on a coffee estate in the central Highlands. Now she is employed in one of the state textile factories in Managua (Source E).

3 In pairs study Source E. Describe the industry Maria works in, choosing the most likely words and phrases from the list below.
a) Does Maria make raw cotton/cotton thread/cotton textiles?
b) Is the source of raw material local/imported?
c) Will the product be used in Nicaragua/for export?
d) Do you think the factory Maria works in is located in a rural area/a small town/the capital city?

e) Is the factory size small/large?
f) Do you think the workforce is mainly unskilled/semi-skilled/skilled?
g) Does it mainly consist of men/women?
h) Is the CAPITAL invested likely to be low/medium/high?
i) Is the factory privately owned/owned by a corporation/state-run?
4 Why is this an appropriate industry for a developing country like Nicaragua to encourage?

Ownership of manufacturing industry in Nicaragua (1984)			
Owned by the State	Large private	Medium private	Small private
31%	33%	22%	14%

F

Nicaragua: sectors of the economy				
	% of people employed			
	1960	1970	1978	1984
Primary sector	60	47	42	35
Secondary sector	16	16	19	15
Tertiary sector	24	37	39	50

G

Effects on employment

5 Look at Source F. What main change in the ownership of manufacturing industry do you think the revolution has brought? Who has suffered as a result?

6 Using Source G, draw a triangular graph to show the pre-revolutionary employment structure. How has the employment structure changed? Suggest reasons.

7 Of the population in Managua, 46% work in the informal sector (see pages 116–117). In pairs:
a) make a list of the jobs they might do.
b) discuss your understanding of the term 'informal sector'.

HAS THE REVOLUTION BROUGHT ABOUT A BETTER QUALITY OF LIFE?

The revolution has had economic effects. But a socialist revolution also aims to improve the quality of life for the poorer people, especially in health and education. At the time of the revolution, the problems were pressing. The government needed to look for short-term and long-term solutions.

Health care

1　Think back to Juan in 1978 (page 160). What health problems did he and his family have? Make a list.
2　In the short-term the government trained *brigadistas* (health volunteers) like Puerita (Source A). Read Source A. A *brigadista* is planning a popular health day in the village. What activities might she encourage?
3　Nicaragua is a poor country. There is limited help from outside. The government wants to improve the health care of its people. They have certain options (Source B).
　a) What are the costs and benefits of each option?
　b) Which option do you think the government ought to choose first? In which order should it put the options? Give reasons for your choice.

I come from a farming family. I work now as a *brigadista*. We have been trained by the government to promote health care in the community.

We have had many national public health campaigns (popular health days) to help get rid of the major infectious diseases. We fought malaria. When the mosquitoes bred we filled in the ditches, sprayed chemicals and used anti-malaria drugs. We vaccinated babies against polio and measles. Our rehydration units prevented babies from dying from lack of water. We went into homes to explain the importance of drinking clean water. We encouraged mothers to breast feed. We have mobilised people to burn rubbish. We use a lot of natural medicines and we train midwives. We want to prevent diseases. If we cannot do that, how can we achieve any of the things the revolution set out to do?

Puerita, one of the health volunteers trained by the government

c) Which option do you think would be the most difficult to put into practice? Give reasons.
4　Developing countries might well wish to set up the system of health care shown in Source C.
　a) What would they need to set up such a system?
　b) If the government was to set up one national health centre, three regional health centres and nine district health centres, where might they be found in Nicaragua? (Use your atlas to find names of places with a large population.)
5　Look at Source D.
　a) In what ways does health care seem to have improved since the revolution?
　b) Source D shows that a rise in population has occurred. What effect do you think this will have on the standard of living? Why?

A health administration plan

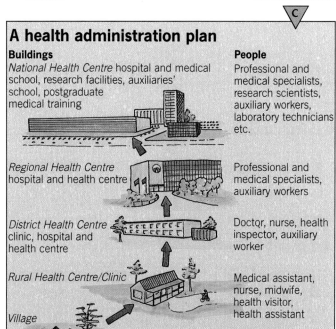

Buildings	People
National Health Centre hospital and medical school, research facilities, auxiliaries' school, postgraduate medical training	Professional and medical specialists, research scientists, auxiliary workers, laboratory technicians etc.
Regional Health Centre hospital and health centre	Professional and medical specialists, auxiliary workers
District Health Centre clinic, hospital and health centre	Doctor, nurse, health inspector, auxiliary worker
Rural Health Centre/Clinic	Medical assistant, nurse, midwife, health visitor, health assistant
Village	Mobile clinics, village and home visits by staff of rural health centre

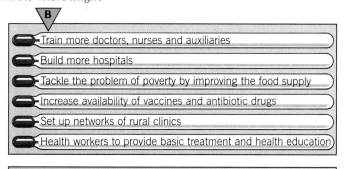

- Train more doctors, nurses and auxiliaries
- Build more hospitals
- Tackle the problem of poverty by improving the food supply
- Increase availability of vaccines and antibiotic drugs
- Set up networks of rural clinics
- Health workers to provide basic treatment and health education

Social indicators: health

	1978	1984
Population	2,545,000	3,110,000
Infant mortality (per thousand births)	121	72
Vaccinations	923,000	2,875,015
Health budget (millions of cordobas)	373	1,528
Doctors	1,309	2,172
Clinics	177	487
Hospitals	40	46
Children treated for dehydration	n.a.	173,081
Polio (deaths)	101	0
Measles (deaths)	1,270	153
Malaria (deaths)	18,418	12,907

Education

A key aim of the Nicaraguan Government is to improve the quality of life through education. How successful has it been?

6 Look at the photograph in Source E.
 a) What problems does the government face in trying to improve education?
 b) Why does Judith Porce think educational standards have got better since the revolution?
7 Look at Source F. What progress in education does it show the government has made?

An interview with Judith Porce

'Some of the children only come to school two or three times a week. To some extent that's an inheritance of the past, when people didn't think education was important. The majority of their parents still can't read or write. We're in one of the poorest parts of Occotal. The families are so badly off that the children often don't have any breakfast. So even when they do come, it can be difficult for them to concentrate. For the past three months though, we've been giving them milk and cereal. We hope that will encourage them to attend more often.

I think things have become much better since the revolution. We have a government that really believes people should be educated – adults and children alike. A lot of new schools have been built and even where there are no new buildings, there are places where classes can be held, like houses and community centres. Because of the economic situation some things are in short supply like desks and chairs. But we can't demand more because our country has other needs which are more urgent.'

The photograph shows children at the San Martin school, to the north of the border town of Occotal. With them is Judith Porce, a primary teacher. The building on the left is the new school on which construction had to be halted because of a cement shortage. On the right is an old wooden hut, which serves as their current temporary classroom.

New Internationalist, February 1986

Social indicators: education	1978	1984
Illiteracy rate (%)	50	13
Education expenditures (millions of cordobas)	341	1,481
% of GNP for education	1.32	5.01
Total pupils	501,660	1,127,428
Adult education enrolment	none	194,800
Pre-school enrolment	9,000	70,000
Teachers	12,706	53,398

J. Collins, Nicaragua, Grove Press

G	1: low importance 4: very important 2: some importance 5: essential 3: important	1–5 score
	● Build own schools	
	● Train more teachers	
	● Send students out from the city to teach skills	
	● Train local volunteers to teach basic literacy	
	● Provide more books	
	● Provide more pens, paper, blackboards	
	● Produce materials that relate to people's lives	
	● Produce materials to explain recent history	
	● Have large-scale advertising campaign	
	● Use radio and TV	
	● Teach literacy in the community	
	● Use the work-place to teach skills	
	● Use trades unions and co-operatives	
	● Provide transport to get teachers to the people	
	● Run evening classes	
	● Use the non-harvest period for the campaign	
	● Use women's associations	
	● Promote national literacy days	

Literacy

8 You are part of the new Nicaraguan Government, which wants to improve literacy.
 You and your colleagues are discussing why literacy is a high priority in a developing country. Is it because it is important:
 ● to communicate government plans to the people?
 ● to help people to make decisions which affect their lives?
 ● to give people useful, everyday, practical skills?
 ● to improve the quality of life?
 ● Are there other reasons?
 Discuss this in groups.
9 You are told to plan a campaign to improve literacy. Colleagues have given you suggestions (Source G). You can add others. Score the importance of each one and choose your priorities. Put forward your suggested campaign plan.
10 Design a campaign poster to encourage people to learn to read and write.

One third of the people of Nicaragua live in the capital city, Managua. These people need homes. Along with health and education, housing indicates the quality of life of the people. In 1972 an earthquake killed about 10,000 people and devastated 250 blocks. The ruins are used by the homeless. Money to rebuild the city went into corrupt politicians' pockets. Speculation in land and housing was common. As Source A shows, Managua inherited an enormous housing problem in 1979.

A

1 Using Source A, describe the housing problem of Managua. Suggest what the reasons for the housing problem might be. The government have discussed the problem (Source B).

Housing in Managua

Households with no home of their own	Households in homes in a bad state of repair	Households in overcrowded single rooms	Households in adequate housing

0   10   20   30   40   50   60   70   80   90   100 %

B

It should be possible for everyone to have some form of housing, no matter where they live or what they earn.

The government should arrange for people to help themselves. We must provide money and building reserves for people to build their own houses. But we still need to build some houses.

We should encourage people to build their own homes with their own hands, using local materials and equipment.

We want people to work together to agree on how they will build their own houses.

Housing is necessary and useful. It is not something which should be bought and sold for profit.

Land is needed for housing people. So it shouldn't be left empty or sold to make money.

To make the most of the little money we've got, we must control the growth of the city. We should fill in the empty spaces and keep building small plots.

Principles

2 The government have developed principles about housing. In groups, match the statements in Source B to the following principles.

- *Land* should be inhabited, not used as a means of making money.
- Limited resources should be *planned*.
- *People* should be involved in the housing process.
- Housing should be for people's *needs*, not for making profits.
- All people have a basic *right* to shelter.
- Dependence on *technology* should be reduced.
- *The State* has an important role in housing.

Practice

3 But have all the principles of the revolutionary government been put into practice? Source C lists what has been done since the revolution to solve the housing problem. In your groups:
a) List the seven principles from question 2 in one column. Match what has been done (Source C) to these principles.
b) Have all the principles been put into practice?

4 Think what you know about the UK government's housing policy. Do you think its aims and achievements are different from those of the Nicaraguan government? If so, in what ways?

Action in housing: a government report

C

- Land has been taken from landowners by the state and given to other people.
- Plots of land have been made available to households.
- Restrictions have been put on selling land.
- The government has built houses.
- Emergency programmes for the barrios (spontaneous settlements) with major problems have been put into effect.
- Resources have been made available for do-it-yourself housing schemes.
- The government is involved with planning and plot layout.
- Illegal land occupation is now legal. The government is reorganising spontaneous settlements.

Power to the people?

Adapted from D. Massey, *Nicaragua*, Open University

D Madres Martires de Pantasma: housing along the main road on the edge of the settlement

E

An interview with Juanita Carlos who lives in Madres Martires de Pantasma, a spontaneous settlement in Managua

" This spontaneous settlement grew up after a land occupation in August 1984. To begin with, there were about 20 people, but as the day passed more and more people arrived. The first occupation took place at nine in the morning. People kept on arriving. By the end of the day there were about 500 of us, all demanding a piece of land. Later, people took land by night. They were worried they might be moved on by the housing ministry. The woman who took possession of the first plot came from the Las Torres barrio (near the lake). Her house had been flooded and she had nowhere to go.

The settlement grew over the next five months. The occupation of lands was directed by a woman called Virginia who was one of the first people to arrive. She organised the distribution of plots. The idea was to have plots of a standard size – 10 × 30m – because they said that was the size used by the housing ministry, but in the end the size of plots varied. People would then clear and clean their plot and build houses using poles, planks and bits of zinc.

In those early days, the police appeared and told the settlers that they couldn't stay because the land was private property. But the settlers said that there had been a revolution by the people and that they were the people. The police went away and didn't come back anymore. Later, representatives from the ministry appeared and told the settlers that this land had many fault-lines and was therefore not suitable for building houses. And they came back again with the argument that the land was the property of some Managua cattle ranchers. The settlers paid no attention to this either. The government seemed to realise it would be difficult to evict them and people began to build their houses with less danger of being moved on. A CENSUS in 1985 showed the settlement had 365 houses and a population of nearly 2,000. A few people come from other parts of Nicaragua, but most are from neighbouring barrios. Among the main reasons people come are lack of housing, not being able to find a place to rent, overcrowding, and young people who want to live away from their families. Another cause is people coming from war zones, though these are few, and those who come to Managua to study. "

5 People in Managua *acted* and built spontaneous settlements.
a) Using Source D and Source E, describe the houses they built themselves.
b) Where did the settlers come from?
c) Why did they come?

6 People built an *illegal* settlement on someone else's land.
a) Should the occupation be made legal? In groups of four put forward the views of the police, the settlers, a ministry official and the landowner.

b) Who should own the land? Do the settlers need the land? Do they have a right to it? What about the rights of the landowner?
c) Did the government's initial opposition to the settlement contradict any of its principles about housing? If you think so, explain why.

14 FAIRNESS OR BIAS?

Do you think this Unit gives a fair picture of Nicaragua – or is it biased? The authors wrote and rewrote their pages. They had to make choices about what to include in the Unit and how to present their work. There was an exchange of letters (Source A and Source B) . . .

Margarita, a member of Sandinista Youth on duty on the Nicaraguan border

 C

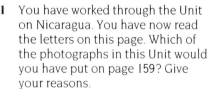 A

Dear Keith and Mike,

I have read through your draft of the Nicaragua Unit carefully and think there is some great stuff here. I particularly like the way you have focused on real people and the effects of the revolution on their lives.

One thing worries me, however. You make very little mention of the war. After all, not everyone agrees with the revolution. The Contras oppose the Sandinistas strongly and have received help from the USA. Perhaps we should stress just how seriously the war is affecting the development of Nicaragua. At least 40% of the government's income is spent on the armed forces and the war. This leaves so much less for agriculture, houses, schools etc. What about making the attached photograph the lead picture for the whole Unit? It highlights the issue of the war, and also emphasises just how strongly committed many Nicaraguans are to their revolution.

Best wishes,

Bob

Dear Bob,

Many thanks for your comments on the Nicaragua Unit. We agree with you. The war has distorted the economy. The war has caused food shortages. The war has caused nearly one-tenth of the people to move to places of greater safety. Rural people worry about the physical threat of the Contras.

But we wanted students to understand the deeper, long-term principles of revolutionary socialist development. After all, the war won't last forever (we hope).

We wanted our readers to appreciate what a revolution might achieve in the countryside, how it has changed people's lives in a poor country, how a socialist government is concerned for the health, education and housing of all its people.

So we accept that the war has distorted the economy. We also realise that the USA has distorted the hopes and needs of the Nicaraguan people. Do you think we should have a map to show how close Nicaragua is to the USA? Should we include the views of Americans who are very worried about the way Nicaragua is going?

In the end we can only rely on the students checking information and views presented to them in this Unit.

Kind regards,

Keith and Mike

B

1 You have worked through the Unit on Nicaragua. You have now read the letters on this page. Which of the photographs in this Unit would you have put on page 159? Give your reasons.

2 It is difficult to show the real world in a school book. What other information do you think you need to get a fair picture of Nicaragua? Follow the newspapers. Study television programmes. Look up reference books.

3 This Unit has investigated some aspects of Nicaragua.
   ● Can you see any bias in the photographs chosen, the written text and the organisation of the Unit?
   ● Authors have views. Can you detect the attitudes of these two authors to what has happened in Nicaragua? Give your evidence.

WHOSE ECONOMY IS IT?

Selling at the Saturday market in St George's, Grenada

CO-OPERATIVES

This book has shown you many ways in which work can be organised. In some cases the State does it, in others, private companies are responsible. Most people work for an employer who pays them a wage or salary. This relationship can be unsatisfactory. This Unit looks at some of the alternative ways work can be organised.

The photograph on page 171 shows women in Central America. They are poor and their future is uncertain. However, they belong to a CO-OPERATIVE, and by grouping together they believe they can have real control over their lives.

The example of La Imilla, Bolivia

1 Study the photograph on page 171 and with a partner discuss the benefits and the problems that working together can bring.

2 **a)** Study Source A. What sorts of skills and technology do you think workers would need to run their co-operative?
b) What do you think were the most important reasons the workers had for creating a co-operative?
c) What help was available to the co-operative members?
d) What opposition might the co-operative face?

Isabella Mendez, a worker at La Imilla co-operative, describes how the co-operative grew up.

❝❝ This photograph shows me at work in the co-operative. Our families own small farms but, for us, there are few opportunities to earn money. In the past, the only paid work we could get was spinning wool. Then along came a new company, offering us money to knit sweaters. We jumped at the chance to earn money, but the wages were poor and working conditions were awful. Some women became ill. When we complained, the company threatened us and we lost our jobs.

We wanted to get more control of our working lives, so we decided to form a co-operative. We make the same things, but we share the running of the organisation. This allows us to develop our craft skills through training.

Things have not been easy. We started with 25 members, but we had trouble raising the money to start producing. In the end another co-operative lent us money. At first we sold goods locally. Later we took them to La Paz. We got other loans so that we could build up our stock with more materials. Other co-operatives advised us about how to improve our book-keeping, health and literacy. These things are important if we are to be successful. Now everyone takes part in making decisions. Our numbers have grown – at the moment we have 44 members.

There is an increased demand for our product. The US is interested in our knitwear.

Now we are making a small profit we must decide what to do with it. Should we try to improve our small farms? Should we buy more land? Should we raise pigs for local consumption? We are not a healthy community. Perhaps we should put our money into improving health-care to prevent unnecessary illness. ❞❞

A

Reasons for setting up co-operatives (%)

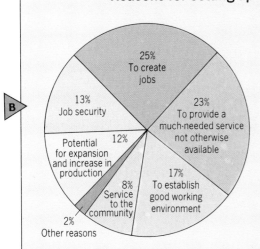

- 25% To create jobs
- 13% Job security
- 12% Potential for expansion and increase in production
- 23% To provide a much-needed service not otherwise available
- 8% Service to the community
- 17% To establish good working environment
- 2% Other reasons

B

A co-operative is a business owned and controlled by its workforce. Decisions are taken on the basis of a vote among all the members. Co-operatives give people greater control over their work by allowing them to have a say in how much gets done, when and by whom.

Why form co-operatives?

La Imilla is one example of a trading co-operative. Other people in other parts of the world have also set up similar organisations. Their reasons may be many and varied.

3 **a)** Look at Source B. In pairs, list the reasons given for setting up co-operatives. Now rank them.
b) Compare the reasons for setting up La Imilla co-operative with those for setting up co-operatives in the rest of the world.
c) What might the risks and problems be in setting up and running co-operatives?

4 For any co-operative to be successful, the members must have certain characteristics which make it possible for them to work together. The words in Source C describe some characteristics.
a) In pairs discuss what each term means.
b) Which characteristics do you think would help a group to be successful as a co-operative?
c) Pick out the ten most important characteristics and rank them in order of importance. Join with another pair to compare your rankings.
d) On a copy of Source C, draw up your profile of an ideal co-operative member.
e) Do you think you have the qualities needed to work in a co-operative?

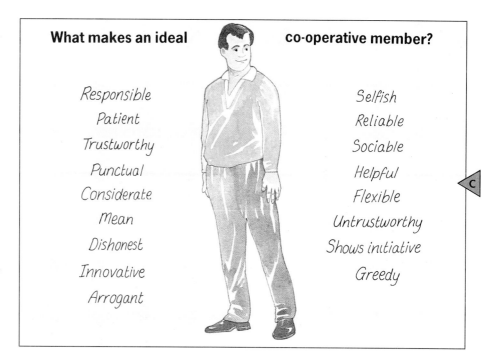

What makes an ideal co-operative member?

Responsible
Patient
Trustworthy
Punctual
Considerate
Mean
Dishonest
Innovative
Arrogant

Selfish
Reliable
Sociable
Helpful
Flexible
Untrustworthy
Shows initiative
Greedy

C

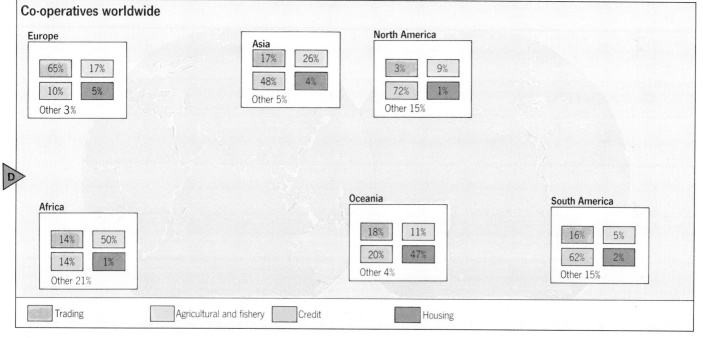

Co-operatives worldwide

Europe

| 65% | 17% |
| 10% | 5% |

Other 3%

Asia

| 17% | 26% |
| 48% | 4% |

Other 5%

North America

| 3% | 9% |
| 72% | 1% |

Other 15%

Africa

| 14% | 50% |
| 14% | 1% |

Other 21%

Oceania

| 18% | 11% |
| 20% | 47% |

Other 4%

South America

| 16% | 5% |
| 62% | 2% |

Other 15%

D

▢ Trading   ▢ Agricultural and fishery   ▢ Credit   ▢ Housing

The world picture

5 Trading co-operatives are only one of several different types of co-operative. Work through the following activities to find out what types are the most important throughout the world.
a) Using Source D, complete a copy of the table on the right. Rank the types of co-operative for each continent. Europe has been done for you.
b) Write down the most important type of co-operative for each continent. Comment on your findings.

Types of co-operative

Area	Europe	Africa	Asia	N. America	Oceania	S. America	Total
Trading	1						
Agricultural and fishing	2						
Credit	3						
Housing	4						

Note: most common = 1; least common = 4

c) What can you say about the pattern of co-operatives worldwide? Use both the rank table you have drawn and the percentages in Source D.

6 Investigate co-operatives in your area. Use local trade directories from your library. Think about the following:
● What sorts of co-operative are they?
● Where are they found?
● What reasons were there for setting them up?

15.2 THE ISRAELI KIBBUTZ

Co-operatives are a feature of many parts of the world. Some of the most famous are the kibbutzim of Israel. Jewish people like Sarah Joseph (Source A) went to Palestine in the 1920s. Read on to find out their reasons for going and what they achieved.

1 From Source A, pick out eight words or phrases which best illustrate the beliefs behind the setting-up of the kibbutz.
2 Draw an annotated sketch of Source B to show how the desert has been changed and made productive.

We came out from Europe in the 1920s. In 1947 the state of Israel was created. We worked to build a nation and change the landscape. We made the desert productive.

We were proud of what we did, but what mattered to us most was that we were creating communities where people could work together. There was no private property – all labour and income were shared. Children were cared for by the group, rather than by individual parents. There was no money. Democratic decisions were taken by the community. Men and women were treated as equals. From an early age, the children were taught the importance of work. Everyone was expected to contribute and pull their weight. If you had a cup of tea in your home, you were anti-social. We tried to make the kibbutz self-sufficient to meet the needs of families.

B Three per cent of Israel's population live on kibbutzim, but they provide 40% of farm output and 7% of industrial goods

Changing times, changing ideals?

The state of Israel is now over 40 years old. It has expanded its territory. The old kibbutzim have changed. New ones have been established for different reasons.

3 Read Source C. In what ways have the kibbutzim changed in the last 40 years?

Conflict

Some of the new kibbutzim are on the West Bank and Gaza Strip (Source D). This is an area of intense conflict because these territories are disputed between Israel and its Arab neighbours. Since 1948, war has broken out four times (see Source E). Each war has resulted in Israel taking over more land, with increasing numbers of Arabs becoming refugees.

4 In pairs, answer the following questions:
a) Why do you think Israelis have set up kibbutzim on the West Bank and Gaza Strip?
b) What effect is the conflict in these regions likely to have upon the kibbutzim there?
c) What effect do you think the Kibbutzim will have on Arab–Israeli relations?

5 Using an atlas and the information on this page, describe the land and environment in the West Bank and Gaza Strip.

6 David Simons left the UK to live and work on a kibbutz. In small groups discuss the following:
a) Do you think you would be able to live and work in a kibbutz like Ashdot Yaaqar?
b) What might be the advantages and disadvantages of kibbutz life and work?

7 On pages 172 and 173, the characteristic qualities of a co-operative member were discussed. What other characteristics would be needed for a successful kibbutznik (member of a kibbutz)?

8 Use your library to investigate other types of communal work organisations – e.g. the Tanzanian Ujaama villages or the Chinese commune. How do these compare and how do they differ from the Israeli kibbutz?

David Simons left a law practice in Scotland six years ago to work on the Ashdot Yaaqar kibbutz.

The kibbutz way of life still attracts people from all over the world. The Ashdot Yaaqar kibbutz is in the Jordan Valley, a few miles south of the Sea of Galilee. Altogether, there are about 280 kibbutzim in Israel.

But these kibbutzim have changed. We've built factories. A lot haven't been successful and have had to close. Some people now have private incomes. Children are brought up with their parents, rather than in dormitories. The older generation say these things go against the ideal of the kibbutz.

But we are still pioneering. We have set up new kibbutzim in the Negev. They have between 60 and 2000 people. This is desert land, where there are real problems of getting water. But we've made the desert productive by using modern drip irrigation methods which save water. We all contribute to the kibbutz in the best way we can. Some of us work on the land or look after machinery, whilst others teach. We have our own flats but still eat in communal dining rooms. There are creches for young children so we can go to work. We still aim for equality between men and women. Some of the children don't stay on the kibbutz when they grow up, but find work in the towns instead.

C

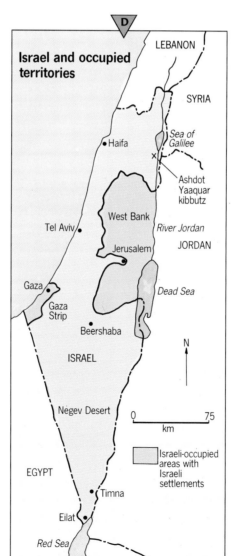

Israel and occupied territories

Time-line of events in the history of Israel

1947 In an attempt to solve a centuries-old dispute between Arabs and Jews over the area of Palestine, the United Nations suggests that the area should be split up between the two groups.

1948 The state of Israel is set up by the Jews in the area advised by the United Nations. The surrounding Arab countries refuse to recognise Israel and launch an attack. A war follows which is won by Israel. As a result, Israel occupies a number of Arab lands. Many Palestinian Arabs become refugees in neighbouring countries such as Egypt, Syria, Lebanon and Jordan.

E

1956
1967
1973
1982 Four further Arab-Israeli wars break out. The result of each is that Israel gains more land and an increasing number of Arabs become refugees.

1988 Widespread violence breaks out between Israeli Jews and Palestinian Arabs. The violence is concentrated in the Israeli occupied areas of the West Bank and Gaza Strip.

15.3 SELF-EMPLOYMENT

Some people do not share the communal ideal and want to develop their own business. They enjoy the challenge of organising their own work patterns. What does it take to be your own boss? Do you have to be a certain sort of person? Are there other influences? Study Source A to find out more.

Developing a business

1 In pairs answer the following questions:
   a) What reasons does Colin give for wanting to be self-employed?
   b) Who does Colin rely on to keep his business running? Explain why these people are important.

c) Do you think Colin is completely self-employed?

2 Draw a diagram, similar to the one on page 173 but this time using ten words to describe an ideal self-employed person. Which words appear on *both* diagrams? Which occur on only one, and why?

Colin – a case study

A Colin used to work for a family firm that built houses in a small market town in Norfolk. He was an apprentice carpenter, but picked up many skills in general house building such as bricklaying, electrical skills, plumbing, painting and decorating. In 1979 he decided to set up his own firm, building houses and doing other jobs in the same town. Here, he explains the advantages – and the drawbacks – of being self-employed.

I like being able to pick and choose the jobs I do. Mind you, at first it was difficult trying to attract customers and making sure they were satisfied. To stay in business I have to do a good job. Luckily, I'd had good practice building my own house in my spare time whilst I was still working for the firm. I take on all sorts of jobs – extensions, re-roofing, repairing churches and building new houses. I sub-contract (give work) to others, especially the bricklaying and electrical jobs. I am self-employed, but I rely on other people.

I take on extra help when I need it. My prospects improved when I bought a van to help transport materials. I've also got better at estimating how much time, labour and materials a job will take. The VAT returns take a lot of time and I have an accountant to look after that side of the business. I can give cheaper quotes for jobs than bigger firms because I have fewer OVERHEADS. Anyway, big firms aren't really interested in small jobs.

I lent Colin some money a few years ago when I first became manager of his bank. I had to feel confident he could pay back the money by making the business profitable.

There were lots of other people who wanted money to start up in the building trade at the same time as Colin. He has been one of the successful ones. There were a number of others whose businesses failed. But Colin looked like a person with drive and ambition. I heard he did a good job for people. It has been a risk, though – sometimes my judgment has been wrong.

Colin really does seem to be on to a good thing. As more people come up from London and the south-east, house prices increase. People can afford to pay for extensions and alterations. The future for his business looks very bright.

How easy is self-employment?

B

" Colin has qualities which will allow him to succeed. But there has to be the right sort of encouragement for small businesses. We politicians can help to provide the right sort of atmosphere. Some small firms can respond to change more quickly than large organisations. Besides, competition is good for business.

We have made grants available to small businesses. We try to encourage individual enterprise, especially in rural areas where variety of employment has been lacking. The government believes small firms will be the major source of new jobs in the future. "

A survey of self-employment

Self-employment in the UK

Year	1976	1979	1981	1983	1985	1987
Self-employed (thousands)	1,952	1,906	2,119	2,221	2,627	2,861
Total UK working population (thousands)	25,774	26,313	26,407	26,272	27,444	27,568

Comparison of the earnings of the self-employed and those in formal employment

Type of employment	Number self-employed in thousands	Average earnings (£) a year of those employed	Average earnings (£) a year of those self-employed
Agriculture, forestry, fishing	310,000	5,250	4,050
Metal goods, engineering and other manufacturing industries	200,000	7,600	4,600
Construction	640,000	7,650	4,950
Distribution, hotels, catering, repairs	870,000	5,300	5,450
Transport and communication	110,000	7,950	5,100
Banking, finance and business services	310,000	8,850	9,350
Other services	450,000	7,100	5,500

Self-employment by region as a percentage of total employment

Scotland	8.0%	West Midlands	8.2%
North	7.7%	East Midlands	9.9%
Northern Ireland	8.9%	East Anglia	12.8%
Yorkshire and Humberside	10.2%	South East	11.3%
North West	9.5%	South West	13.6%
Wales	12.7%		

Since 1979 a Conservative government has been in power.

3   Many self-employed people have an entreprenurial spirit, (individual business enthusiasm) but the government also tries to help them (Source B). Use a library to find out more about the help the government gives to self-employed people.

Source C tells us a great deal about self-employment in the UK. It gives details of:

• how self-employment has changed since 1976.

• how many people are self-employed in different occupations.

• how earnings of the self-employed compare with people employed by others.

• how self-employment varies regionally.

4   With a partner, use Source C to draw a set of graphs which illustrate this information. Present them as a wall-display. Beside each graph add a brief statement about what it tells you. (Think carefully about the best sort of graph to use for each piece of information.)

5   How typical does Colin seem to be of the self-employed in the UK?

6   Make up a questionnaire which you could use to interview a self-employed person in your area. Possible questions could be about:

• the background leading to self-employment.

• why self-employment was chosen.

• the activity and its location.

• the effects – whether the person prefers self-employment to their situation before.

7   Find out how important self-employment is where you live. You could start by investigating how many people in your class have parents, relatives or friends who are self-employed. You could then do a survey of the whole school.

177

Is there strength in numbers?

Some people cannot or do not want to join a co-operative. Some do not want to be their own boss. But many still want to join together in organisations which look after their interests. Trade unions have helped employees to get their needs listened to. They have fought to improve working conditions.

1 Look at Source A. List the reasons given for joining a trade union. What other reasons might there be?

2 Work in small groups. Using all the information in Source A discuss in groups whether the following statements are true or false:
a) Trade union membership increases when unemployment increases.
b) Trade union membership decreases when Conservative governments are in power. (Refer to Source A on page 44.)
c) Female workers are more likely to be in a trade union than men.

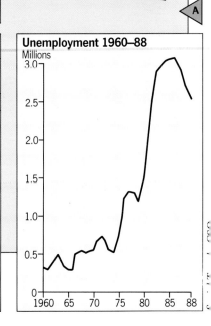

> ❝ I joined the union because I wanted protection against unemployment and because I hoped it would get me better pay. Also, I think government policy in industry is biased towards the management. ❞

A

Trade union membership in the UK

Year	Membership (millions)			As a percentage of all employees		
	Men	Women	Total	Men	Women	Total
1951	7.7	1.8	9.5	56	25	45
1961	7.9	2.0	9.9	53	24	43
1971	8.4	2.8	11.1	59	32	49
1976	8.8	3.6	12.4	61	38	52
1977	9.1	3.8	12.8	63	39	53
1978	9.2	3.9	13.1	64	40	54
1979	9.4	3.9	13.3	66	39	55
1980	9.2	3.8	12.9	64	38	53
1981	8.4	3.8	12.1	59	38	53
1982	8.0	3.5	11.5	55	34	52
1983	7.7	3.5	11.2	54	33	52
1984	7.6	3.4	11.0	53	31	51
1985	7.4	3.4	10.8	50	30	50
1986	7.2	3.3	10.5	49	29	49
1987	7.0	3.1	10.1	48	27	46
1988	6.6	2.9	10.4	47	26	45

Unemployment 1960–88

Millions
3.0 – 2.5 – 2.0 – 1.5 – 1.0 – 0.5 – 0
1960 65 70 75 80 85 88

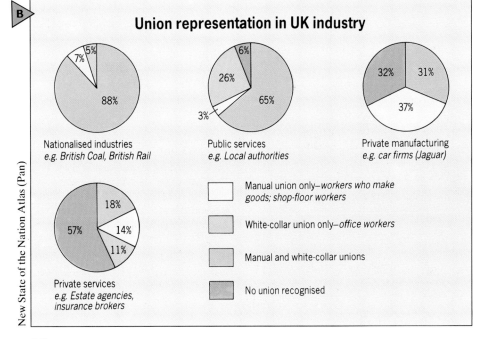

B

Union representation in UK industry

88% 7% 5%
Nationalised industries
e.g. British Coal, British Rail

65% 26% 6% 3%
Public services
e.g. Local authorities

37% 32% 31%
Private manufacturing
e.g. car firms (Jaguar)

57% 18% 14% 11%
Private services
e.g. Estate agencies, insurance brokers

☐ Manual union only–*workers who make goods; shop-floor workers*

☐ White-collar union only–*office workers*

☐ Manual and white-collar unions

☐ No union recognised

New State of the Nation Atlas (Pan)

Different unions

3 Look at Source B and in pairs answer the following questions with reference to: a booking-clerk at Euston station; a secretary in an estate agent's office; an assembly-line worker at Jaguar; a school playing-field worker.
a) Which of these workers is most likely to be represented by a trade union? Which worker is not likely to be represented? In each case say why.
b) Which type of union is each worker most likely to be in (e.g. manual, white collar)?
c) What sort of organisation does each work in (nationalised industry, public services, etc.)

4 When you leave school and get a job, will you join a trade union? Give reasons for your answer.

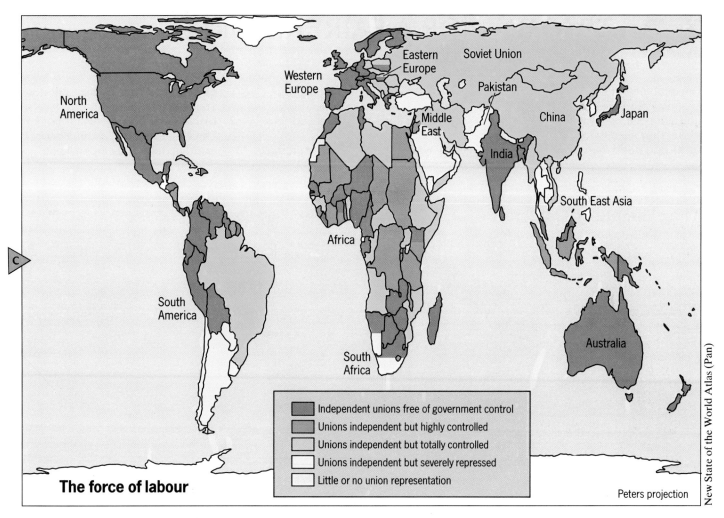

The force of labour

		Independent unions free of government control
		Unions independent but highly controlled
		Unions independent but totally controlled
		Unions independent but severely repressed
		Little or no union representation

Peters projection

Trade unions throughout the world

Type of economy	Area/country	Independent unions free of government control	Unions independent but highly controlled	Unions independent but totally controlled	Unions independent but severely repressed	Little or no union representation
Market capitalist economies	North America Western Europe Japan Australia South Africa					
Centrally planned economies	USSR Eastern Europe China Others					
Economically developing areas	Latin America Africa Middle East India Pakistan South East Asia					

Everyone has the right to work, to free choice of employment, to just and favourable conditions of work and to protection against unemployment.

Article 23 of the United Nations Declaration of Human Rights

D

Workers united worldwide?

People in the UK are able to form and join trade unions. How does the UK compare with the rest of the world?

5 Carefully study Source C. Using the information it gives you, copy the table and complete it.

6 **a)** Under separate headings, list the main areas that have the following: independent trade unions; trade unions under tight government control; governments which do not want trade unions to exist at all.

b) What other information would you wish to know about trade unions worldwide to give a fuller picture?

7 Read Source D. In groups, discuss whether a revision of the United Nations declaration should include the words 'Everyone has a right to join a trade union.'

One problem for people in the economically developing world is to find someone to buy what they grow or make. They need to trade. How can they break into world markets?

1 Look at Source A. In small groups answer the following questions:
a) What sorts of products do Traidcraft sell?
b) Which countries do the products come from?

c) What sorts of organisations does Traidcraft deal with?
2 Discuss whether organisations like Traidcraft can bring about a fairer world in trade and employment.

The example of Traidcraft

In 1979 Traidcraft was set up. Its aim was to import goods from the economically developing world and sell them in the UK. Traidcraft works for fairer trading.

I work for Traidcraft because I know the profits they make go directly to the workers in the countries which produce the goods. You might pay a little more for the product, but we are helping the workers there.

The shop I work in stocks a variety of goods. Over 75% of them come from overseas. These are mostly food, coffee, tea and craft products like those shown in the photographs. We also sell products from the UK including cards and recycled paper products.

We know we are helping people in the developing world. We only buy from organisations which are set up for the benefit of their workers. They have to pay wages and provide working conditions which are above average for the locality. The products they make can be sold here and we don't have to pay agents or service fees. We encourage our suppliers to process and package their goods too.

A

The problems

3 Look at Source B. What seem to be the main problems facing economically developing countries?

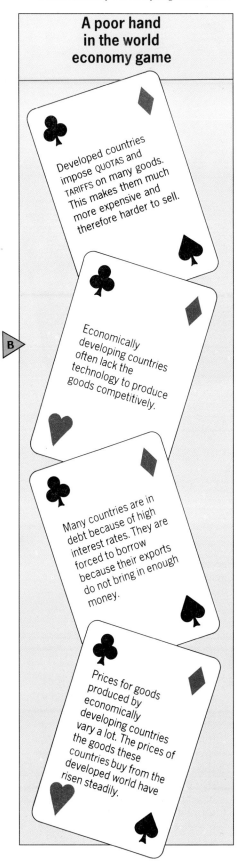

A poor hand in the world economy game

Developed countries impose QUOTAS and TARIFFS on many goods. This makes them much more expensive and therefore harder to sell.

Economically developing countries often lack the technology to produce goods competitively.

Many countries are in debt because of high interest rates. They are forced to borrow because their exports do not bring in enough money.

Prices for goods produced by economically developing countries vary a lot. The prices of the goods these countries buy from the developed world have risen steadily.

B

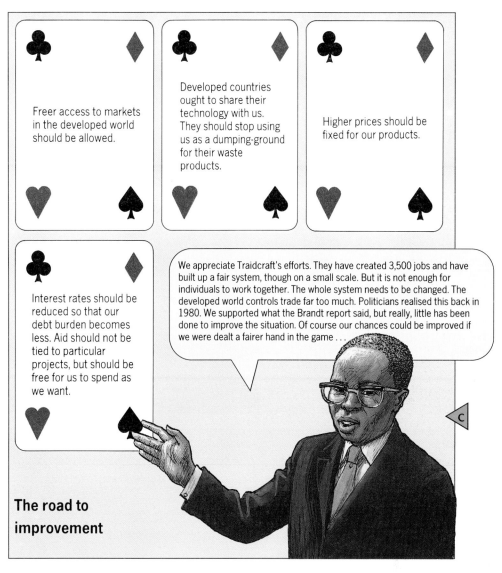

Freer access to markets in the developed world should be allowed.

Developed countries ought to share their technology with us. They should stop using us as a dumping-ground for their waste products.

Higher prices should be fixed for our products.

Interest rates should be reduced so that our debt burden becomes less. Aid should not be tied to particular projects, but should be free for us to spend as we want.

We appreciate Traidcraft's efforts. They have created 3,500 jobs and have built up a fair system, though on a small scale. But it is not enough for individuals to work together. The whole system needs to be changed. The developed world controls trade far too much. Politicians realised this back in 1980. We supported what the Brandt report said, but really, little has been done to improve the situation. Of course our chances could be improved if we were dealt a fairer hand in the game . . .

The road to improvement

C

The Brandt Report suggested that there is a moral responsibility to solve the problems of the poor countries, and remove the injustices that have held back development, by worldwide co-operation. It recommended that all developed nations should meet the target of giving 0.7% of their GROSS NATIONAL PRODUCT as official development assistance and that the quality of this aid should be improved so that more is readily available to the poorest countries. To deal with global trade, a new organization, which might be called the World Development Fund, should be set up. This would co-ordinate the financing of the development programme and would provide the opportunity for all countries to co-operate on a more equal basis. As yet there has been limited action in this direction.

Aspects of Social Geography, J. Geddes and K. Muir (Edward Arnold)

D

4 Traidcraft and the politicians in developing countries both have the same aims – working for a fairer trading world. But they want to achieve their aims in different ways.
a) In groups look at Source C and discuss how the two groups differ.
b) Which view do you favour most and why?

What about the Brandt Report?

5 The Brandt Report was published in 1980. Source D comes from a book published in 1987. Has the situation changed since the report was published?

6 In small groups, discuss whether we in the economically developed world have a 'moral responsibility' to concern ourselves with the problems of the poor countries.

What should be done?

1   Get into groups. One person should take notes. Discuss your reactions to Source A and Source B. Think about what is happening in each, whether it gives a positive or negative impression and how similar the pictures are to each other. How might the people in each picture benefit from a fairer world?

March against unemployment, 1981

Harvesting the coconut fruit in Quelimane, Mozambique

2   Most people's idea of a job is of routine work from 9 to 5 which brings in a regular income. In this Unit you have learnt about some jobs that are rather different. How do you see *your* future? Which of the ways of organising work that you have read about most appeals to you? Give reasons. Or are you more attracted by the idea of a more conventional job? If so, say why.

GLOSSARY

Balance of trade   The difference between the value of *visible exports* and the value of *visible imports*.

Bureaucracy   A centralised system of government designed to process a large volume of administrative work. A badly-run bureaucracy can lead to a slowing down in the running of government through unnecessary official procedures.

Capital   Wealth created for use in the production of further wealth. Examples of capital are money, stocks and shares, machines and buildings.

Capitalism   An economic system where the majority of capital is owned by private individuals rather than by the State.

Cash crop   A crop grown with the object of producing a surplus for sale or barter. This is in contrast with a crop grown for use by the farmer and the family.

Census   An official count of a country's population, usually collected on a regular basis by a government.

Centralisation   The concentration of people and capital in few, rather than many locations.

Choropleth map   A map which uses shading to show density (e.g. of population) in an area.

Collective farm   A farm owned by the State and permanently leased to a large group of farm workers. The workers run the farm themselves, but are influenced by planning decisions made at local and national levels. The kolkhoz farms in the Soviet Union are examples of collective farms.

Colonialism   Rule by one state over another, usually less economically developed state.

Common Agricultural Policy (CAP)   A policy of the European Community which aims to help and control farming in the member countries.

Command economy   A system in which the State controls wealth and property and makes decisions about their use and about the distribution of income.

Communism   Communist governments believe that *capital* should be owned by the State rather than by private individuals. The governments of the Soviet Union, Eastern Europe and China can loosely be described as communist.

Conglomerate   A business made up of many companies whose products and activities may all be very different.

Consumer   A person who uses goods and services.

Co-operative   An association of people organised for their mutual benefit in the production and marketing of goods or services.

Corporation   A united body or group, joined together in trade or business. A corporate strategy is the plan of the group.

Current balance   The total exports of a country minus total imports.

Demand   The willingness and ability of *consumers* to pay for a particular good or service.

Development   In the narrowest sense, the characteristics of a country's development are those of economic growth, as measured by its GNP. A wider definition includes social, cultural and political changes.

Dictatorship   A form of government in which one person has sole and complete political power.

Economically developed countries   Countries which have become wealthy by developing farming, industries and services (the *primary*, *secondary* and *tertiary* sectors and economy). These countries have a high GNP. The UK and Japan are examples of economically developed countries.

Economically developing countries   Countries with poor living standards which are trying to increase wealth by developing farming, industries and services. These countries have a low GNP. The Gambia, Nicaragua and Sierra Leone are all economically developing countries.

Employment   Regular trade or profession, in return for money.

Enterprise zone   An area where the government gives tax concessions to firms and removes various planning restrictions. The aim is to attract new business to the location. Enterprise Zones are usually in urban areas with a high unemployment rate.

European Economic Community (EEC)   An economic association of West European countries, also known as the Common Market or EC. The aim is to promote common trading, economic and social policies beneficial to all member countries.

Exports   Goods sold abroad – either *visibles* or *invisibles*.

Glasnost   A Russian word meaning 'openness'. The General Secretary of the communist party, Mikhail Gorbachev, sees increasing glasnost in all aspects of Soviet society as important.

Green Belt   A zone of farmland, parkland or open country which surrounds an urban area. The zone is protected from new developments by permanent government restrictions.

Gross Domestic Product (GDP)   Total value of goods and services produced by a country in a year, not including foreign investment.

Gross National Product (GNP)   A way of measuring a country's wealth. It represents the total output of goods and services produced by the country in a year, plus the value of foreign investments.

IMF   The International Monetary Fund, an international financial institution set up in 1945. The aim is to strengthen international trade. A fund exists out of which member countries with temporary *balance of payments* deficits can borrow money.

Imports   Goods purchased from a foreign country – either visibles or invisibles.

Industrial estate   An area of land planned for industry by one owner or a local council.

Inflation   A situation where prices rise steadily. This leads to a decrease in the value of money, as it can buy fewer goods.

Informal work   Work done (paid and unpaid) without the official knowledge of the government and therefore without formal control and payment. The revenue of this informal economy cannot be measured accurately as it is outside the power of the tax authorities.

Infrastructure   The facilities which provide a fundamental framework for an economy, e.g. roads, power supplies, sewage.

Inputs   The resources needed for industrial or agricultural production, such as raw materials, labour and *capital*.

Intervention price   The price at which the EEC buys surplus produce when the market price falls below a certain value (8% below the target price).

Isopleth   A line drawn on a map connecting places of equal data value.

Market economy   An economic system in which the bulk of the outputs is produced for exchange, and economic decisions are freely taken by businesses and consumers The market price is the price at which goods are offered for sale.

Management buyout Payment by managers of a factory to the owner in order to buy the factory and run it themselves.

Mixed economy An economic system in which capital is owned partly by private individuals and partly by the government.

Multinational (Also known as transnational) A large company which operates in several countries and directs policy from a headquarters in one of these countries.

National grid A network of power lines connecting major electricity power stations.

Nationalisation The process of placing industry under state ownership and control.

National Park A large area of landscape of great natural beauty and interest which is set aside for conservation. National Parks are protected by government legislation.

NIC Newly industrialising country; a country that has recently developed its farming, industry and services. South Korea, Hong Kong and Taiwan are examples of newly industrialising countries.

Outputs Products from a given system. For example, in agriculture the inputs of land, labour and capital are used to produce wheat or dairy products or oilseed rape.

Overhead costs Costs which do not vary with *output* and cannot be charged directly to any unit produced. They include rent of premises, salaries of staff and electricity costs.

Perestroika A Russian word meaning restructuring. There has recently been much emphasis on the need to restructure government at all levels by the general secretary of the Communist Party, Mikhail Gorbachev.

Primary employment Economic activities concerned with the exploitation of natural resources (e.g. agriculture, fishing, forestry, mining and quarrying). The output of such primary production often needs further processing.

Politburo The principal policy-making committee of a communist party.

Private limited company A company that is not allowed to offer shares to the general public or the stock market or to have more than a small number of shareholders (20 in the UK).

Privatisation The transfer of assets from the public sector to the private sector.

Producer An organisation or firm responsible for converting *inputs* into useful goods and services.

Profits Money left over when wages, interest, rent, raw materials and other payments have been paid by a business. Profits are the financial reward for taking risks.

Quota A restriction in the minimum or maximum level of production or trade. For example, an import quota restricts the volume of a commodity that can be imported into a country during a period.

Rationalisation A process of reorganisation in an industry to achieve greater efficiency. It usually involves a concentration of economic activity and cutbacks on workers.

Redeployment Transferring employees to a new location of work, or assigning them a new position at work.

Renewable energy Energy produced from sources that will never run out. These include solar energy, wind energy, wave energy, tidal energy, hydro-electric power, fusion energy and geothermal energy.

Science park An area, usually linked to a university, where scientific research and commercial development are carried out in co-operation.

Secondary employment An economic activity involving the manufacture of goods from raw materials. Building is an example of secondary employment.

Socialism A political and economic system in which the State owns and controls most capital and industry. A socialist government aims at equality of wealth and is against profit for its own sake.

State farm A farm run by a state-appointed manager and worked by labourers.

Superpower One of the most powerful countries in the world with great economic resources, political influence and military power. The USA and the Soviet Union are at present the two principal superpowers.

Supply The amount of commodity which sellers offer for sale at a specified price.

System A group of elements connected together to form a working unit.

Takeover The acquisition of one firm by another.

Target price The highest price at which a crop is traded within the *European Economic Community* in any year.

Tariff A tax or customs duty charged by a government on its imports.

Terms of trade The relationship between the average price of exports and the average price of imports.

Tertiary employment Work in the service sector of the economy. It includes activities associated with commerce and distribution (wholesaling and retailing) as well as transport and entertainment services.

Threshold price This is a limit set by the EEC, below which the price of a crop of any member country is not allowed to fall.

Trade union An organisation of employees which seeks to secure economic improvements for its members.

Work Employment at a job or occupation; either *formal* or *informal*.

World Bank An international organisation set up in 1945 to assist economic development. The World Bank forms part of the United Nations and gives loans, usually to developing countries.

YTS Youth Training Scheme – a government-funded project, aimed at providing 16 to 18 year olds with work experience.

INDEX

Designed by Derek Lee
Edited by Kate Harris and Frances Benn
Picture research by Caroline Thompson
Production by Lorna Heaslip
Maps and diagrams by John Booth, Jerry Fowler, Jillian Luff, Malcolm Porter, Tim Smith, s + m Technical Services, Gillian Tyson
Cartoons by Rolan Fiddy
Other artwork by Gay Galsworthy

The authors and publishers are grateful to Christine Wise for her detailed comments on the manuscript

Typeset by the Dorchester Typesetting Group Ltd
Printed in Hong Kong by Wing King Tong Ltd

Acknowledgements

Every effort has been made to contact the holders of copyright material but if any have been inadvertently overlooked the publishers will be pleased to make the necessary arrangements at the first opportunity.

Maps on pp. 6–7, 27, 71 and 124 are reproduced from the 1990 Ordnance Survey 1:50 000 Landranger and 1:25 000 Pathfinder maps with the permission of the Controller of Her Majesty's Stationery Office © Crown Copyright.

Photographs The publishers would like to thank the following for permission to reproduce photographs on these pages:

Key: T = Top C = Centre B = Bottom R = Right L = Left

Action Aid, 135, 142–144; Aerofilms, 9T, 25; APA Photo Agency, 146T, 156L&R; Banque Nationale de Paris, 132BL; Frances Benn, 74, 75, 99L; Anne Bolt, 171; Des Bowden, 107T, 119; Photograph by Derry Brabbs from *Rural England* by D. Mercer & D. Puttnam, Queen Anne Press, 64; British Airways, 29TL; British Coal, 39; British Library, 122; Britain/ Israel Public Affairs Centre, 174T, 175; BMIHT (Rover Group)/*Coventry Evening Telegraph*, 74B; BUPA, 23; Cadbury 47, 50; J. Allan Cash Photolibrary, 1, 26T, 28CR&BL, 43CB, 68, 69, 72C, 115L, 136, 138, 166, 174B; Kim Seong-Su/CIIR, 157; Central Electricity Generating Board, 40L, 43TL; Mrs R. Chappell, 26B; Bruce Coleman, 156C; Compix, 114TR; Courtaulds, 131; Coventry City Council, 76, 77; Prodeepta Das, 51L&R&CR; Reproduced by kind permission of The Viscount Daventry, 123B; Development Education Centre, 139, 140, 145; Dundee Project, 56; English Life Publications Ltd, 123T; *Farmer's Weekly*, 63, 126B; Val Wilmer/Format, 11; Jenny Matthews/Format, 164T, 170, 172; Maggie Murray/ Format, 182B; Nance Fyson, 8B; Tom Hanley, 147; Robert Harding Picture Library, 43CT, 85, 129; Ronald J. Harrison-Church, 112; Holt Studios/Primrose Peacock, 59; Geoff Howard, 83, 92L, 94; Hulton-Deutsch Collection, 127TR; The Hutchison Library, 28TL&CL, 69, 80R, 89, 151; Japan National Tourist Organisation, 86, 92R, 93; JAS Photographic, 78R; Korea National Tourism Corporation, 154R; Korea Overseas Information Service, 148B, 154TL, 158; Leicester Royal Infirmary, 20, 22; Susan Meisalas/Magnum Photos, 165; Chris Steele Perkins/Magnum Photos, 162; James Nachtwey/ Magnum Photos, 168; John Mannion, 8T, 28TR, 40B, 73R, 78L, 80L, 127BL, 178, 180L; Fiona Marsh, 30T; Doreen Massey:Nicaragua/OUP 1987, 169; John Massey-Stewart, 103T; Mike Mayes, 125, 176L; NCR, 52L; NEC OITA Japan, 87; NEC Semiconductors (UK), 91; Laurie Sparham/Network, 9B; Mike Abrahams/Network, 107B, 114BR; Mike Goldwater/ Network, 159, 160, 164L; John Sturrock/Network, 182T; Peter Stalker/*New Internationalist*, 167; Novosti Press Agency, 99R, 103C, 104/5; Oldham Local Studies Library, 121T; Christine Osborne, 116L, 120; R. Berriedale-Johnson/Panos Pictures, 51CL; Julia Martin/Photo Co-op, 7; Popperfoto, 102; The Post Office, 2; PowerGen, 35; Quadrant Picture Library, 29TR; Redwing Holidays, 28BR, 29B; Carlos Guarita/Reflex, 121B; Science Photo Library, 43TR&BL, 127BR; Sierra Leone High Commission, 114TL, 115R; Keith Smalley, 60, 65; Society for Cultural Relations with the USSR, 32, 33, 95–8; Tony Stone Worldwide, 30C, 40T&CT, 72L&R; Jim Styles, 4; Suffolk Record Office (Suffolk Photographic Survey), 126T; Tesco Group Training Services, 14, 15; Caroline & Stewart Thompson, 13, 54C; Topham Picture Library, 127TL; Traidcraft, 180TC&R, BC&R; Tropix, 109, 114BL, 116R; UNIFEM, 146; Veeder-Root, 52R, 54T; ZEFA, 18, 30B, 40CB, 73T, 132TL&R&BR, 176R.

Front cover photograph: Nance Fyson
Hong Kong: selling freshly-caught fish and shellfish on the waterfront.